MA AND ME

Please Enjoy My [illegible]
of Love

Myrna L Brandt

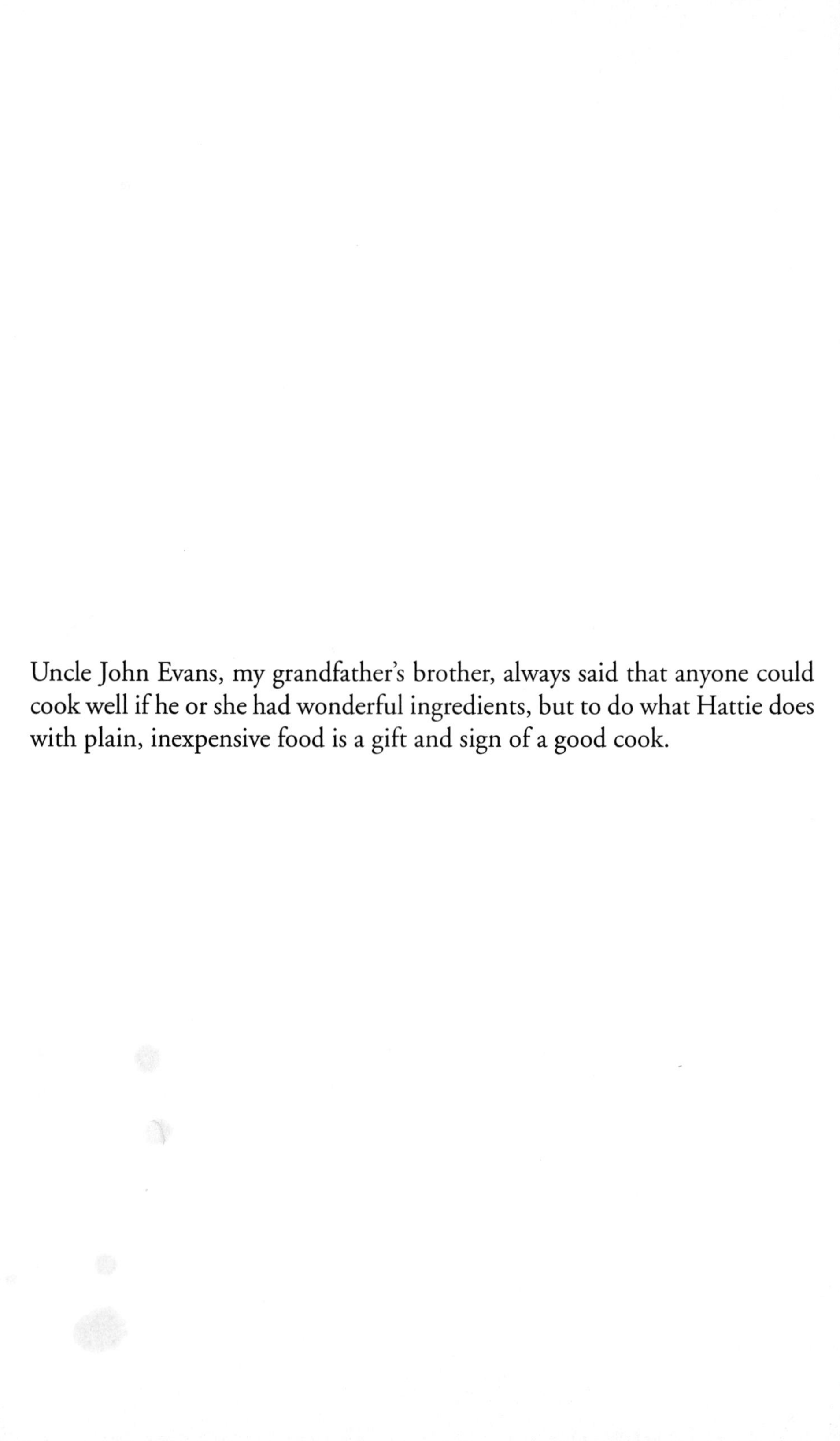

Uncle John Evans, my grandfather's brother, always said that anyone could cook well if he or she had wonderful ingredients, but to do what Hattie does with plain, inexpensive food is a gift and sign of a good cook.

MA AND ME

A Family History and a Country Cookbook with Recipes From the 1800's to the present

Myrna Ruth Brandt

Library of Congress Control Number: 2007902210
ISBN: Hardcover 978-1-4257-6637-5
Softcover 978-1-4257-6601-6

This book was printed in the United States of America.

To order additional copies of this book, contact:
Xlibris Corporation
1-888-795-4274
www.Xlibris.com
Orders@Xlibris.com

32565

CONTENTS

ENTERTAINMENT

DEDICATION

I dedicate this book to Ma, who taught me so much. She did that with kindness and gentleness. Ma calmly motivated me and, when necessary, disciplined me. She encouraged me to find myself. I didn't inherit her patience and endurance, but my grandmother was a caretaker, and I hope that some of that did rub off on me.

MRB

ACKNOWLEDGMENTS

Thank yous go to so many people, family and friends alike. Thanks go to my family, who has helped with their memories. I especially thank my mother, Marjorie Meddings Evans, for her memories of family connections; she was able to remember so many details. She put up with phone calls late at night to pick her brain, and to spell names and words for me. She was a great support and help. Mother is very meticulous about keeping records, so she had phone numbers and addresses that allowed me to contact family members. Thanks, Muzz.

My cousins supplied information I didn't have and I'm not sure I could have gotten without them. Thanks go to Vasso Stenta for sharing her mother's (Aunt Theresa's) recipe of orange and applesauce cakes. She filled me in on her family lineage. Thanks to Joan Krause (Aunt Annie's granddaughter), for sharing family ties to the family on Smith's Island, her hometown. Joan's grandchildren are the fifth generation of Ma's stepchildren. Thanks to Nevitt Evans (Aunt Maggie's son) for supplying so much of the Evans information. I was so glad to speak to him and find that his memory was still working. Thanks, Nevitt. At the end of this great effort I was sad to find that my great source of information, Nevitt, had passed away. I then turned to his children Nevelyn, John and Nevitta and they were able to fill in the last bit of that part of the family tree. Thanks kids! Bill Blake (William Blake's son) is also good about keeping records. He has the Blake family "Bible", and he was interested enough to keep in touch with people on the Eastern Shore. I am grateful to him. He provided me with family names, and dates and, like the rest of the family, encouraged me to write this document of this far-reaching family. Writing this book has let me get in touch with my family members. I stopped procrastinating about calling and visiting.

Thanks go to my daughter Nicole for reading my manuscript and giving me feedback and, most of all, her work to do all the final editing from Susan. Both she and her brother have helped me with my recipes. George is my computer guru and gets all kinds of calls for help in a panic. He set up the program for me to record my recipes. George scanned many more pictures that are in this publication. George, this is your mother. Thanks! Thanks go to George Sr. for his help with spelling many words as I worked on this book and for listening to many of the chapters I read out loud to him.

` My friend for more than 25 years is Dr. Morris Rubin, a psychologist and Doctor of Education. He encouraged me to write and pursue this my second book. He has been a good friend and, like my grandmother, thinks I can do anything I put my mind to. I would not have tackled such a job had it not been for his prodding and for the computer. The equipment allows me to write down my thoughts, then arrange the order and add more thoughts and corrections as I see fit. My friend told me to do it and that I could and so I did!

Many thanks go to Susan Muaddi Darraj at Essex Community College. She is a writing teacher and a professional editor. Susan was able to smooth the rough spots of my writing and make my words read the way I intended them. Much appreciation goes to my niece Alice Buscio for her artwork. Alice drew, in the Entertainment section of the book, the place setting. Alice is a gifted, artist and everyone who sees any of her work admires her cartooning. Thank you so much, Alice, for your contribution to this work of love and family.

The recipe section of this book took a long time to assemble and a lot of patience to make sure they were accurate. I have to thank many people who helped me to edit them. My Cousin Peg's daughter, Mary Elizabeth (Missy) Mc Fayden-Pusey, a newlywed and a teacher. She took time to do some editing just before her wedding. My friend, travel companion and contributor to my theater life, Pat King, also contributed. Many thanks, Pat. I went to many of my Haddon Fortnightly friends, most of who are retired teachers. Constance (Connie) Moncrief, a sweet lady who has been a good friend, but don't tell her I said so; Constance (Connie) Kaczorowski, a new friend, but she pitched right in when I asked for her help; Florence Merker, someone who always appreciates a hug took her time and gave her much appreciated efforts; Joan Neilson, a busy, busy woman who takes on many responsibilities, but quickly said yes when asked; my good friend Dorothy (Dot) Conover, a dear woman who is going to live to be 100 years, but never live long enough to be old; and Margaret (Marge) Triplo, a friend I made many years ago in the theater as well, and I still call her "friend" she is teaching and took time to edit my recipes. (Busman's holiday[1]) I asked my long-time friend Madge Hempsey to also help. Madge and I have been friends for many years, and she took time to lend a hand when I asked. Thanks friends, I couldn't have done it without you. Brava!

A very special thank you goes to my nephew Richard Kniffin. Rich was able to save my recipe file when my computer when crazy. All the many hours that it took to compile, review, and edit would have been lost if not for his intervention. Thank you, thank you, and thank you.

---

1 The old phase referring to a bus driver taking a holiday driving somewhere.

INTRODUCTION

Dear Family,

I have always wanted to record the stories Ma told us about her life but just never got to it. Her life, it seemed to me, centered so much on food because of taking care of so many people, all of whom came from poverty. She was always finagling how to feed them. Ma, as all her children called her, was born on the Eastern Shore of Maryland on April 12, 1881. She was my fraternal grandmother and taught me how to cook and handle food. We often had a house full of guests, mainly relatives, so I also learned to cook for a group and how to entertain. Ma had a very interesting life that contributed to her recipes.

Ma did use a cookbook for some of her recipes, but she mainly just cooked. Before I was married and getting ready to leave home, I got her to give me some of her recipes that came from her head. I put the recipes on file cards, which I still have. The cards are stained and worn from use. I want to hand these recipes, and many of my own, to my children for them to use as often as I have.

I am writing this book for my children, George Nicolas Brandt Jr. and Nicole Ruth Brandt Weal. I reached a point in my life when I thought it was time for me to write down my family recipes, so the children would know how I made some of their favorite foods. I also decided to share this book with my nieces and nephews and other family members who have enjoyed my food for a lifetime.

I was so influenced by my grandmother that it occurred to me to combine her story and her cooking into one volume. This way, everyone could learn some history of the family as well as generational cooking. It just followed that the two ideas went together: Ma's life and a cookbook. So here it is. This book records more than one hundred and fifty plus years of family history and recipes. This is not a history book but a record of stories told to me by Ma and her family. If anyone finds an inaccuracies in these stories, this is the way I remember all pf those tales told over and over so many years ago. Forgive the variations. While you read the book, I hope you'll get a sense of where we came from and how we got to where we are now. Enjoy!

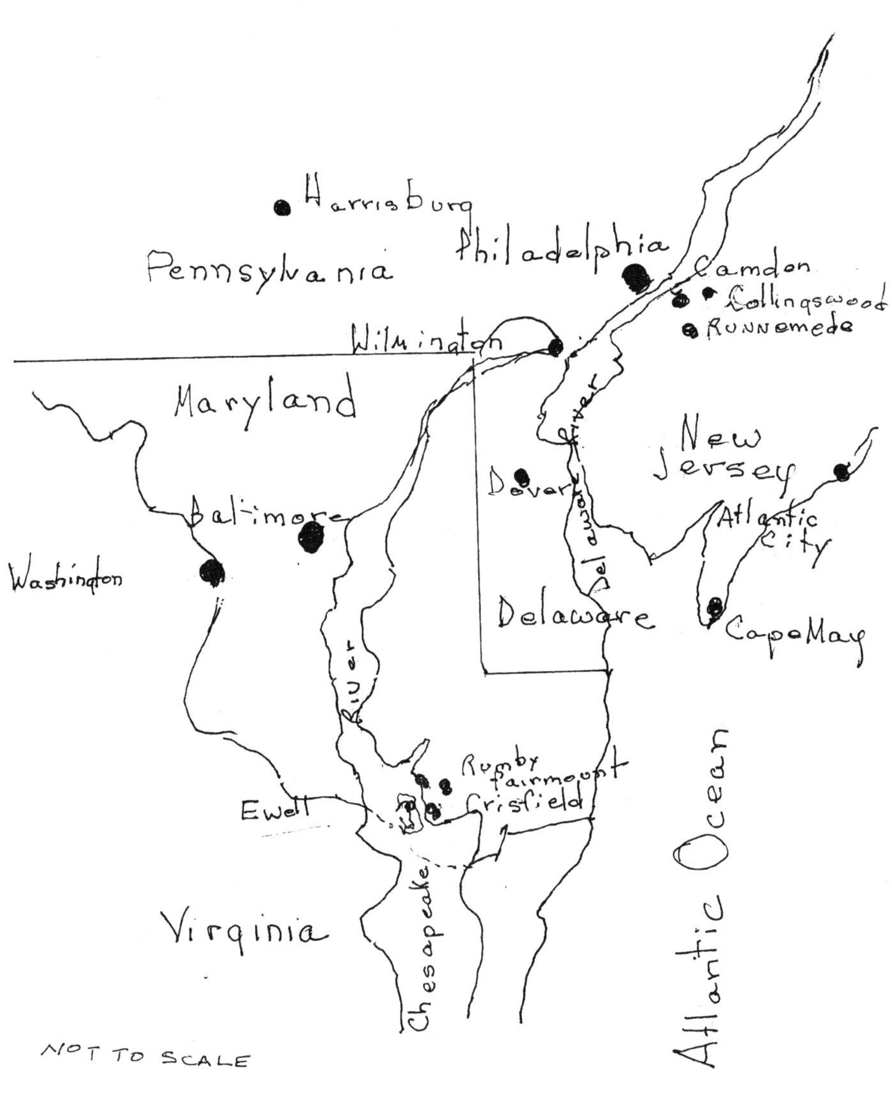

This is the road Ma followed as her life changed through out the years.

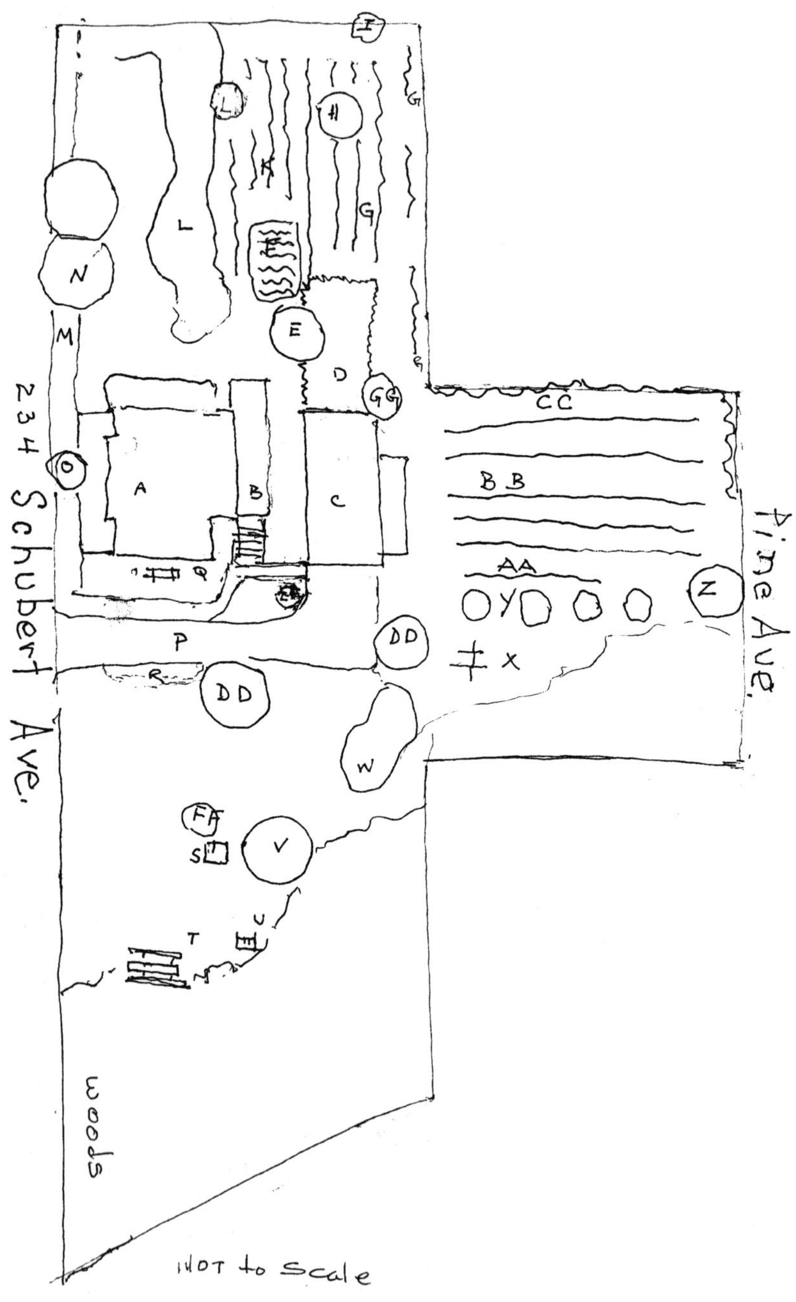

Plot of Runnemede Home and Garden

PLOT OF RUNNEMEDE HOME AND GROUNDS

A-Home
B-Back porch
C-Chicken house/ garage
D-Chicken yard
E-Apple tree
F-Strawberries
G-Berry bushes
H-Pear tree
I-Persimmon tree
J-Damson plum tree
K-Tomato, pepper, eggplant garden
L-Shrubs and flower garden
M-Banks
N-Willow trees
O-Maple tree
P-Driveway
Q-Bench swing
R-Rose garden
S-Arbor
T-Picnic table
U-Fireplace
V-Mulberry tree
W-Pond and rock garden
X-Children's swings
Y-Poplar trees
Z-Black walnut tree
AA-Asparagus and rhubarb plants
BB-Green beans, peas, corn garden
CC-Grape vine
DD-Wild Cherry Trees
EE-Pie Cherry Tree
FF-Queen Ann Cherry Tree
GG-Quince Tree

PART ONE

The Story

CHAPTER ONE

Remembering My Childhood Home

Six people lived together in an old house in Runnemede, NJ: Ma, Aunt Ruth, her daughter, Alvin, her son, and Marjorie, his wife, Alvin Jr., my brother and myself. Runnemede lies in the southwestern part of the state, not far from the Delaware River, and across the river from Philadelphia, Pennsylvania. Dad worked on the house his whole adult life to improve it and make it comfortable, unique and easier to work and live in. Dad's designs in the house included designing and making a moving chair from the first floor to the second. He used airplane steel cables, gears, pulleys, a motor, and a fold-up seat from an old Packard limousine. Although the chair was built for Ma after her heart attack when she was 75, my mother still uses the chair to get to the second floor.

Another idea was kitchen cabinets that came down to you. The cabinets were driven by hydraulics using air compression and counterweights. My father built a saucer-shaped disk in the ceiling of the family room with indirect lighting and an air-conditioning vent in it. Layers of chicken wire and pounds and pounds of plaster went into it to make the shape. The disk is still in place. Dad constructed a moving platform that went from the basement to the first floor so Ma could go down to her summer kitchen.

He thought of these things, and designed, constructed and installed all of his inventions. For several years, we did all of our cooking and ate our evening meals in the basement while Dad redesigned the upstairs kitchen. He poured and sanded the marble terrazzo counter top all in one piece, including the sink. It was quite a job. In working on the counter, he found he was allergic to the dust of the epoxy base he was sanding to create a smooth surface. He had to take time out to design a suit he could wear to allow him to work on the marble and yet breathe fresh air. Using what was available, he constructed a suit with a helmet. He was able to use a vacuum cleaner to pump air into his space suit. What a sight! He sure followed in Ma's footsteps for creativity. He finally finished the kitchen, and it was used for many years. The kidney-shaped sink that sat in the counter had to be replaced with a stainless steel one because the sink Dad constructed sprang a leak. The counter tops were replaced many years later with a Formica covering.

Like his mother, Alvin had very little formal education; he did not finish the eighth grade, and was self-taught. Dad was a sponge who read constantly, but I never saw him read a novel. He read everything about history, science, politics and current events. He remembered almost everything he ever read and could recall and apply it. He also had perfect pitch, which made him cringe at modern singers' inability to hit the notes true as they sang. They got close to the note and then tried to slur it, if they could hear or read it, which was not often. I too am sensitive to music and it is painful to listen to discord if you can hear it when you have perfect pitch.

I remember hearing a story about Dad. When he was young, there was so little money that Ma could only afford to have one outfit for him to wear to school. Each day, when he came home from school, he had to remove his school clothes and put on play clothes so that Ma could wash, dry and iron his outfit to wear again the next day. She even washed his shoelaces. She was fierce about cleanliness. I, too, always had to change into play clothes when I returned from school, but I owned more than one outfit. Ma made most of my clothes. I tried to get my children to change their clothes too, but was not always successful. I don't know if the idea of school clothes and play clothes still continues but, in Dad's time, it was a necessity.

When I was about fourteen, Dad built us a freezer. Freezers were not made for the home then, but since he worked with commercial refrigeration, he knew how they were made. It had a Formica-type material on the outside of a wooden frame, which was filled with fiberglass insulation. A sheet metal interior was formed to fit inside the frame. Dad worked in heating also, which meant sheet metal workers were available to him. There were doors on the top that we could slide back and forth. It was very large and held a lot. He also got an old water air conditioner from a funeral home. It was no longer being used, as he was installing a new unit. He installed the old one in our home so we had a fully air-conditioned house, something no one else had in the early 50s.

The house was heated by coal for years until Dad converted the heating system to oil. Playing in the coal bin in the basement was something we, the children, did. We didn't care if we got black from the coal dust. A large truck would pull up into the driveway. A long metal shoot was attached to the truck and the other end was put into the cellar window. The loud noise of a ton or so of coal racing down that metal shoot onto the floor of the basement was deafening.

When Dad was a boy, the radio was just coming onto the scene. He was fascinated with the primitive crystal radios and would build them. When I was a child, the radio had come into it full bloom, and everyone owned one or more. Dad still remembered the early crystal radio and rigged up a crystal set and put an earphone at each of the beds in the house. You could put the rather large, bulky, black earphone under your pillow and have it handy to listen to music as you went to sleep. We kept the radios for years and years under our pillows.

When I was a kid, we had well water pumped into the house. How we used the water was important. It was a shallow well and we valued the water, because the supply was not guaranteed. A well was dug by Dad a couple of times because it was running low and the water would mix with sand. If the pump stopped because of a storm, or an electric blackout, we were without water. We often stockpiled a supply of water for such emergencies. In the winter, it was not unusual to be without electricity for two weeks. We had a gas stove so we could cook, and it offered some heat. If there was snow, Ma would melt it for us to use. Dad sometimes was able to get water from the well by a hand pump. Yes, we respected water.

Eventually, city water had to be hooked up because the supply of well water began to run very low. We all thought that it was sad because we enjoyed the well water so much. It contained no chemicals and was so sweet and cold that we hated to see it go. When the family from Philadelphia came to visit, the first thing they asked for was a glass of well water. It was so much better than their water at home.

Ma, however, believed in washing everything very well, especially her chickens. She said they were the dirtiest animals because they would walk in their own manure and used that same dirt to dust their feathers. Now, the commercial farm chickens never see or touch the dirt, because they are raised on a wire grid. Ma kept chickens for eggs and for eating.

What an experience it was to watch the birds being killed. Dad would put their necks on a tree stump and chop their heads off with an axe. Sometimes, the headless chicken would run around until it fell over. When Ma slaughtered them, she did it by wringing their necks so that they didn't run around. Next they were dipped in boiling water to soften the feathers in order to be plucked. The next step was to take a few sheets of newspaper and roll them up into a tight torch. It was lit and the flame was passed over the body of the chicken to remove any small pinfeathers. Then the fowl was opened at the rectum and the entrails were removed. Sometimes a stewing hen would have eggs forming in her. Ma paid much attention to this hen and cooked the eggs inside the chicken.

Next she headed to the kitchen to run a bath for the creature. She scrubbed the bird with soap (her homemade sometimes, because "the filthy bird was not going in her pot" until it was cleaned and rinsed very, very well). Just think—all of this time, effort and energy just for a chicken dinner. Of course we always had plenty of fresh eggs.

Each week, Mr. Haines came in his old truck filled with assorted grains. He was the grain man. When I was small, he would let me carry some of the small bags of grains for the chickens. I thought I was just grand, helping the grownups. The chicken feed came in different combinations. Ma would use one of these special mixes when the chickens were sitting on their nests waiting for her chicks to hatch. The baby chicks ate another combination. All the grain came in muslin fabric bags. The muslin was printed in colorful calico prints. When Ma would find a pattern she liked, she requested more of them so she could make dresses, blouses and the aprons she always wore. One year, she saved all of her feed sacks for months, all the same pattern. She made floor length, matching dressing gowns for us three women as a Christmas present. Mother, Aunt Ruth and I all kept these robes for many years.

Ma penned up a rooster in an old car along with a couple of other chickens. Ma did that in order to feed them and restrict their activity to fatten them for slaughter. Once, when I was quite young and wanted to see the chickens in the car, I climbed up on the running board to peer in the window. Sadly, I held onto the handle of the door, which then opened. I fell on the grass, face down, and the rooster jumped on me and began to peck my head. I screamed, and Ma came running out of the house and saved me from the rooster. He was slaughtered that day, and didn't get a chance to get any fatter.

I remember we had a very large and old apple tree. One of the limbs spread out over the chicken yard. I loved to climb trees, and since we had a lot of them on the one and a half-acre property, I climbed many of them. I climbed the apple tree all the time. One day, I went out on the large limb over the chicken yard where I, unfortunately, fell off the limb into the chicken yard.

Ma had to wash me off, outside, with the hose, because I was such a mess. Luckily, I didn't break anything, and I didn't climb out on that limb again. Ma's dog "Spot" would get into the chicken yard sometimes and rub herself with the chicken manure. When she would try to come into the house, Ma would chase her outside and shame her as to what a bad dog she was. She would take the soap and water to her and scrub her down then spray her with the hose like me. Even though Spot was humiliated by the experience, she would return to the chicken yard when she got her chance.

When Ma didn't want to take care of a yard full of chickens anymore, after many years of keeping 50 to 60 of them, she killed them all over a summer and froze them in her new freezer. We ate chicken for a long time. I will never forget the smell of the hot, wet, chicken feathers, and the newspaper singeing the birds.

Ma used the gnarled apples from the old tree as flavoring in her food. We kids ate them as snacks. They were small, very hard, very juicy and tart, and we loved them. Many a summer day, the three of us, Ma, Alvin, and I, sat under this old tree. (That tree had to be removed when, years later, it was hit by lighting.) As another way of entertaining us, Ma would read to us and tell us stories to keep us quiet and still. We would play hard in the morning and early afternoon. Then, late in the afternoon, we were scrubbed, freshly dressed and our hair was brushed. My long hair was often pulled into twin braids. Sometimes the braids hung down each side of my head or they were crossed on top of my head. We had to be kept from getting dirty again so that when our parents came home from work, we were clean and settled down to greet them.

Speaking of trees, in the front yard on the banks, there were two beautiful weeping willow trees. They were beautiful to watch, as the breezes would make the limbs sway. They hung over the bank and cast a nice shadow over the lawn in the afternoon. We climbed them, of course, and would lie on the bank beneath them. They also served another purpose. Ma was very patient and consistent. We were not awfully mischievous children, but we could stray from the rules sometimes. Ma would give us two opportunities to mind her chiding. If, on the third time, she had to scold us for the some offense, our punishment was to go to the willow trees, break off a switch and take it to her. She would strip the leaves from the small flexible branch and give us a swat or two across the backs of our legs. She never did it in anger, nor did she yell. It was all done in a calm, matter-of fact manner. We cried and pleaded not to have to get the switch and not to have to bear the stinging on our legs, but what was to be was to be. She did not have to punish us this way very often, but when she said she would, she did. That was the end of that. I still loved the willow trees and was sad to see them die after a number of years of them swaying to the breezes there on the bank. Willow trees don't have long lives. Neither do poplar trees, which Aunt Ruth planted in a row down along one of her vegetable gardens. They grew tall, narrow and majestic. Neither one of these trees have a long life unlike the old oak trees that grow in my yard, some of which are over 100 years old.

CHAPTER TWO

Ma's Kitchen

In the summer Ma, Aunt Ruth, we kids and sometimes my Father would go to the neighbor farmer's fields and pick what was left after he had harvested the crops. We harvested just one crop at a time and there would be an abundance of that crop. Ma made interesting dishes from the vegetables. She tried to be inventive. Have you ever had carrot pie? It is good!

There was an abandoned pear orchard at the top of the hill, near our home, and Dad would take the old car, with running boards, up to the hill with Ma and the rest of us. We would fill up baskets with the fruit and pile them in the back seat and the trunk of the car. Dad would take Ma and the pears home in the car and we would walk down the hill to catch up with them.

They always went to the local farms and bought baskets of peaches in August. Ma often canned 100 one-quart jars of whole peaches. Leaving the stones in the peaches, whole, gave the fruit a wonderful flavor. Peaches were often purchased in two conditions. Some baskets were very ripe or they were not perfect and had to be processed right away. Sometimes with the soft fruit, Ma would sit up until one or two in the morning in order to go though all the fruit. She would find the ones that had to be used right away and processed them that night. The rest were canned as the days followed and were used to eat out of hand and make desserts.

One of the special breakfast dishes we had each August was Peach Bread. Ma took white bread and buttered slices of it and put them butter side down on baking sheets. Then she covered the bread generously with peeled, sliced peaches. Then they were sprinkled with a mixture of sugar and cinnamon and baked in the oven for about 20 minutes until the fruit was hot, the sugar melted, and the bread brown and crisp on the bottom. My addition to Ma's Peach Bread recipe is to add blueberries with the peaches or just blueberries alone. What a treat for Sunday morning breakfast, when the bread tasted like a hot fruit Danish. We knew it was August when we woke up to the smell of Peach Bread.

The better baskets of fruit that could last a few days were canned for jars of perfect fruit. Ma used her perfect fruit for gifts and special occasions. She used the pears we picked for canning as well, since they were cooking pears and not very good for eating out of hand. Each year, she would sweet pickle a few jars of peaches and pears, which were saved for holidays and company. The pickled fruit was served as a compliment to the meal. It was always a special treat when we had Ma's pickled fruit. Apples were also bought from the farm. They were not perfect and were cheaper, but for the purposes of cooking, canning, and baking, they were fine. Ma made applesauce for canning, apple pie, dumplings, fried them and stewed the apples.

Each August, Ma's kitchen was busy, from morning to night. There was water boiling in large pots. The water was needed to sterilize the jars and the lids. The sink was filled with peaches or tomatoes and boiling water was poured over them. Tea towels were put over them as they steamed for a few minutes. Cold water ran freely in the sink to stop the steaming and then the water was drained. The sink was filled with cool water to make the fruit easier to handle then the skins on the fruits easily slipped off. Next the fruits were cooked in large pots until they came to a boil. When they had simmered for a short time, they were ready to be put in the sanitized jars and capped. The kitchen was sticky, hot, and filled with jars and cooking food. The smell of fruit, sugar, and spices filled the air. The "pinging" sound was the signaling that the lids on the jars were sealing. The next morning if a jar didn't seal, the fruit had to be reprocessed or used. The jars had to sit in the kitchen until they cooled and sealed before they could be moved. Each jar then could be cleaned of any syrup or juice, and the rings tightened and moved to shelves in the large closet in the basement. Ma canned about 100 quarts of tomatoes and approximately 50 pints each year. I know that Ma canned many more fruits and vegetable in her early days, but by the time I was aware of her summer job, she had slowed down. She was also able to preserve many vegetables in the freezer, which was preferred to canning things such as green beans.

Ma would put cabbage down in a large crock with salt and vinegar to make sauerkraut. Some summers she made crocks of pickles. Soda pop was not readily available, but Ma would make root beer and Dad would use the capping machine to seal the bottles. Then we had to wait for a few weeks so the soda would develop the carbonation. The root beer was so good. It was a real treat and worth the wait.

Ma made her own pickles, relishes (chow-chow, pepper and corn relish), jams, jellies and preserves. There was a permanent supply of these things on the breakfast room table. The assorted jars and bottles were left there to be used during each meal, along with salt, pepper, butter (only home made), margarine, a glass cruet of vinegar, and a small cut glass toothpick holder with wooden toothpicks and a supply of paper napkins.

I remember when margarine first came on the market. It was packaged in a sealed plastic bag. It looked like lard because of its pale color and consistency. In the center of the bag, there was an orange-colored pellet. You squeezed it until it popped, then you kneaded the color into the white margarine. When it was thoroughly mixed, you put the bag into the refrigerator to chill. My brother and I were permitted to knead the bag.

Something that was always around the stove was a small, old saucepan with paraffin wax in it. The pan would be heated to melt the wax whenever Ma made a jar or two of jelly from some small quantity of fruit she might have. The one-inch layer of melted wax was poured on top of the jelly, then cooled and the jar was topped with a lid. This sealed the air out of the jelly. You would slip a knife down between the side of the jar and the wax, then lift the wax to one side so it could be peeled off. The wax was washed and added to the saucepan to be used again.

Ma used cooking as entertainment for my brother and myself. We were born before the invention of TV, when children had to be kept busy with many things. Ma taught me to keep a clean kitchen and clean hands and to never, never put the spoon in my mouth and then back into the pot. Both of us always kept a good supply of spoons handy, ready to be used when we cooked. She always tasted the food as she seasoned and cooked but she used a clean spoon for each taste. I have seen TV commercials where someone tastes the food with a large spoon and then puts the spoon back in the pot. Yuck! Ma would have not liked that. When Ma let us cook with her, we had to scrub our hands with soap and hot water and clean under our fingernails with a wooden toothpick. Next, we donned an apron, to cover our clothes. If you put your fingers in your mouth or in your hair, you had to wash your hands before continuing to work with the food. This habit was ingrained so deeply that today when I cook for a large crowd or prepare a lot of food, my hands get chapped from the constant washing to remove food from my hands and after I have put my fingers in my mouth.

One story Ma told was when she was first married and raising her 4 stepchildren, there was a church function. The adults were fed first and then the children. Ma was shocked and discussed as people just wiped of their dish to feed the children on. Ma said. "Oh no, that would not do for my children," and wash a dish for each of her children. This was Ma!

Ma used to tell us that she would give us a lump of bread dough so we could make our own rolls. By the time we had kneaded it, dropped it on the floor, and rolled it around, the dough was gray. We wanted to make sure we got "our own" roll, so she would mark them. She said that there was no fear of the rolls being eaten by anyone else.

My brother and I learned how to set the table and had plenty of practice because each evening the table was set for at least six, sometimes as many as twelve. We waited for our Mother to come home from work at 6:30 so we could eat dinner at 6:45. Yes, the table was set everyday, and the family gathered around it each evening. After being called to dinner, we said grace and then all the food was passed around. We all joined in as we talked about the events of the day. Many topics were discussed. Politics and current events were especially high on the list. When I was thirteen, we got a TV so we would watch the fifteen minutes of national news but this would only help to prolong the discussion. We never discussed or even mentioned anything that was considered inappropriate to talk about at the table, such as bodily functions, descriptions of illness, details of a gory crime and other unacceptable topics. Too bad that these restrictions have fallen by the wayside in many American homes. Manners that were forbidden at our table are common behavior today. Men always removed their hats when entering a building. No man would ever have sat at the table with a hat on, and never come to the table without a shirt on! You never fixed your hair at or around the table or near food or its preparation. Ma never appreciated anyone washing their hands in the kitchen sink unless it was while we were cooking. The bathroom, not the kitchen, was for bathing and washing your body and hair. Pots, pans and utensils were used only for the preparation of food and for no other purpose. All of these things I have seen violated in today's world and people accept it as permissible behavior. It wasn't in our home.

On the table each evening, we always had meat of some description, sometimes a little of various leftovers from previous meals. Food was never wasted. The exception was macaroni and cheese, which was the main course. Potatoes, one or two vegetables, and Ma's homemade bread, rolls, cornbread, or biscuits and butter were always included in the menu. Sometimes, often in the summer, we would eat a fresh salad. As I noted, the standard items were always on the table. We often had a side dish on the table such as applesauce, rhubarb or cole slaw or hot slaw. Coffee, milk and, for me, water, all completed the meal.

Ma always served dessert with dinner. She would make pie, puddings, custard, or a cake, but very often she would offer fruit, fresh if available, stewed dried prunes, applesauce, or she would open one of her jars of peaches or pears. Some of our favorite desserts were apple fluff, canned or fresh applesauce sweetened, and a meringue folded in the sauce. Gingerbread, served warm with apple fluff, was so good on a cold day. One of our favorites was canned figs. We each got one fig in the syrup. It was something we didn't have often, because figs were expensive. I wanted to eat the whole can. When the apples were in season, Ma peeled and scraped them with a spoon to make raw applesauce. She also added a little sugar and cinnamon. Whipped cream or clabber was served with it. Aunt Ruth loved clabber, but I never cared for it. It was milk that was allowed to sit out on the counter until it soured and thickened. The solid part was served with sugar sprinkled on top. Each night, all week long, we all sat down to this kind of evening meal. It was quite a spread! Saturday night was the only easy night. Sometimes, dinner would just include soup left over from Friday night and sandwiches. On Sunday, the banquet like meals would start again. Ma cooked like this until she was nearly eighty-six years old.

You could get bunches of bananas at the store for very little money if they were over-ripe. When Ma would get this over-ripe fruit she would sometimes make a banana pudding with a meringue top. Other times, she would make banana fritters and serve them with warm cornstarch pudding as a topping. Ma used this dish as a dessert. However, my family liked it so much that they wanted it for breakfast. I serve it with bacon, sausage or ham. It is very rich.

Ma's fritters were really a pancake batter to which she added fruits or vegetables. She made blueberry pancakes and used some of the blueberries to make syrup to pour over the cakes. My husband's father, Arno, made blueberry pancakes for dinner for his family of eight children each Shove Tuesday. Mother's tradition on this holiday was to make an English-style pancake. It is a very thin pancake topped with butter, sprinkled with sugar and fresh lemon juice squeezed on top. The cakes were then rolled up, and you cut down though the roll. Buckwheat cakes were another childhood favorite. Mother and I were the only ones who liked to butter the cakes and topped them with ketchup. (Don't say "eww" until you have tried it.)

The milkman delivered milk each morning. There was a metal rack on the front step were Ma would leave the clean, empty bottles and a note if she wanted anything other than her normal order. The milk came in glass bottles with cardboard lids. The milk was not homogenized, so the rich, whole cream was on top of the milk. You could see where they separated. Ma would skim the cream off the top and save it until she had enough to make butter or whipped cream. In the winter, if the bottles of milk sat outside too long, the milk would freeze and the cream would rise up out of the bottle. We children thought that was very funny. I remember Ma making butter from the cream. She would put the cream into her electric mixer and beat it. The cream would first turn into whipped cream and, as it continued to beat, it would separate into small chunks of fat. The whey had separated from the fat. She would then put it all into a cheesecloth bag and hang it up for the buttermilk to drip into a container. She would lightly salt the butter and refrigerate it. The buttermilk was used in cooking. She also made cottage cheese with the milk that she let sour and become thick. She would hang it in cheesecloth bags out on the clothesline until the liquid had dripped out and the milk had turned into curds.

Usually on Fridays, the menu consisted of soup and bread pudding. All the vegetables, starches and bits of meat leftover from the week's dinners were the base of her pot of hearty soup. The pudding was made with stale bread, cookies, cake, biscuits, the last of the cottage cheese, the end of a jar of jelly or preserves, any leftover canned fruit or some fresh fruit, some eggs, sugar and milk. If coconut, nuts, raisins or other dried or canned fruit were available, they went in too. No two dishes were ever alike but they were always hearty and good.

Because Ma came from a very sparse life and lived through the Great Depression, she learned to use everything that she could come by. Ma learned to economize very well. When her grandchildren, my brother and myself, were born after the Great Depression, she had another generation to feed, raise and teach. I remember that we were not very affluent. The adults all worked, and Ma even sold things from home, such as a line of clothing, but there was still not much money to have extra luxuries. So, when we got any treat we appreciated it. Tastykake cakes and pies were just five cents, and we thought they were the greatest things, but we could not have them too often because we couldn't afford them. Dad worked on the WPA in the 30s, digging roads and earning the high wages of $5 to $6 a week. When we were young, I recall that Dad made just $40 a week as an electrician. Five cents was a lot of money then. Ma made small pies for us to take in our school lunch and we thought we were being deprived because we couldn't have a store-bought pie. Stupid kid! Candy bars were five cents also, so we had to settle for penny candy. Off we would go to the little grocery store near by to make the hard choice of what one or two pennies could buy.

MY TURN IN THE KITCHEN

Ma and her daughter Ruth would travel to the Eastern Shore and Smith's Island to visit family and friends in November almost every year. They would be gone for a couple of weeks. People did this a lot in those times. That is why we often had relatives visiting for a few months at a time. Ma's Aunt Lucy stayed with us for a few months a couple of times. The last time she came to see us she stayed for two years. There were only a few major highways then, and it could take a good part of a day to go 175 miles. To come to our house by train or bus, our company had to go into Philadelphia, and it then took another hour from there by car or bus to get to our home. Now, we can get to Center City Philadelphia in 20 minutes and down to Crisfield in about three hours.

In my eleventh year, when the women went to Maryland, I planned the meals and cooked them for my parents, who both worked. I would have a meal on the table when mother came home from her job as a salesperson in Gimbels department store in Philadelphia. Dad worked in commercial heating, air-conditioning and refrigeration as an electrician, so he went to work early and got home in the afternoon shortly after we arrived home from school. Mother and Dad were kind and complimentary about my cooking, even though some of it was not very good. They did not discourage me.

I found that I was a natural cook. I learned well, and could imitate Ma's recipes. As I got older and Ma was unable to cook for the large family parties as easily as she had before, I was the only one she would let help her in the kitchen. As more time passed, I often made her traditional dishes like steamed fruitcake, chocolate potato cake and handled most of the preparation for large groups.

THE GARDEN

Aunt Ruth was a gardener. She loved it. She taught herself how to grow wonderful flowers, shrubs, trees, vines, fruits, and vegetables. She studied organic gardening and she was devoted to its methods. What food scrapes and peelings were not given to the dogs went to her compost pile. All the grass clippings as well as what was left of the plants after the crops were harvested went into the compost pile. One year, she had a large pile of horse manure put in the back of her garden. She covered it with tarpaper and dirt. She let it set like this for a year or so. The manure turned into beautiful, sweet smelling-soil to be used in the garden. I remember one February when Aunt Ruth had the yard covered with horse manure. It was supposed to make the grass grow better. The manure dissolved into the ground, as well as grass seed that was sown, with the rain and the snow. Unfortunately, we had warm weather that week and all you could smell inside and outside the house (for that matter, the whole neighborhood) was the very strong smell of the horse manure. She was so embarrassed by the smell, but we did have beautiful, thick, dark green grass that summer.

Each summer, we had a supply of Aunt Ruth's wonderful Jersey beefsteak tomatoes, yellow miniature plum tomatoes, peppers, corn, eggplant, peas, green beans, wax beans lima beans, rhubarb, asparagus, onions, garden lettuce, cabbage, kale, and collard greens. She had blueberry, raspberry, blackberry, boysenberry, and gooseberry bushes, as well as those wonderful, sweet strawberry plants. We had about 150 feet of purple Concord and white Niagara grapevines. Damson plum, pear, cherry, (pie and Queen Ann) and quince trees were spotted all around the house. As children, we had a good supply of snacks each summer. Ma used the grapes to make juice. Some of the juice was made into jelly. The whole grape was made into grape jam. The pulp was ground up with the skins for the base of the jam. In an old cookbook Ma gave me, I found a recipe for grape pie. It is still a big hit when I can get enough grapes. If I get a lot of grapes, I make several pies and freeze them. It does take a little work to make this delicious treat, but it is well worth the effort.

There were wild cherry, mulberry and persimmon trees on the property, and also a very large patch of wild blackberries. I had purple feet all summer from walking in my bare feet over the mulberries and wild cherries that dropped from the very large trees.

Ma went into the blackberry patch to pick the berries one summer. She used the wild fruit to make her wonderful duff, a steamed pudding. She disturbed a hive of bees. They stung her so badly that the only way she could get relief from the stings was to sit in the bathtub with cool water and Epsom salts. Thankfully she was not allergic. Years later, my mother had the same incident happen to her as she gardened, but she had a bad reaction to the bees and is still afraid of getting stung. As a child it seemed I was stung each summer. I was stung a coupe of times on my feet because I was always in by bare feet. It didn't seem like summer if I wasn't stung and Alvin didn't get poison ivy.

Other things that grew on the property included patches of wild strawberries, which were small but very sweet. In the spring, Ma would pick young lambs quarter, dandelion leaves, and dock, all wild greens. She steamed them with a bit of butter. They were very tender with a slight bitter taste. With all of these fruits and vegetables available all spring, summer, and even into the fall, Ma was kept busy cooking, canning, pickling, preserving and freezing.

You must realize that Ma did all of this preserving during the summer as the crops came off and still cooked a full evening meal every day. Plus she feed herself and the two of us children including any company that might be with us at the time, breakfast and lunch. Yet she had time to take care of us as well.

Dad also built a very large dehydrator in the kitchen. It was under the counter like a large appliance. Ma dehydrated fruits and vegetables and stored them for the winter. She also dehydrated some of Aunt Ruth's beautiful flowers. We used them for arrangements, decorations, and for making gifts such as flower arrangements under glass.

CHAPTER THREE

The Beginning

Hattie Smith Beauchamp was born on April 12, 1881 to Virginia McDaniel and George Beauchamp; she was their first child. Were most of the family made their living on the water, George was a cobbler. The literal French translation of Beauchamp is "beautiful field." In this part of the Eastern Shore, this beautiful name is pronounced Beechman. If you ask me why, I must say, "I haven't got a clue!" One explanation might be found in one of the old-time sayings the county people used when someone was acting above themselves in either word or action. It was said that they were "putting on airs!" Maybe pronouncing this name with a French flair might have seemed like "putting on airs."

When I try to put the date of Hattie's birth in perspective, I realize that the Civil War was just over, the Native Americans were being put on reservations out west, and many Americans were clamoring to "civilize" the wild, wild west. There were only 38 states in the union and President James Garfield was in office the year of Hattie's birth. Sadly, he was assassinated that September, and Chester Arthur became President to fill out the four years. Think about that in relationship to today. She lived to see me as an adult and to relate all the experiences she did. I am attempting to recall and record them all.

The second child born to the Beauchamp's was Margaret (Maggie), then Harold. Finally in 1890, six months after Linda was born, their father, George died of typhoid fever, and he was 32 years old. Hattie was just 9 years old.

Virginia was left with four children all under 9 years of age and there was no such thing as welfare to help them. Furthermore, women did not work outside the house.

One of Virginia's cousins lived in Fairmont, just a few miles from Rumbly, Maryland, where Hattie was born. The cousin needed help with her young children so Hattie was hired. She was sent to live in Fairmont to live with them and to help run the household. She would get up each morning and start the fire in the kitchen stove and the fireplace, pumped water and carried it to the house to be put on to heat. She would shuck a couple of bushels of corn for the pigs, and then start breakfast. If time allowed, she grabbed some breakfast for herself. Then, and only if she finished her jobs each morning could she go to school. She would run the mile and a half to a small one-room schoolhouse by the side of the road. Ma said she was always afraid she would be late. Sometimes she was, but she was able to finish the fourth grade.

With the little bit of formal education Ma got, she learned to read everything. She was a great speller, and her handwriting was beautiful. She knew a lot about history and kept up with the times. She knew the latest politics, news, fads and fashions. She read all the time, both books and newspapers. Hattie kept herself informed and educated by her own means. She lived in a time in history that she saw such an unbelievable change in society. Being born after the Civil War, living though the Gibson girl fashion to the mid 1960s, so much happened. She witnessed electricity come and grow into electronics, SkipJack sailing ships to space ships, buggies to Buicks, deaths from simple colds or viruses to antibiotics. Ma lived though it all and grew and learned and adjusted to the changing technology, ideas and morals of society. She was not a stick in the mud. She was a progressive. Ma was against the death penalty; she thought that criminals should work and earn money that would help keep them while they were jailed and the rest of the money to go their victims. She believed a woman should have equal rights and chances and that she should have a choice to determine what she does with her own body. She felt that a woman should be responsible for herself, but it was her choice to do with her body as she saw fit. She said she would never have had an abortion, but she didn't feel she had the right to make that decision for others. She did see women get the vote but not the right to choose. Being from a Southern state to favor the right to vote for everyone in the 1940s and 1959s was progressive, to say the least, but that was her feeling. Unfortunately, these ideas did not set well with all the members of the extended family and that would be one of the topics of heated conversation at family gatherings.

Back in Fairmont, as a child, when she returned from school she had to help the women of the house and tend to the children. She helped to get the evening meal and then cleaned up after everyone. After all of this work, the little child could study her lessons and go to bed. (Remember she was nine years old.) For all of this work, she received room and board and three dollars a month, which was sent to her mother.

After working there for awhile, the cousin's husband fondled her. He was the local minister, and he had her in his carriage as he went visiting his parishioners. She had to fight off his advances until they got back to the house. She never went with him again and, when she could reach her mother, she told her what happened and that was the end of that job.

Next she was sent to Smith's Island, Maryland, an island in the Chesapeake Bay. It lies twelve miles off the coast of the Eastern Shore, Maryland at Crisfield. Rumbley is about 30 miles from Crisfield, which was a long carriage ride from home. Then there was the 12-mile voyage over the turbulent waters of the Chesapeake Bay to Smith's Island. She was sent again, away from her mother and her siblings, to work in a person's home, doing menial tasks as well as taking care of children. She was very good and loving to the children, something she was always great at doing all of her life. She was able to give a lot of love, patience, kindness, joy, innocence of childhood and understanding, the things she needed herself. As she grew, she worked for several other people on the Island.

One of the stories she used to tell us showed how some people treated children who were in their employment. Many adults didn't place much value on them because they were only children. This particular woman was very rough on this little girl who had come to work in her home and made her work very hard. One day Hattie was sitting on the back step of this house where she was working. She was playing and joking with one of the children she was responsible for. Just being kids! The woman of the house didn't like what she was doing, so she walked up behind her, reached over her and hit her square in the face. What a shock! Blood squirted out of Hattie's nose and went down the front of her dress. She was yelled at and told to go clean herself up. She did that, but she rolled the bloody dress up in a ball and hid it under the porch steps. She said that she didn't know why she did this, but she thought it was the right thing to do. Her mother was able to visit Hattie and when the woman complained about her and what trouble she was, Virginia knew that Hattie was a mannerly, hardworking, child who gave no one a hard time. Because of this reputation, her mother was surprised at this report. Virginia asked what Hattie had to say for herself. Hattie ran and got the dress and unrolled it for her mother to see. Hattie went home with her mother that day.

Virginia loved her children, but it was very hard to find the money to raise them. Fishing, crabbing, and oystering was the local income in this tiny village on the Eastern Shore and, for that matter, the surrounding area. The land was used for farming, mostly personal farming, and they sold what they had excess of.

Virginia's sister, Mary McDaniel, married a man by the name of Daniel Blake, Uncle Dan. They had 3 children, Fred, Arintha (Rinthe), and Daniel Arthur (Arthur). Hattie and her brother and sisters were their first cousins. A few years after George died, Virginia's sister Mary also died, so she decided to marry her brother-in-law, Daniel Blake. Now Hattie and her sibling became half brothers and sister to their first cousins. As time went on, the Blakes had three more children, Rozzie, Medford, and William Ethridge (Bill). So their children were, as they use to say "yours, mine and ours", ten children in this family. The "cousins" were the oldest of the children, so they were addressed as Cousin Fred, etc. The new Blake children were the youngest of the family and were addressed by their first names. Ma was addressed as "Sissy" by her younger Blakes' siblings and, years later, their children called her "Aunt Sissy." Her brother, sisters and their children called her Hattie and Aunt Hattie as did her cousins (stepsiblings).

The second Blake family was growing not too many years before Hattie, Maggie, Linda and Harold were having their own families. For this reason, the uncles and aunts were not much older then some of their nieces and nephews.

Meanwhile, back to Smith's Island. Hattie had a job with Cap'n Ellsworth Thomas Evans and his wife, Kitty Guy. The Evans couple had three children, Emory, Annie, and Edna. Hattie grew very fond of the children and the wife. The Cap'n was not very visible as he was usually on his SkipJack sailing ship out on the Chesapeake. He fished, crabbed, oystered, and transported crops in the summer and other cargo in the winter to Baltimore, Philadelphia, and other points north.

Mrs. Evans became pregnant again and was very ill. She suspected that she might die and made Hattie promise to take care of her children if she did. Hattie loved them all and made a promise she would need to fulfill. Ellsworth was born prematurely and his mother died shortly after. Ellsworth was so small that he had to be carried around on a pillow for several months. Remember that this was at the end of the nineteenth century. Hattie felt that the only way she could fulfill her promise, to care for the children, was to marry their father. Young and single females could never live alone in the home of a widower. Hattie did not love him, since she hardly knew him. He, of course, needed someone to take care of the children, and a sweet, innocent, beautiful, blond-haired, young girl of 17 was a very welcome prize. Cap'n Tom was 34 years old.

Hattie had fallen in love with a man on the mainland. He was helpful to her and her family, which became important when her husband didn't provide very well for her. Mr. Bradshaw owned a general store and was able to supply them with the necessities they needed to survive. When Hattie decided to make this great sacrifice to marry a man she had little feeling for the mainland gentleman was crushed. I don't believe he ever got over it. I know Ma never did. He married, and Hattie and his wife became lifelong friends. I believe the wife knew of the love between the couple and honored it. Ma's friends never had children, and he seemed to think that the sun rose and set with his wife.

Even as a child, I remember seeing Ma and him together as older people and I always sensed an unspoken attachment between them (his wife was still living). He treated me as if I was his grandchild. I remember going to his beautiful home and to his store in Crisfield. I got bags of goodies, as much as I wanted. I remember seeing the locomotive arriving on the tracks in front of his store, and it was the largest thing I had ever seen. The train stopped there because it would otherwise go into the bay. The tracks ran right down the middle of town. I had never seen such a thing.

Hattie married Cap'n Tom. Their wedding day was June 1, 1898. She wore a blue dress, with mutton leg sleeves and a long sash. Because she was marring a widower, she thought that blue was more appropriate than white. She carried flowers that were cut from the garden and fields. The bouquet contained white roses, calla lilies, orange blossoms and baby's breath, tied up with a big blue bow. I was married sixty-five years later on Ma's anniversary. I wore white and my attendees, Aunt Ruth and my sister-in-law, Martha Lee Davis, wore blue. On their arms, they carried calla lilies. I carried a bouquet of white roses, gardenias and blue baby's breath. The bouquets were tied with blue ribbons. Ma was very honored that I based the theme of my wedding on hers. She was not able to go to the ceremony but was present at the reception, which was held in her yard.

As Hattie became a new wife and mother, she became more aware that Cap'n Tom was not a domesticated man. He had few graces, manners, and could not read or write. One of the first things she did was to teach him how to write his name. "How can a man conduct business if he cannot sign his name?" she said. She taught him how to read basic words. Though the years, she taught him some graces, but not many.

Hattie set to working with her new stepchildren. Ellsworth had to be nursed to survive. This caring he never forgot, and would brag how she worked so hard to see that he lived. He always gave thanks to his Ma; after all, she was the only mother he ever knew. Hattie became Ma to all the children. The oldest was only four or five years younger than she was, but they always treated her as their mother until they died. Hattie had to become a farmer to support her new family. Most of the people had gardens and a few animals. She learned to cook, can, and pickle. She had an ever-plentiful seafood supply, rockfish, oysters, blue crabs, both soft and hard shell, and clams, were some of the choices, as well as many fish and waterfowl, which are now not available in the Chesapeake River.

In 1903, as two American men made their way from San Francisco to New York in the first automobile trip across America, Ma worked day to day with no electricity, autos, phones, or any modern conveniences. This twenty-two year old young woman was raising her four stepchildren, tending a few animas, keeping a home, sewing, cooking. preserving, growing her own vegetables as the world, in a new century, was growing outside her grueling, small, simple life.

Smith Island supplied the main land with picked crabmeat, fresh hard and soft-shell crabs, and oysters, whole or shucked. The most expensive restaurants in the cities of Washington, Baltimore, Annapolis, Wilmington, Philadelphia and even New York depended on the island seafood for many years.

Ma kept chicken and pigs and at slaughtering time, in the fall, she processed a whole pig. Some of the different uses of the pig were pickled pig's feet, souse, sausage, and scrapple. The feet were scrubbed, soaked, and boiled with spices and vinegar, then set aside so the spices and vinegar could penetrate the bony, fatty feet. The gelatin in the bones would cause the juices to thicken into a gelatinous substance. Souse was made much the same way but chopped onions were added to the odds and ends of the pork, like the tongue, and when cold, it could be sliced. I remember Aunt Ruth saying that she hated pig-slaughtering time. A man would come to the island to do the killing. The pigs would squeal and squeal as if they knew their fate. She said that when she got older, she often left the island until all of the slaughtering was done.

By the time I was around, I saw Ma make these things, but she used meat bought for that purpose. Her scrapple was anything but scraps. She would use the less tender or less expensive part of the pork, and a pork roast and liver was always used as well as a whole chicken. The meat was cooked in water in a large pot until it fell off the bone. The meat was removed from the broth, cooled so it could be pulled off the bones, cut into pieces, then put into the manual meat grinder. Ma's little fox terrier dog, Spot, would sit under the table as Ma or one of us would turn the handle of the grinder that was clamped to the edge of the kitchen table. The juice would drip out of the machine and on to the floor. Spot was in dog heaven as she lapped the juices up off the floor. After the meat was ground, it was returned to the broth and brought to the boil. Then Ma carefully and very slowly added white corn meal, spice, and flavoring into the hot pot until it thickened. The mixture was poured into pans to set and cool, then placed in the refrigerator. What a wonderful fall or winter treat.

I liked the scrapple cold, served on buttered bread and topped with ketchup. Ma usually sautéed the meat in butter until it was brown and crisp on each side. We would have it for any of the meals and ate it with ketchup. The scrapple had no preservatives and had to be used in about a week. I still like scrapple but the store-bought type isn't even close to Ma's special homemade kind.

Ma's sausage consisted of ground pork fried with added spices. She sometimes added the spices to the raw meat and formed them into patties. She often made pickled pigs feet and souse when we were kids. These special items were used for lunch or as snacks.

When Ma lived on the island, meals were hardy and she used what was available, something she continued the rest of her life. One of the things some islanders ate for breakfast was fried bread and yellow longhorn cheese melted in their coffee. It was all served with homemade preserves. Bread dough was fried in small pieces until it puffed up and browned. They made the coffee very hot and dropped chunks of cheese into the cup for it to melt. In a few minutes the cheese became soft and could be spooned onto the fried bread and topped with preservers, syrup or molasses. Yum! This is something that would stick to your ribs, especially when you had to get up early in the morning and head out by four AM on that cold river and bay. The men pulled crab pots up from the bottom of the water or pulled oyster racks up to dump the shells on the decks of the boats. It was very hard, backbreaking work and the fishermen had to be fortified with fuel for such work.

After ten years of marriage, Hattie and the Cap'n had a child of their own, Virginia Ruth (Ruth). Next came Homer William (Homer or Bill), then eight years after Virginia, Alvin Strauss was born. The first two were born on the island, but Alvin was born in Baltimore. Her husband's children grew up on the island. Two moved away to other parts of Maryland and married, and had children. Edna married and became a Sommers. Annie and Ellsworth stayed forever on the island, where they married and had children. Annie married Daniel Sommers and had three daughters, Lucille, Nina Ruth, Eloise, and one son Eugene. Ellsworth married Ada Middleton and they had a son. Most of their children lived and died on the island too. Some left the island and made their lives on the mainland.

CLOTHING IN A LIFETIME

Ma sewed very well, by necessity I am sure. All the children she had to take care of forced her to learn to sew. Some of the stories she told were about the mode of dress people wore throughout her lifetime. I remember her describing the Gibson girl era, when the dress sleeves were very puffy at the shoulders, but tight from the elbows to the wrist. It took six or seven yards of fabric to make each sleeve. Remember the fabric was only 24 to 36 inches wide in those days. There were yards and yards of fabric in the gathered skirt that had extra fullness at the back. The skirts reached to the floor, sometimes with a slight train in the back. Ma said that a horsehair brush binding was put under the hems of the dress to keep the hems from rubbing on the floor and wearing out. The binding was changed if it wore out. Cotton, wool, and linen were the fabrics she used for most dresses, because silk was much too expensive. The dresses were used for many years and the women did not own very many. Cotton was used for the day dresses. Wool, for the winter, and cotton and linen, for the summer were used for best dresses. If you have ever seen the inside of the old homes, there is very little closet space and what is there is shallow. This was because they didn't have a lot to put in them.

Under her dress, a woman wore several petticoats, long bloomers, a chemise that was worn under the corset, and a camisole that was worn over the corset. Stockings and high-buttoned shoes were all a part of this ensemble. The underwear was made of cotton, and it had to be starched and ironed. The petticoats and camisoles had rows and rows of ruffles. If they could afford it, they also featured rows and rows of lace. The underwear was often embroidered. Ma wore layered clothing all of her adult life. As the skirts shortened, the layers of clothing still persisted. Aunt Ruth was a young woman in the time of the flappers, in the 1920s, but even then, women wore many layers of clothing.

Ma talked so much about her long dresses and her leg of mutton sleeve, so called because of the shape, that I could just envision her. She would be bright and sparkling with her 18 inch waist, corsets, blond hair piled atop her head, swinging that skirt around with a layer or two of petticoats, working and tending to her children and home. She was still feisty in her 60s when I remember her, and she was that way until her death at 86, still taking care of her home and family.

Up until the 1960s when Ma died, each morning she would arise and put on an undershirt and long—legged panties. Then she put on a full, boned corset that was laced and hooked. She wore nylon stockings that were hooked to the corset. Then she donned a full slip, a cotton dress and a full apron that wrapped all the way around her, covering her dress completely. The dress and the apron were starched and ironed each day. She wore laced-up black; chunky heeled shoes, summer and winter. In the summer, her shoes for dress up were white, chunky-heeled, laced-up shoes. She wore a wristwatch and, when she dressed for a special occasion, she would wear a small brooch and maybe small, clip-on earrings and a strand of pearls.

Ma's hair was blond and it stayed blond all of her life, except in the front, where it turned white as she aged. She always had long hair and she wore it in a French twist in the back and fluffed up in the front around her face. I think she wore it this way most of her life. I know she braided it at night to sleep in, and each morning she brushed it very well, piled it up on her head, and affixed it with hairpins and bobby pins. She used a very fine hair net to cover the front of her hair. She used to talk about her Aunt Mary's hair being auburn and long, and she would comb it with her fingers and pile it on her head in the Gibson girl style. Women prided themselves on long, lovely hair in those days. Summer and winter, Ma dressed the way I have described every day. She stayed dressed that way all day and never took any of it off until it was time to go to bed. The only exception was that she would take her apron off after dinner when she wasn't planning to work anymore but I never even saw her take her shoes off unless she put on slippers. This was just a way of life. I know I would never be able to live that way and I don't think women ever will again. I live and work in T-shirts, jeans and walking shoes. I cannot imagine myself in a matron dress even at the age of 85. I am sure I will be dressing casually in my everyday life and dress in modern dress for other occasions forever.

CHAPTER FOUR

Camp Meetings

Two weeks of camp meeting were held each summer on Smith's Island. A large tent was erected on an empty lot somewhere near the church in Ewell. There are two towns on Smith Island, Ewell and Rhodes Point. There is a third part, Tylerton, which used to be called Drum Point, a separate island off Smith's Island but one that is considered part of the island. For the two weeks, religious meetings were held daily in the tent. People came to the island and stayed with family and friends or some people offered bed and board in the resident's homes. Ma always had people often the quest Evangelist to board in her home. The table was set for the three meals for a house full of guests. A morning meal might consist of large platters running over with fried oysters or soft-shell crabs, pork chops, ham, and eggs. Homemade rolls or biscuits and often her cinnamon buns were added to the abundance. Homemade fig preserves from wild fig trees that grew on the island, honey, jellies and preserves, were all on the table. This meal was topped off with pots of coffee. Lunch featured more platters of food and soup. Dinner included dishes running over with vegetables, potatoes, fried chicken, and baked fish, roast beef, or pork, as well as homemade breads and desserts. Pies, cakes, puddings, and fruit were some of the choices. Ma prided herself on setting an impressive table.

Two of the stories I remember about camp meeting were these. On the first Sunday dinner of camp meeting, her table was laden with food. One of the dishes was a big platter of fried chicken. She called everyone to dinner and, as she entered the dining room before the company, a neighbor's cat was in the middle of her table, chewing on a chicken leg. Her cats were never allowed to jump on the table or counters. She quickly picked the cat up and threw it out of the dining room door, then hurriedly put the leg back on the platter just as everyone came into the room. She saw to it that she got the leg and no one ever knew about the cat. The other story was about one of these camp meeting dinners when my grandfather was home. As everyone gathered around the table, preacher and all, Cap'n Tom drew himself up and announced, "Hattie, where's your butter knife?" Hattie had no butter knife, and he knew it. Hattie was so embarrassed and mortified! After this incident, Hattie insisted that he buy her a butter knife. The question from grandfather was used in the family when any issue of etiquette arose; "Hattie, where's your butter knife?" was the joke. We always had a butter knife in my childhood home.

In the 1950s, I remember going to Smith Island to camp meeting. We dressed up in hats, gloves, high-heeled shoes and matching bags like everyone did in those days. It was so hot and humid, and there was no breeze. The island is like that in the summer if there is no air coming off the water. The island is surrounded by marshes and is barely above sea level. This does not make for a cool summer. But the experience was interesting, and the family was still feeding everyone very well.

I remember that the families often built their homes next door or close to each other. When Ma, Aunt Ruth and myself stayed for a week or so, we each stayed in a different home. At night, we would get into our nightwear and visit with each other in one of the homes. I just thought that it was so neat. Running from house to house in the dark in my jammies! It was so comfortable and cozy to sit up late, visiting with family, listening to stories and reminiscing.

Many houses had a summer kitchen, a building separate from the house, which sometimes included a wooden walkway between them. The small building was a shell, with just the 2x4-stud construction uncovered inside. It had large windows, a basic kitchen and a large table with many chairs. The canning, pickling, and preserving was done here in the summer, and crabs were also boiled here. We would often have an evening of blue hard shell crabs, fresh from the bay. The table was spread with a thick covering of newspapers. The cooked crabs were piled in the middle. There was a pitcher of ice tea, saltine crackers, tools for cracking the crabs and small bowls of vinegar on the table. You cracked the crabs and picked the meat out dipped it in the vinegar, and put it on the cracker, then you washed it down with sweet iced tea. Many paper napkins were available for this messy job. Of course, the women were so proficient in the picking of the crabs because many of them worked in the crab shanties, picking crabs for the cannery. I, who had to be shown how to pick the crustacean, was very, very slow, but I loved the adventure.

To have a crab boil today costs a fortune, especially when one buys a bushel of Maryland blue hard crabs. I don't enjoy cooking the crabs, because I have to throw them in the boiling water while they are still alive. Crabs need to be alive in order to use them, even the soft-shell ones. You have to clean them while they are living, then cook them. I lose my appetite after this experience. I watched Ma do it but have never followed in her footsteps.

I go back to Maryland in order to get soft crabs that are cooked properly. They clean them well, drench them in flour, and pan-fry them in butter until they are brown and the legs are crisp. To cook them any other way would be to do the lovely creatures an injustice. Ordering crab cakes in local restaurants are disappointing because they are made poorly in most every other state other than Maryland. Others do not know how to treat the crustaceans well. A simple recipe of crabmeat with an egg, some mayonnaise and a little flavoring, sautéed in butter as patties, is the best way to taste the delicate flavor of crab. Only someone who has never tasted crab cooked to perfection would smother the delicate crab flavor with filling, bell peppers, pimento, and breading. With the high cost of blue crab, it is a waste to distort it with extra frills that camouflage and overpower the great and delicate flavor.

Camp Meeting is still held on Smith's Island each summer and is still quite an event. People come from near and far to meet on the Island for this summer ritual.

CHAPTER FIVE

Christmas

Christmas was a fun time. The preparation for the holidays started in September and continued through December each year. First, the damson plums were put down to ferment so that we'd be able to eat them on Christmas morning with Ma's hot rolls. When the plum tree no longer bore fruit, she used large black grapes for fermenting. She had a gallon jug in which the fruit was layered with sugar. The jar was sealed and put in the back of a cupboard to age. Every week or so, she would stir the fruit. What a treat we had on Christmas morning! We children were able to have only a small bowl of fermented fruit. We were children and the fruit had developed an alcohol base; even after we added some water to the juice, it was still strong, so we never had much at one time.

Each fall, the house was torn apart. All the curtains were taken down, the rugs rolled up and the furniture moved. Then, sometimes the hardwood floors were sanded and refinished but definitely waxed and polished. Walls and woodwork were scrubbed and also painted every few years. Everything was cleaned, polished and returned to its place for the winter arraignment. Fresh window decorations were put up along with newly covered pillows everywhere. The decorative objects, such as the dining room centerpiece and candlesticks, were changed each season.

In the spring, much of this ritual was repeated. Ma said they did this on the Island each year. In the spring, the floors were left bare with straw mats scattered over them. Heavy drapes and rugs were used for the winter. The rugs were hung over the clothesline and beaten with a rug beater to remove the season's accumulation of dirt and sand. I also remember Ma talking about the wooden kitchen floors, which were cleaned, with milk. Milk was mopped onto the floors to clean them and to give them a coating from the fat in the milk. Then straw was spread over the floors to catch any drippings. It was a simple task to sweep the straw out to clean the floor and to sprinkle it with a fresh covering.

When I started to keep house, I thought you only cleaned twice a year because that was all I remembered. Ma said she didn't have much of a childhood and that she wanted us to be free of daily chores. I really did not see the day-to-day maintenance of the house. What did I know? Cleaning was not part of my childhood, but I soon learned that you had to clean more than twice a year.

Before Thanksgiving, the fruitcake was assembled and baked, which was a three-day event. Mother brought the candied fruit home from the markets in the Reading Terminal in Philadelphia. The candied orange and lemon rinds, pineapple slices, and citron peels were all whole rinds or large chunks of fruit. We had to cut up all the pounds of candied fruit along with a couple pounds of raisins. Then came the nuts. The walnuts, pecans, almonds, Brazil and hazelnuts all had to be cracked, picked, chopped, and measured. Then all the fruit and nuts were drenched in a cup of flour and mixed well in a large, black roasting pan. It was set-aside until the next day. The next morning, we would get up and mix the batter that was poured over the fruit and nuts, and then the mixture was stirred with a large spoon. The batter was large; it contained nine eggs and filled the electric mixer's large mixing bowl. The batter was then poured into a large pan with a jar inverted in the center. The pan was then put inside a large pot with hot water filled halfway up the baking pan.

The cake steamed like this for five hours. Hot water had to be periodically added, so we did not stray away from the kitchen for very long. After the steaming, the cake was removed to the oven, where it baked for about an hour, and then it had to cool overnight.

The next morning, the cooled cake got a bath of rum and brandy, which was then covered tightly and set in a cool, dark place. It was basted with a jigger or two of rum and brandy each week until it was cut on Christmas Eve, after the tree trimming. I still follow this tradition and, although I used to make three of these cakes each year for the family, I had to find a less time-consuming recipe. I still make the yearly treat and, sometimes, I make extra to share it with the family.

Thanksgiving comprised of a typical dinner of turkey, stuffing and a table full of vegetables. Ma and Aunt Ruth were back from Maryland by Thanksgiving, and they brought home lots of fresh seafood with them. We usually had fresh oysters on the half shell or sometimes the oysters were scalloped with large thick Undeea crackers and baked. What a treat! Pies, cake, fresh fruit and nuts were served for dessert. Ma sometimes made her own mincemeat; I have made it also. The homemade mincemeat is a lot of work, but the result is delicious. My maternal grandmother also made her mincemeat from scratch. The old recipes actually called for meat and suet.

Following Thanksgiving, the preparation for the Christmas holiday really started. Cooking, sewing, ironing the linens, and changing the furniture to accommodate the Christmas decoration all took place. Of course, homemade gifts were in the works all year long, all planned to be ready for Christmas.

Sometime after Thanksgiving, cookies and Ma's favorite chocolate potato cake were made. The cake was very rich, like the fruitcake. Served in thin slices. The cooked, white potato in the cake keeps it moist. Between the cake and the icing, the recipe calls for seven ounces of baking chocolate. Wow!

A large tree was put in the dining room in the corner about a week or so before Christmas. The decoration took several days to do. First, the lights went on the tree. We knew we were growing up because we were allowed to put the tinsel on the tree. Aunt Ruth said that each strand of tinsel had to be put on separately. The tinsel was made of metal so it would hang very well from the branch if it were unobstructed. You started at the back and center of the tree, and worked out, around and up the tree. Sometimes, we kids got tired and bored, so we often threw the tinsel in clumps on the tree. Of course, the adults had to take it all off and put it on one strand at a time. Then the balls and other decorations were placed all over the tree and a star on the top. It was always a beautiful tree.

In the adjoining room to the dining room, a four-foot by eight-foot plywood platform was set up for the trains. In the living room, the fireplace featured stocking hung and fresh evergreens from the yard decorated the mantle piece. The stairs to the second floor in the living room were often covered with the fresh greens, and pinecones we gathered from the yard and ribbons and sometimes tinsel. Centerpieces for the dining and living room tables were all homemade from winter cuttings. Sometimes, a wreath or a group of branches were made from the garden greens to hang on the front door. Each year, Aunt Ruth would gather her clippings and make a blanket to put on Uncle Homer's grave. On few Christmases, the family let me paint the glass in the front door with a Christmas decoration. I used Bon Ami cleanser powder made into a paste to cover the glass. I would draw a picture in the cleanser and painted the glass with poster paint. I painted the pictures on the inside, so I had to paint the picture in reverse by putting the details in first. Then the background colors were filled in around them. I loved doing this; it was a lot of fun. In the fall, in town, the storekeepers let school children paint the large store windows with Halloween pictures using the same technique. This tradition went on for years. As an adult, when we had a business in town the school children still got permission to paint the windows yearly.

One Christmas, the family wanted to surprise my brother and me. After we had finished the tree and trains were set, we had our fruitcake and went to bed to wait for the morning. All night, the adults worked to undo most of the tree in order to put the newest thing, bubble lights, on the tree. Bubble lights look like multicolored candles set on a holder. The candle part is glass filled with colored liquid. The light is in the holder. When the heat from the bulb reached the right temperature, the liquid began to bubble. They were fascinating to watch. After putting on the new lights, then they had to put everything back on the tree. Dad removed the train platform with the Lionel trains, and put a new one up with HO trains. He laid the track and made a brand new platform for the trains. They had just gotten to bed when we were waking up.

In our Christmas morning tradition, the first thing to do was to eat breakfast in the breakfast room. It was a big breakfast. To eat eggs, ham or bacon, juice, the fermented fruit, hot biscuits, jellies, fruitcake, cookies, and coffee was typical. Dad was allowed to retrieve our stockings from the living room and we would unwrap each of the small gifts while we waited for breakfast, but we were dying to get to the dining room and the presents. Ma said that when she was a child, they got just a stocking with just one small toy, maybe a small sack of hard candy and some nuts. That was all there was. For just a short time, when her father was living, he would light the small candles on the tree to the children's delight. It was, of course, unsafe for the candles to burn for long. When my mother was a child, her old stocking was hung on the foot of her bed. Then, in the morning, a new sock with a few gifts as well as the mate to the sock was found in the toe. Sometimes they would get a tangerine in their stocking for a really rare treat. My children found their stockings outside their bedroom door. This allowed them to wake us up to tell us that Santa had left gifts at our door as well. It kept them from rushing down the stairs without waking us up. We would open our stocking gifts while still in bed, so we were able to wake up and go down to have our traditional breakfast before the gifts were opened.

The Christmas that the adults changed the decorations and set up new trains, we were able to see the train as we came down in the morning, because that is the room the back stairs came into. We were so surprised to see the trains. We played with them and opened our stocking as we awaited breakfast. Then we ate and headed to the dining room for the gifts. The waiting was excruciating; we wanted to move but the adults all had to have their cup of coffee as well as some cookies, maybe even a box of candy, to take in to the ritual. A trash bag and a knife or two to open the packages very carefully were also necessary. The paper would be carefully folded to be reused the next year. Whoever got to the box of paper first got the best choice of holiday wrappings. All of these things had to be assembled before we were allowed to enter the dinning room. We children thought that everything was a surprise to everyone, so we just waited.

Dad, of course, had gone into the dining room first and turned on all the lights on the tree. We never could understand why he got to see everything first, but that was the way it was. The bubble lights were such a surprise and a wonder as to how they worked. I still have the special lights and they still work. The base of the tree was piled high with wrapped gifts, as it was each year. If we got a bike or something large, it was often held until all the gifts were unwrapped and a space was made for the final surprise. We would take turns opening our gifts, one at a time, so that everyone could see what each person got and from whom. Sometimes the gift unwrapping had to stop in order to tend to the dinner cooking for that evening, and to get another cup of coffee or a trip to the bathroom, sort of like a seventh-inning stretch.

Of course, if there were family members visiting over the holiday, they were included with gifts under the tree as well.

The unwrapping took hours. We admired each other's handiwork of handmade gifts. We all made many of the gifts and we waited all year to receive some of them. Ma dressed dolls for me and made me clothing. Mother knitted sweaters, socks, bed socks, wraps and stoles. Aunt Ruth painted pictures on canvas and other things and Dad built things for us, even toys. As we children grew, we were able to add to the homemade gifts also.

Mother worked in a department store in the city, and she brought home all kinds of things. She was able to get first choice on sale items. There were many items that were broken or had missing pieces. They were going to discard these items so she would ask if she could have them. She brought them home and Dad was able to repair or make parts to fix them. I remember one of her coworkers worked in the lamp department and Mother brought home a beautiful, clear glass table lamp, but the base of it was broken. Dad took a large, square, glass ashtray, turned it upside down, and drilled a hole in the center so the cord could run down though the new base. He screwed it on to the column and we had a lovely and much admired table lamp for years. The same person gave Mother a bunch of small and medium lampshades of different shapes and sizes. They were discontinued floor samples or bent shades that were not going to be sold. We had new lampshades for years. So mother shopped all year long for bargains to be saved for Christmas. Everything, no matter how small, was wrapped and put under the tree. The little trinkets and odds and end of things that she found in her travels were saved and wrapped just for the sake of having the joy of opening packages.

We often had a large roast or a fresh ham for Christmas as well as vegetables; often collard green from the garden and fresh bread filled out the meal. Pumpkin, mincemeat, apple, lemon meringue pies were served along with more fruitcake, potato cake and cookies. You needed to rest after all the excitement, work and eating. The adults, of course, were excused after having had little or no sleep in order to surprise the children and getting everything ready and just right for Christmas morning.

It often snowed in December but it sure did in January and February. Ma would make hot chocolate for us and we would go out to gather fresh snow for making snow cream. Ma would wait until the second snow of the season, something about the air being cleaner. She would give us a large pot or bowl and send us out to find a clean spot for gathering. We then pushed the top of the snow aside and filled the bowl with cold, clean, dry, white snow. We would rush the snow into the house where Ma had made custard. She folded the snow into the warm custard until it was the consistency of ice cream. We would eat it and be so thrilled; to turn snow into ice cream was quite an experience. It was never very good if it was frozen to eat later. It had to be consumed when it was freshly made. We thought it was such fun, but the adults seemed indifferent to our excitement; we just didn't see why they weren't as interested as we were.

Ma told us when she was a child that people could skate on the Chesapeake River. They traveled the twelve miles from Smith's Island to the main land on skates and often pulled a sled with children or other items on it. She said that they could skate all the way to Baltimore. I could picture people in their long clothing, hats, scarf, gloves and muff gathered on the ice. They could go long distances on their skates. I remember in the 1950s, even the '60s, the Coast Guard had an ice cutter that went up the Chesapeake River to break up the ice so the large ships were able to sail North. People were used to being frozen in on the island. For years, they would stockpile canned goods and other necessities for such an occasion. They often had to wait for the cutter to free up the waters around them so the boats could get out and away to the main land.

Ma also reported that one winter it snowed so bad that the first floor of the house was covered with the drifting snow. They had to get out of the house via the second floor. As a child I remember snow every winter and lots of it. Today, if we get a dusting or two, we are lucky. I remember a winter when I was young and the farmer down the road had to bring a large team of horses to pull Dad's car out of the long driveway. The snow was that deep, and it was far too much to dig out. I always wore matching leggings to my winter coat to school during all of my grammar school years. It was cold, gray and snowy most of the winter.

Many winters, our children were not able to make a snowman or throw snowballs because of little snowfall. Now they say there is no global warming! You had better check the weather patterns on the East Coast for the last hundred years before you accept that fable.

CHAPTER SIX

More Memories

I have commented on Cap'n Tom's rather antisocial personality. Ma said she thought he loved the water and his ship above everything else. He spent most of his life on his ship. He did not financially support his family very well. When he occasionally came to port to visit home, Ma said that one time he brought a fifty-pound sack of flour after being away for three, or four months. Ma would say she wondered what he thought they had lived on while he was away and whether he thought they would live only on the sack of flour for the next three or four months. She would insist that he give her money for living expenses. He would turn his back to her and take out his purse, take some money out and hand it to her with his arm stretched out behind him as if he begrudged her the money. She never knew how much money he earned or had. Ma often told this story.

I don't think grandfather knew how to interact with people. He had not been educated and he spent most of his time alone. He was probably overwhelmed with children and a wife. Ma was a cheerful, verbal woman and I'm sure he was a duck out of water amid all the confusion of a busy household. I think he was a kind man but he didn't have the graces to deal with home life.

The story of this tight hand on his wallet became the family's reference point of honor. Hattie had stood up for the children, his children and herself by speaking up. She was a fighter and never just a quiet downtrodden woman.

She had to fend for herself for many years, not to have learned the importance of being up front and protective of herself and others.

Hattie was a woman before her time. She was pregnant with Alvin, times were rough, and she just could not bear the stress of trying to make ends meet. Her stepchildren were grown and had moved on with their lives. She felt that she needed a place to have more opportunities to make a better living for herself and now her third child. She left Cap'n Tom, took the two children and moved to Baltimore to be with her mother and family. Hattie became the mother of many members of her family, including her own mother who had lost her second husband. Some of the other members of the family were not doing very well either. They all needed a solution to the problem. Ma had taken her life and her children's in her own hands. She was determined to make a better life for them all. Ma got the idea of opening a grocery store. The whole family moved in together in a building with a storefront. Ma opened the store many hours a day and she baked and cooked all night to have pies cakes, soups and other food to sell the next day.

Some customers couldn't pay for the merchandise, but she saw that they didn't go away without something. She carried what they called "A Book"; each purchase was written down in "A Book" under the customer's name. At the end of the week, part or the entire bill was paid. Some could not pay at the end of the week, so the tally kept going until they could pay the bill in full. Some were never able to do so.

Ma told us the story about a signal she and her family had between the store and the living quarters upstairs. It was the way she would call up to them if there were any trouble in the store. One day, a young man entered the store. She had seen him nervously pacing outside. He seemed on edge, and his hands were in his pockets. Ma saw another man pacing outside. This young man said he wanted some sandwiches and cake and to make it snappy. Ma immediately called up the stairs in her secret way and the whole family came down the stairs. Her mother, two brothers, her children and an assorted cousin or two descended the stairway into the store all at one time. This sight overwhelmed the young man. Ma approached him with the food in a large bag and handed it to him. She said, "I know you are in trouble and have no money, but I am sure your mother would treat my son well if he was in your situation." The boy took the food; not saying a word, he slinked out of the store. She always remembered this incident and how she knew she had avoided being robbed by using kindness and reminding the young man of his mother.

After a few years, Hattie found that Baltimore was not a place that the family could stay in for a long time. So the family, Ma, her mother and the three children moved even farther north to Philadelphia where Hattie's sister Linda lived. She had married a detective on the Pennsylvania railroad. I always heard, growing up, the family speaking of him and how it was thought that he had been murdered because of the work he used to do. But I don't know the details, as those things were not spoken about in front of me. This couple had two sons Edward and Granville, whose father, Granville Dougherty, had been killed on the railroad. After Uncle Granville died, Aunt Linda raised her boys by herself. She never married again. Her boys were Alvin's age and they played together along with Aunt Rozzie's daughter Katharine, who lived in Philadelphia also. Aunt Linda lived for many years in Philadelphia until she moved to California in her later life to live with Edward and his family, where she died at the age of 88. Edward became a Presbyterian minister and Granville worked for the national grocery store chain A&P for many years until he joined his brother in the Whily Missionary group. Both brothers worked in California for the ministry until their deaths. Many of their children work for them today.

Eventually Aunt Rozzie and Uncle Ernie Herzzog lived with her brother Bill, his wife, Mary and their children, Marbell, Margaret, (Peggy) and William, (WIB) in Philadelphia for many years until her husband's death. Then Aunt Rozzie and her daughter lived together until her death. Katherine married twice but had no children.

In the meantime, Hattie's mother became very ill. She came down with what was called pleurisy in those days, and Ma worked day and night to keep her from swelling up and dying. Today, we have diuretics and antibiotics, but there was no treatment then. The disease caused you to fill up with fluid and drown in it. After a period of time with taking care of children and her mother and working to support them Ma, no longer was able to stave off death. I remember her saying that she got in the bed with her mother and straddled her to push the fluid away from her heart. Virginia died after much struggle.

Ma and her family were used to a meager lifestyle, but she had to work all the time as she continued to take care of the family. Ruth took care of her brothers as her mother went to her customers to sell corsets. The times were not very kind to this young woman. She, at one point in her life, had to beg to feed her children. If she couldn't sell corsets to the rich women and maybe make a fifty-cent profit, she had no money that day. One time, there was not a penny with which to feed her children that night, so she dressed up in an old coat and pulled a scarf down around her face. She walked to a distant neighborhood and knocked on doors to beg for an egg or any small amount of food to feed her children that night. Everyone had very little also, but she was able to gather a bit of food for her children that night.

She was always looking for ways to feed the family. She would not waste anything, including food. Ma's jellies and preserves were made of the leftovers from the produce store blocks away from where she lived. Each Saturday evening, she would set out to get to the stores just before they closed. She took her children's red wagon to carry home the produce that the vendors would give her. The spoiling fruit would not last until Monday (stores closed on Sundays in those days). So they figured she might as well have it because they would throw it away otherwise. Again, Ma would stay up all night, paring and saving the best parts of the fruit to turn them into a sweet treat. Ah! The good old days!

It was now just at the beginning of the Great Depression and Ma helped many a man who was walking from place to place, looking for work. Sometimes they were going from city to city. She would find men at her back door. She would invite them in and make them a large plate of pancakes, as many as they could eat, topped with her jellies and preserves. This was topped off with a hot pot of coffee and she would send them on their way; even though she didn't have much, she felt she had enough to share some of what she had with others who had less than she did. I remember a time when she told us about one of her pancake breakfasts. One of these strangers got into her jelly cupboard and opened jar after jar, putting his hand in the fruit to eat some from each container. She was so angry because she just couldn't understand why, after her kindness, he would do such a thing. However, she kept on feeding the weary travelers, in spite of the one ungrateful guest.

Ma also did piece work for a manufacturer of infant clothing in Philadelphia. She did hand smocking on baby dresses. Smocking involves gathering of fabric in a small pattern, usually across the bodice of a frock. It is done with the same colored thread as the fabric or with a complementary color. For each piece she did, she was paid a small amount of money. She was able to do this at night after she had worked all day. I remember when there was a child born into the family, she always would make a beautiful smocked baby dress as a gift. That may be why that I still have the smocked dress I made for my daughter. I was always impressed with her beautiful work. She had no pattern and just created the design as she went along. I, however, had to use a pattern. Smocking is a tedious job and has to be done just right so that the tension in the stitching is even.

Hattie's youngest child was a teenager when they moved across the Delaware River to Collingswood, New Jersey. While in Philadelphia, about 1930, Hattie had worked on the very rich Main Line of Philadelphia, where she sold corsets to the women who lived there. When she moved to New

Jersey, she continued to service her customers and made new ones in New Jersey. Hattie believed that wearing a corset was healthy for the back and that is gave a woman good support. Thank goodness, somewhere in the 1960s, girdles were a thing of the past because corsets and girdles were the most uncomfortable things anyone had ever invented. Today, women would die if they had to wear such things all day long.

Hattie had to take trolleys and a ferryboat across the Delaware River to get to her customers and then back home. Hattie lived with her three children very near the Cooper River. The boys, along with their dog, spent many hours building rafts, sailing, and swimming in the river.

As a teenager, Dad spent a few weeks in the summer on his father's boat. Dad often talked about his experiences and how they lived on the boat. Grandfather, Cap'n Tom, was evidently a good cook. Dad talked about his oyster stew and the fried soft crabs his father cooked for him. Grandfather was in touch with his family as they lived in Baltimore and Philadelphia, but he never lived with them after Hattie left him and moved to the city. Dad was about 18 years old when they got the news that his father had died from a stroke aboard his beloved SkipJack sailing ship. Grandfather was 72 years old at his death. Sometime after his death, Ma, Aunt Ruth, and Dad went to Crisfield to claim Grandfather's ship and found out that it had sunk.

It was another old SkipJack that had disappeared, one of many that has found a home at the bottom of the bay. SkipJack, "Bug-eye" a slang name, sailing vessels are still built today and used for oystering on the bay. The flat bottom, motor-driven fishing boat had taken the sailing boat's place on the Chesapeake Bay for other fishing or crabbing. Sometime ago, they made a law that oysters could not be harvested with a motorboat, the old beautiful sailboat with two masts and distinguished by the fact that the masts slanted toward the aft. The random pass of the sailing ship allows for better conservation of the sweet shellfish.

Dad was fascinated when we discovered an old SkipJack in a lake at Smithville Village New Jersey near Atlantic City. When Dad saw it, he seemed to have recognized an old friend. It sat in the lake for many years, but it was not taken care of and finally disappeared. It was a pretty ship to look at, and I am glad I got to see the kind of ship my grandfather lived and died on all those years ago.

In mid 1930s, after the family had lived in Collingswood for a while, they moved from place to place. Ma said they were moving to keep ahead of the sheriff because they often could not pay their rent. The country was now in the depths of the depression. They stayed in homes in Camden, New Jersey, for a period of time. When they moved into one of these row homes, they found that it was not very clean. With a bucket, a scrub brush, and a five-cent bar of soap, Ma took this place in hand and scrubbed it from top to bottom, including the front porch, steps, and sidewalk, to the curb. Ma always said that you could be poor, but you didn't have to be dirty.

She found a brown print fabric in the Woolworth five and ten-cent store. It cost only ten cents a yard, so she bought many yards. Ma covered the little bit of furniture she had with the fabric. She made covers for wooden orange crates to make tables and bookshelves. She even made bedspreads for the beds. Ma was resourceful. She said the little city home looked cozy and inviting. Of course, it was not the current decorating fashion in those years. Usually, each room was a different color and coordinating, or using a common theme of color or pattern throughout the house, didn't come into style until many years later. Leave it to Hattie!

I remember that in, our dinning room, one of the walls had three windows in it. Once Ma requested that Mother, who worked in a large department store in Philadelphia, buy her yards and yards of cheesecloth. None could understand why she wanted so many yards of cheesecloth, other than it was cheap. She cut the fabric into three long pieces and dyed each length a different color: gray, peach, and light blue. When the panels were dyed and dried, she twisted the strips together and draped them over the tops of the windows to make a valance. The rest of the fabric fell to the floor on each side of the room. Ma's valance was very colorful and set off the sheer, white curtains under it. This was in the late 1950s long before free form swags came into fashion. She sure was ahead of her time. Ma made new pillow tops and curtains all throughout the house. I remember that she made summer bedspreads for Aunt Ruth and her own bedrooms. She used a printed fabric for the curtain and cut out the patterns from the fabric and appliquéd them on a colored sheet. This made lightweight summer bedspreads. It was so pretty, and she didn't spend much money.

Across the street from their Camden home was a field that was made available to the residents of the city for gardening. Aunt Ruth began her love for the garden here, with her small plot of ground. Ma, as always, used her preserving techniques to preserve any food from the garden not immediately used. Everyone worked on the plot of ground, even my mother, because by now Alvin had taken a wife, Marjorie Meddings. Alvin and Marjorie meant when they both joined a social club. They were married on April 18, 1936. Mother and Dad were no longer able to afford the apartment they lived in. They moved in with Ma and Aunt Ruth and Uncle Homer, Dad's brother, in the Camden home.

Early in the year 1937, they found a home in Runnemede, New Jersey. It was run down and was being sold for taxes. The cost was 400 dollars, but adding the taxes due brought it to a total of 1,000 dollars. Imagine! It took years for them to pay that 1,000 dollars off, but of course they did. The property was entered from the back of the lot on Pine Avenue, because the road that ran in front of the building was just a cow path. The property included a big house and a two-story garage. The house was cold and uninsulated. I was born that October of 1937 and they told me that they had to burn 12 tons of coal that winter to keep them and me from freezing. There was just one large heating vent in the first floor and they spent much of their time huddled around it. Once Dad pulled down the walls inside the house to do them over as well as to insulate them, he found beer bottles inside them. The previous owners had dropped bottles in the walls. Dad took baskets full of bottles out to the front yard, dumped them there and covered them with dirt. The bottles helped make beautifully rounded banks that are still there in the yard. The old garage was eventually torn down and a new one erected. Years later, a foot-thick wet March snow caved in the roof of the garage so that the building was razed for a third garage to be built on the same location. At one time, the building was used to house Ma's many chickens.

More property was bought around the house, and it eventually amounted to one and a half acres, having over a four-hundred-foot front. The house was built in the late 1900s to early 1920s, and a couple of the stories about the property were told. It seems that during Prohibition, "rum running" trucks and cars were housed in the garage and on the property. The "Revenuers", a name given to the newly formed Internal Revenue Department, were known to have hidden in the woods around the house and watched the comings and goings to catch the crooks. The other tale that was told was about a man who hung himself on a maple tree in front of the house. There are still maple trees in front of the house on Schubert Avenue. During the 66 years Mother has lived there, the cow path eventually became a county road. The farmland all around the home became the site of many homes, a regional high school, and stores and businesses at each end of the road.

TRAGEDY STRIKES

In August 1938, an awful accident happened that would affect the whole family for the rest of our lives. Homer, Hattie's oldest son, was an avid motorcyclist. Both he and his fiancé, Bella, loved to travel on his motorcycle with her in the sidecar. One day, a little more than a week before their wedding, they were traveling close to Atlantic City on the White Horse Pike when a older man, traveling without his glasses on and in an old truck that was in disrepair, pulled out in front of them. Homer tried to stop but could not. Bella flew out of the sidecar and hit the windshield headfirst; she was killed instantly. Homer flew over the truck and hit a telephone pole. He lived ten days in the local hospital and then died on his wedding day.

I recall seeing the old family movies for years, films of his competition and motorcycle stunts, films of him traveling in motor-cades in the South Jersey area. I remember seeing the large, ornate black leather belt he had won in his many competitions. There was also the film of the funeral, with more than a hundred motorcyclists in the parade of mourners going to the grave sight. Homer was much admired, loved and honored. He was a slim, slight man with dark brown curly hair like his father. He was the tallest of the family being about five foot 11 inches; his brother was only five foot five inches tall. The family mourned him for their lifetime. Ma talked about him all my life, as I was just nine months old when he was killed. He was really remembered in August each year. Ma ate little and cried a lot. Maybe the canning of the fruits and vegetables gave her strength enough to get though that hellish nightmare she never got over. Dad and Aunt Ruth were forever changed by the event, and motorcycles were frowned upon forever in our house. In those days, there was no inspection of vehicles, seatbelts, or helmets; any one of these may have changed things that fateful day.

CHAPTER SEVEN

Potpourri

Thoughts come to me, and though they don't seem to fit into other ideas or stories, they do tell a part of the story. I have accumulated them in this chapter. Music was a big part of our lives, and I wanted to write about it. I have also written about sewing, which was an important part of Ma's and my life, as was school. "Time" is a melancholy memory of Ma and myself.

MUSIC

I don't recall Ma being very musical. I know she would sing to herself, sometimes whistle and, when the family would have sing-a-longs, she would join in, but she played no musical instruments. Ma did not keep the radio or phonograph on all day either. These things were only used at a specific time or to tune in a certain program, usually in the evening. We grew up listening to the sounds of the world around us. My environment was fairly quiet, because we grew up in the country. An occasional automobile or truck would rumble down the dirt road in front of our home. Once in a while, you would hear an airplane fly overhead. But there were the sounds of dogs barking, chickens clucking, roosters crowing at different times of the day. For years, we also had a nanny goat, and she would often bray. The trees rustling, children laughing and yelling, or a mother calling her children to come home were the everyday sounds we heard. There were great lengths of time when there was just silence.

Aunt Ruth and Mother both read music and played the piano. They had an old upright piano they brought from Camden to the Runnemede home, which is the same piano I used to teach myself to read music at the age of ten. When I was about 13, Aunt Ruth bought a rebuilt grand piano to replace the old one. Aunt Ruth loved to play it and she often did. Because I showed so much interest in music, the family wanted to give me lessons. There never seemed to be enough money in the budget to afford them until I was about 14 years old. Mr. Van Os came to the home and for $2.50, gave me music lessons on the piano each week until I was 18. He would write the melody of popular songs from memory in a book and add the chords for the left hand for me to practice. I still have these books filled with the old standards. When my children wanted to study music, I took them to my former teacher and he taught them as well. Unfortunately, they didn't have the devotion to practicing as I did, for I often played for hours at a time. My children seem to think that if they could play the melody that was sufficient. George, Jr., was gifted with music like his grandfather. When he knew a piece, he would sit down and play it, while transposing the song into any key that he wanted. Mr. Vas Os saw great potential in George, but George didn't care about the piano very much, so the lessons stopped, much to the teacher's regret.

As I said earlier, Dad had perfect pitch, but he couldn't read music; he played by ear. Dad worked at Wurlitzer in Philadelphia as a young man and bought himself one of their beautiful accordions. I remember him playing the accordion all my life. He would sit and play for hours. Ma's only objection was that she wished he would just play the entire song through. Dad often spent so much time trying to perfect the harmony of the song that he would play a phrase over and over again. First, he would try a phrase in the major, then the minor. Next, he would go for an augmented or a seventh chord or maybe an augmented seventh combination. He wanted to hear that blend of the sounds just right. He played with a band his uncle pulled together, but did not continue for very long. He was just not happy with the other musicians' willingness to play mediocre music. It was O.K. with them. He wanted the sound to be on key at all times and they didn't seem to hear the clunkers. When Dad retired, he bought an electric organ and took lessons from an old girlfriend of mine who taught the organ and piano. He enjoyed learning a new skill, but still looked for the harmony, or making the instrument blend the sound just right to his ear.

My brother, Alvin, played the clarinet and sang in the school choir during both high school and college. As an adult, he now sings barbershop harmony with a choral group, as well as in a quartet. When he was a teenager, he practiced his clarinet in the living room, and more than once, he would suddenly stop playing. When anyone would check to see why, he or she would find that he had fallen asleep with the instrument in his mouth. That's what you call devotion.

I was taught classical music in grammar school, and I listen to it at home. I remember when Dad brought home a wind-up Victrola record player with a stack of records he got somewhere. It was a console, and we had to stand on a stool to reach the top. The lid lifted up to reveal a turntable with a large round head that had a needle in it on a long metal arm that you set on the edge of the record. After winding the crank in the side of the wooden case, you would release the metal level that would set the record spinning. The wonderful, but slightly tiny sounding music would come out of the holes in the front of the cabinet. There were Caruso records and other famous singers from the early 1900s as well as great classical music that we would play for our amusement. We thought the old records sounded strange, but fun. We had a wind-up Victrola record player in grammar school as well. I remember what a great honor it was to be chosen to stand up in front of my second grade class to turn the handle so we could listen to music.

When I was a teenager, Dad got a wire recorder for us to use. We recorded family gatherings and then replayed them to everyone's great amusement in order to hear what we all sounded like. I remember that once, one of my aunts refused to believe that her voice really sounded the way it did. This was a new phenomenon at that time, the first time that people where able to record themselves and then hear their own voices.

Then rock and roll came along. One of my girlfriends and I loved to record the latest music from the radio. We would replay the wire over and over so we could dance to the music. Bill Haley and the Comets with "Rock around the Clock" was repeated at nauseum. Poor Ma, who had to listen to this racket as we delighted in the repeating noise! However, she never complained except to remind us, on occasion, to turn down the volume. I never cared much for rock and roll, surely not for Elvis and never hillbilly music, which was also popular in the 50s. At 17 and 18, I started to go with an older group; they were 20 and older and were fans of the "big bands", so this music appealed to me more. Today, after listening to big band, rock and roll, rockabilly, hillbilly, folk music, folk rock, disco, and new wave, to name a few, I still fall back on classical, the 40s standards, jazz, Dixieland, and ragtime, and I pick and choose the modern music.

My children loved to play their tapes and the radio very loudly, and I was not as patient as Ma was. I refused to live with the walls vibrating. You could always tell when I was out of the house by the level of the stereo. I would drive up and open the car door to blaring music. As I would open the front door, I would call to tell them that I was home, and the music was immediately turned down. They have survived, but I worry about their hearing! These children were the first to have the recorders and radios with earplugs. Even though I wouldn't let them have them because of damaging their hearing they still listened to their station at a mega noise level.

I don't play the piano anymore, even though I have a baby grand and see it every day. I do listen to music on tape, CD and sometimes the radio.

I do find it annoying to go shopping or to go to a restaurant and other public places and have to be accosted by sound. Out of the ceiling comes loud, what some people call "music"; I, however, call it noise. I do not find this to be so in Europe; they seem to think that people can shop, eat, and be in public without being "entertained" by some unsolicited choice of noise. Here, in America, people feel that they need to be surrounded by noise. But I still do not need to have music or any sound coming out of the ceiling or the walls to be happy. I still enjoy the quiet, even silence. It was a gift from my generation and those before me.

SEWING

Ma started me sewing when I was just five years old. I cut an A-line dress out of one of her muslin feed bags. I then sat on her lap as she pumped the petal on her treadle Singer sewing machine and I guided the fabric through the feed of the machine. This is my first memory of sewing. Sewing was a necessity in our home for both clothing and home furnishings. Ma made most of my clothing and she even tore apart old clothing to make use of the fabric for my new garments. I learned to sew very early, so by the time I got to high school, I was an accomplished sewer and was able to take first prize in a dress designing and sewing contest in my first year. It was a dark blue dress made of a sheer fabric with a gold pattern on it, so it had to have a lining. The dress also had a jacket, which was quite an undertaking for a freshman since most of the class had never read a pattern. I learned to use the fabric to its best advantage, so I usually didn't need as much fabric as the pattern called for. I usually had fabric left over even though I didn't buy the amount called for on the pattern. This was Ma's thriftiness again: save, save, save.

When I married, I made my own wedding gown and my bridesmaids' gowns. I had little to start my home with, so I covered old furniture and made curtains and continued sewing when my children came along. I made clothing for them both, and each year made all of Nicole's special holiday dresses. It was like sewing for my dolls again. I made my own doll clothes and then made my daughter's doll clothes.

I learned to knit, crochet and embroider from my mother. I taught myself other handicrafts through the years. I tried many different crafts, but sewing, crocheting, needlepoint, cross-stitch and quilting are the crafts I prefer.

I have begun a quilt with handkerchiefs from Ma, Aunt Ruth, Mother and myself. Mother gave me all of the smaller hankies she had, and I have assembled them as a top for a lightweight quilt. I am going to work with Nicole to finish it, as my eyesight is not as good as it once was. It will also be the joining of the generations to create this item to be treasured for years. Fabric hankies are something that are no longer fashionable for today's women, but Ma always carried one in her apron pocket or tucked in her bosom. Aunt Ruth also always carried one. For that matter, Mother still does. Handkerchiefs were washed and ironed along with the rest of the laundry. A handkerchief supply was something you always had. It was a usual gift for birthdays or other holidays. Crocheted or tatted edges, embroidered corners, and lace were some of the decorations. The hankies were made of cotton, linen and for decorative purpose, silk. They were stored in a handkerchief box that was scented. These little fabric pretties were tucked in bosoms, under straps of underwear, up sleeves, and in pockets, ready to stop a runny nose with a dainty pat or to catch a sneeze.

Tissues don't have quite the romance of the old flirting technique by which a woman casually removed the hankie from her bosom and nonchalantly dropped it on the floor. The lady made sure that it was noticed by the gentleman, who would quickly retrieve her hankie. Then a whiff of the fragrant, lacy hankie passed his nose as he returned it to the lady, his way of flirting back. This was the plot of many an old silent movie. Paper tissues have done away with this tradition. Too bad!

As a memory for my son, I plan on using my father's neckties to create another quilt. Using my hands has been something I have done all my life with the influence from my two grandmothers, mother and aunts as they all sewed, crocheted, knitted, or tatted and used their hands in some creative way. I have pieces from my grandmother Meddings, Ma, Mother and

George's mother, Mildred Brandt. It was something so many women did as just an everyday thing. I am always appreciative of handiwork and encourage everyone to have a try at something. Mother has spent time teaching me and all of her grandchildren how to knit and I am sure she has shown her great grandchildren. Using my hands to create things still continues to be a relaxing and interesting thing for me to do. I still whip up curtains, valances, pillow tops and there is an new afghan made for each room each time it is redecorated. Nicole is beginning to take an interest in finding a craft, something to do with her hands, as a tool for relaxing. The tradition goes on.

SCHOOL

School was a highly honored institution in our home even though none had very much formal education, as Ma's lack of formal education made her very aware of how important education is and wanted her grandchildren to get every bit of it they could. The example of reading and enlightening oneself was very evident in our household; everyone did it as no one had very much formal education. With the evident intelligence of the family around me, I often wonder if they had had more schooling, just how far they would have gone in life.

My brother and I went to Grace Downing Grammar School. My children went to the same school and so did some of Alvin's grandchildren. We started in the public school and I went from kindergarten to the fourth grade. The neighborhood that we had to enter to get to our school bus was not very good, and we were often beaten up. Because of that, Alvin and I were sent to a private school. We went until I finished the eighth grade. The classes were small and the education was much more advanced than the public school, which propelled us ahead in our education. I was studying Latin, algebra and early European history in the eighth grade.

We went to the private school for four years. We did have to play with some of the children from the neighborhood after school and it was difficult. Once a 12-year-old boy had my brother, Alvin, who was 7, pinned down on the ground and was punching him. I clobbered him in the head with my metal lunch box. The boy stopped and let my brother up but continued to bully him whenever he got the chance. Even some of the girls were nasty. I remember defending myself with punches and hair pulling. For this reason, we didn't have many childhood friends. We made friends in school, but I only had 8 children in my class. We depended on Ma and each other for our entertainment and to keep busy. Alvin kept busy with activities in high school and I went to work when I was very young. I had one girlfriend with whom I still have contact, Lee Koring Wilkenson.

We attended high school a few towns away as there was no local school in the early 1950s. Alvin went to the Air Force Academy after high school. He did not finish, but did some local schooling after he left Colorado. I was the first to graduate from college in the family; even then, I did that as an adult. College doesn't seem to be the goal of most of Alvin's and my own children, even though most have gone back to school after high school, for different reasons.

Originating from a family of uneducated watermen, our extended family has reached all levels of education, availing us of jobs in many different fields. I think of Grandfather Tom, Ma, her parents and siblings and what they might think of their descendents nearly 150 years, a century and a half after their births. I think they would not be surprised but very proud.

TIME

For some reason, the concept of time was hard for me to grasp as a child. Twenty minutes after and twenty minutes before the hour was just not computing! I must say that there were only the hands on a clock to tell time with in those days. (I have heard that some children today, when confronted with a clock face, cannot tell time because they are only familiar with digital timekeepers.)

The family tried to help me to learn to tell time. One way that Ma would do so was when she and Aunt Ruth were out in the garden, she would send me in the house to see what time it was. Ma saved the small pieces of cardboard that came between the layers of shredded wheat biscuit cereal and I would take one of them and draw the clock face and take it to the women in the field. They would tell me what I had drawn. Eventually, I learned to tell time. Such a simple thing to learn, and yet it had been so difficult.

Today, time is very important to me. I like to know the time of day it is. It allows me to feel comfortable in the scheme of things. I do plan a day allowing myself time to accomplish what I have planned. Sometimes, time gets away from me, and I lose my place.

Ma used to say how time was "going by so fast" and I could not understand what she was talking about. To me, time moved so slowly the days were long and getting from one summer to the next or from one Christmas to the next was endless. I never thought that I would become another year older, let alone ever grow up to become an adult! But time has gone by and now that I am in my later years, I must agree with Ma, that time goes by so fast.

Ma found it lonely as she grew older because the old friends she had made as a child, the siblings who were younger than she, stepchildren, her own son were all dying and leaving her here by herself. She said that she was losing the people she could reminisce with, the people who had lived their lives with her and with whom she had experiences. She loved her living family but missed her peers who were leaving her here alone. I also see what she meant as I have lost some family and friends myself.

Time is important because we don't know how much we have left of it. We often do waste so much of it when we are young. We don't value it as we do when we begin to mature. I like to use my days to their best advantage because I don't want to miss much when I am gone. The message I got as I grew up and watched the people around me was to "keep busy." No one seemed to be just bumming; they would be doing things with their hands, such as sewing, knitting, reading, keeping notes of ideas, or anything, building or designing something. It took me years to let myself just do nothing and enjoy the quiet time. My mind was busy but my body was still. Daydreaming is the art of the thinker. We visualize our ideas, plans, and dreams. We see what we want to accomplish and then comes the time to do the work. I try to follow my heritage of using time wisely.

CHAPTER EIGHT

A Few More Family Characters

AUNT RUTH

Aunt Ruth was a special person. She was very lovable, and she had her own special personality. Ruth stood on her own and didn't seem to be bothered by people and what they thought. She did her own thing at her own time and speed. Ruth had her own ways of doing things and you could not distract her or make her move any faster than she wanted to. She was funny, quiet, kind, smart, pretty, and well dressed; she was good with figures, loved to garden and paint. She was like a big sister to me and we were pals. She taught me manners, how to carry myself, how to sit like a lady, and, when I was old enough, how to take care of my hair and to use makeup.

Aunt Ruth never married, even though she had a gentleman friend all of my life. Her brother, Homer, as I have said, was a motorcycle fan. He raced them and drove them in motorcycle caravans on trips. He belonged to a motorcycle club, which is how she met one of his friends, who was also a member of the club. James Alfred Volz (Al) and Aunt Ruth became friends sometime in 1937.

After Uncle Homer and his fiancée were killed on his motorcycle in 1938, Ruth and Al began to see more of each other and became sweethearts. This relationship lasted until her death in 1974. They never married after nearly forty years of a friendship and of dating consistently. They were together at least each Wednesday, Saturday, and Sunday evenings during all those years.

Both Ruth and Al each had their own homes and each had their mothers living with them. I believe that they felt a great responsibility to their parents and neither was willing to give up their home and family to make one of their own. They both seemed to be content with the arrangement they had developed. Sadly, while I was writing this book, Al passed away at the age of 94. He was Runnemede's oldest resident, having lived in the town for 90 years, longer than anyone. We miss Al. He spanned my whole life and that of my children.

Ruth retired from the Internal Revenue when she was sixty-two after being a cashier there most of her adult life. At home she worked in the house as well as the yard and did everything but cook. When Ma passed away, Aunt Ruth took over cooking for Mother and Dad and I taught her. She would call me on the phone to ask how to fix something she had never tackled. I taught both Aunt Ruth and Mother because Ma and I were the cooks and they had no experience. I taught them Ma's recipes. Aunt Ruth could cook basic food but nothing fancy, so the three of them—Aunt Ruth, Mother and Dad—never went hungry. However, she never truly liked to cook. Dad learned to cook after his retirement, and he and Mother cooked together.

I remember when I was a teenager, my cousin Peg came from Philadelphia on one of her weekend visits. This summer Saturday, we were all fixing ourselves a light lunch. There were lunchmeat and the fixings for sandwiches on the table. We had all hurriedly whipped up a sandwich with lettuce and slices of Aunt Ruth's wonderful Jersey tomatoes. As usual, Aunt Ruth sat down to the table last; she always had one more thing to do before she could come to the table. As she started to assemble her sandwich, she realized that all the sliced tomatoes had been used. She began to slice one for herself. We were all busy talking, until Dad noticed Peg looking at Aunt Ruth in a strange, questioning manner. We also looked and noticed that as Ruth began to slice the tomato, her head must have started to itch because, not wanting to put her juicy fingers to the temples of her head, she began to scratch her head with the heels of her hand. She sat there with one hand on either side of her head, with the knife in one hand, the partially sliced tomato in the other, with the juice running down her arm, rubbing her temples. Dad said to Peg, "Don't mind her, Peg. She's O.K.," as he began to jerk his head to the side, "It is just a family trait." Peg caught on and everyone burst out laughing. Aunt Ruth didn't miss a beat and went along with the joke, exaggerating her movements, as she finished cutting and assembling her sandwich. We all had a good laugh about it for years.

Aunt Ruth was as honest as the days are long, to use an old saying. We knew she did not tell lies. Everybody's birthday was celebrated each year with gifts, a special meal of their favorite foods, and a cake, candles and a Happy Birthday serenade. Each March 22, when Aunt Ruth's birthday arrived, Alvin and I would ask her how old she was. In those days, a lady's age and weight were something that was never discussed. Her answer to us each year was "Sixteen." We knew that this never could be right and we would beg her to tell us her age, but she would still say "Sixteen." We just could not figure out the puzzle. She didn't lie but she wasn't sixteen, so for years the game continued. It wasn't until we were much older that the puzzle was solved. She was sixteen, but she never would say how many more years past sixteen she was. Our faith had been restored. Aunt Ruth was born in 1908.

Aunt Ruth was my maid of honor in my wedding party and she was delighted. Unfortunately, she developed ovarian cancer in her early sixties and died much too soon. She did live to know my two children. They remember her stopping by the back yard in her car, where she would call them to the fence and give them candy or a few small packets of sugar or whatever she had with her, for a little visit with her little children she loved. This is how I remember my Aunt Ruth.

ABOUT AUNT LUCY

When I was about 12 or 13, Aunt Ruth had just learned to drive and she brought a Crosley station wagon, one of the first very small cars in America. It stood out among all the full-size cars that were typical of the automobiles in the 1940s and 1950s. People would stop and stare at this little car as Aunt Ruth traveled to and fro. Uncle Harold, who always loved to joke, had his picture taken in front of the little car with one of his legs raised. We all laughed at this bit of humor.

One summer, Ma, Aunt Ruth and I packed the little car to the roof with our luggage, a vacuum cleaner, cleaning supplies, food and other items to make the trip from New Jersey to Fairmont, Maryland, to stay a week with Aunt Lucy and Uncle Will Ford. Aunt Lucy was the other sister of Virginia and Mary Mc Daniel, Ma's aunt. The Fords had two sons, Wallace and Louis who married and his wife, Ruth and he had one son Louis. Lucy and Will lived in Fairmont all their married lives. Uncle Will was a house painter. I remember his eyes; the lower lids were red from the effects of the paint. (Remember that paint had lead in it in those days.) Their home was an Italianate-style Victorian home. It had two large rooms on each of the first two floors, running from the front to the back of the house. A large hall with a stairway that went to the third floor separated the rooms. The house had a flat roof and was symmetrical with a door in the center of the house. The windows went almost from the 15' high ceilings to the floor. As you entered the house, the room to the right was their living and dining room. A fireplace was in the dining part of the room towards the back of the house. The room to the left of the hall was originally the formal living room but they were not using it at that time. The kitchen was a small room added to the back of the house at the end of the hall.

Upstairs, the only two rooms were bedrooms. The room we slept in had two double beds and a single one. There was a small closet in the bedroom that was just the depth of the wall and about the width of the door. We had a washstand with a pitcher and bowl and towels on it. Under the bed was a chamber pot to use during the night. In the morning, it was carried downstairs and out the back door, down a path to the outhouse where the waste was deposited. I did not see the resident's bedroom but I know it had a register in the floor over the dining area to allow the heat from the fireplace to travel up to heat the bedroom. The fireplace was the only source of heat in the house.

We had gone to Fairmont to give Aunt Lucy's home a thorough cleaning because she could no longer do so. She and Uncle Will must have been in their late eighties. We took extra wands to the vacuum cleaner to reach to 15-foot ceilings. The stairways were quite difficult to do. The three of us had quite a job to do in this old home that was in need of much housecleaning. We spent the week doing just that.

It was the first time I had crab stew. Aunt Lucy made a large platter of hard crabs cooked in a stew fashion with potatoes, onions, and dumplings. What a feast! Though picking the crabs that were in gravy was messy, they were delicious and worth it.

Her neighbor across the street lived in a very large Victorian home that had been staffed with servants in times past, so it had the kitchen in the basement. I was invited to tour the home. I entered by the kitchen entrance after passing through a arbor of grapevines. The home was laid out with beautiful furniture, and antiques. I was allowed to travel to the attic, which was a treasure chest of old toys, books, furniture, and other items. I was just 12, but I knew that I was looking at valuable historical items. The woman of the house took me on the grand tour of the home and it was like touring a museum.

She then took the three of us to her daughter's home down along the Chesapeake River and it was like a movie set. The long driveway to the house from the road was lined with trees on both sides of the drive. The large old trees near the home were hanging with moss and the grounds went down to the river. They had two large Great Dane dogs that walked with us over the grounds and then into the very old home with low ceilings and country colonial furniture. I was so impressed by my exposure to these two estates that it directed me toward interior design.

Up until that time, I had wanted to be a dress designer. After my visit I spent many hours with a Sears catalog, designing houses in my imagination and furnishing them from the catalog. In those days, the catalog contained kitchen and bathroom fixtures, building supplies, doors, windows, hardware, etc. You could order all the materials to build and furnish a home from a Sears catalog in the 1950s. So I designed to my heart's content.

As an adult, I graduated from the then-Philadelphia College of Art, now University of the Arts, with a degree in Interior Architecture. My interest in this field of study may have started in Fairmont, Maryland, with our trip to clean an old Victorian home. After Uncle Will died, Ma took care of Aunt Lucy, who lived with us for two years towards the end of her life. Unhappily, Aunt Lucy became very forgetful. Both she and Aunt Maggie lost their appetites. If Ma had not just put healthy meals in front of them and encouraged them to eat, they would not have eaten very well. Both of the women would have been happy to live on coffee, bread, butter, and jelly. Ma gave them meat, vegetables, and fruit.

I remember Aunt Lucy forgot to bathe or change her clothes, so Ma would take her clothes at night and wash them and return them without saying anything. She would escort Aunt Lucy to the bathroom and run a bath for her to see that she bathed. We teased her about telling and retelling her stories but she would repeat them again the next day just the same. She thought that she was being very scandalous by shyly saying that she was going to the A & P. Then she would laugh. How shocking! Ma made us children respect her, and not make fun, be unkind or rude to her. She always said that young people forgot that, if they were lucky, they would get old someday, too. As a result, it would behoove us to be respectful. Ma was the ultimate caretaker. Aunt Lucy stayed with her son and his wife at the very end of her life, and she lived to be 96 years old.

YOUNG FAMILY FROM THE ISLAND

When I was about sixteen, my cousin Joan Middleton and two other Smith Islanders moved to New Jersey. They had graduated from high school and thought they could do better securing a job closer to the city than at home. Lee, the brother of Ginny Evans, one of the girls, worked at a large newspaper, so she and her cousin, Shirley Evans had a family member to depend on. This Evans family was not directly related to our family. There was three Evans families who were traced back to the 1600s. Joan was able to connect with Ma, her great-grandmother, and us. They made the big move North, took an apartment in a near-by town and all set out to find a job. They too lived in Collingswood for a time. They were all successful and began their new lives away from home.

When I was eighteen or so, I began to pal around with them. On a Friday, when we all got home from work (I was working at this age), Dad would take me over to their apartment and I would spend the weekend with them. We would go out on the town on Saturday night and pal around on Friday night and Sunday morning. At nineteen, when I got my driver's license I would drive us around and hit all the nightspots. We had so much fun. They were a little older than I was, so I could pal around with an older group, the college group. We went to the Pocono Mountains one long weekend and stayed in a resort. It was a nice way to grow up with family and friends and do it in a group. We didn't do anything too darning, but we did meet men and honed our skills by dating and interacting with males.

I remember one time I stayed with Joan and Ginny, and we cooked dinner. Our menu was fried pork chops with gravy, corn, lima beans, and potatoes. I don't think we planned this meal to well, but it was tasty even if it was rather loaded with starch!

All three girls met their mates on the job and did marry and have children. Ginny and her family live in Tennessee. Shirley still lives in New Jersey and Joan, who is now Joan Kraus, lived close by and was a grandmother. Unfortunately, while I was writing this book, she passed away. I miss her and am sorry that she did not see this book completed. My dear cousin Peg will not either, much to my chagrin.

MOTHER'S FAMILY AND WASHINGTON, D.C.

Marjorie was just twenty years old when she married Alvin. She was the oldest child of Fredrick Charles (Charlie) and Isabella (nee Miller) Meddings. They had come to America in the early 1900s from Birmingham, England, to Gloucester City, New Jersey. Grandpop's three sons by a previous wife, Fredrick (Fred), William (Bill), and Alfred came to America one at a time. Fredrick, the oldest, came to be with his family after serving in the military in the First World War for England. He worked for Campbell Soup Company until he retired. He married Nellie Payne and had one child, Irene. Nellie died and Fred remarried and had two sons, Alfred and Fredrick. Alfred and family moved to the town next to us, and his children went to high school with my children. They didn't know they were cousins until I told them. Regrettably, Uncle Fred didn't stay close to the family, and that is why the cousins didn't know each other.

Grandpop's brother William, as well as Grandmom's mother, Rebecca Cope, also came to America. His brother Sam stayed in England and brothers Leonard and John went to Australia. Great-Grandmother's last married name is the only name Mother remembered because she had married three times. Grandmom's sister, Rose, and two bothers, Henry and George, all came to the United States with them. Grandpop's other two brothers moved to Australia and New Guinea.

Grandmom Meddings had another sister, Louie (Lou), who did not come to America and she lived out her life in England, where she married and had two daughters, Doris and Louise. They married and each had children. Doris and her husband Samuel (Sam) Ford had a son, Allen, and a daughter, Christine. Louise had two daughters, Hazel and Irene. They are all married and have children. The family is still in the midland area of England where we have visited them and they have also come to the U.S. to visit.

Uncle Bill worked in the building trades, as did his father and his brothers. He eventually moved to California, where he married Aunt Dora and had two daughters, Marjorie and Betty who still live there. Uncle Alfred was a plaster; he married and had one son Alfred who followed in his father's footsteps. Uncle Alfred lived in New Jersey all his life and his son also moved to California, where he still lives with his second wife. His children still live in New Jersey.

Grandmom and Grandpop Meddings had four children together. Marjorie was the first, then Rose, Isabelle and Walter, the youngest. They lived in Delaware Township, New Jersey, for many years, next to what is now known as Route 38 in Cherry Hill. The "cherry hill" was a place where mother and her siblings played and slid down on snowy days, right across where the highway is now.

They made this area their own little community by building their homes next to each other. Grandpop was a Master bricklayer and he built his own home. Uncle Henry made the blocks to build Aunt Rose's home, but built his own home with brick. He and his wife Sally lived there with their nine children. The homes were built at the bottom of Cherry Hill.

Grandpop also brought his pigeons with him from England. He raced them and raised them for eggs as well as to eat them. Some of Grandpop's long distance racing records still stands for his pigeons. The depression came, and the demand for brick laying was scarce, which affected Charlie. They lost their home sometime in 1935 or 1936, and they and the other three children moved to Silver Spring, Maryland.

Grandmom and Grandpop Meddings lived in the suburbs of Washington, D.C., and I remember visiting them as a child. Not only did Grandpop raise pigeons for racing and eating, he also raised rabbits for eating. I did have rabbit for a meal. It was sad to pet the rabbits in the backyard and then have rabbit for dinner. Mother was raised on pigeon eggs and squab, but I don't recall having them myself. When I was in Paris, France, a few years ago and I asked for beef in a small restaurant, using the little bit of the lanuage I knew, the waitress brought rabbit. It took me awhile to figure out what I was eating, but I knew it was not beef. I think the waitress, who spoke no English, thought she would fool me, but when I let her know after I had eaten it that I knew what it was rabbit and that I had enjoyed it, she blushed.

When I got older, Mother's sister, Isabelle's children and I would go into Washington to visit the National Monuments. I climbed the Washington Monument (the needle) and though I would have a heart attack. That is a lot of steps! Each time I would visit the family, we would travel to the city and make a tour of the different sights. I enjoyed my cousins and we had a good time exploring the beautiful city of Washington, D.C. When our children were young, we stayed a few days in Arlington, Virginia, and spent each day visiting all the museums and monuments in the capital. I finally got to visit the White House. Washington, D.C., is a city full of beautiful monuments to honor our county.

When my grandparents moved to the Washington area, Grandpop found work there and they continued to live there until they died, Grandpop at the age of 86 and Grandmom at the age of 76. Aunt Isabelle married Cotti King and had five children. They lived in the area for a lifetime. Aunt Rose married Edward Roberts and had four children. She moved around but eventually settled in the Tampa area of Florida and spent the rest of her life there. Walter married and had four children. He lived in Maryland for many years, then moved back to New Jersey. Walter, who is Mothers only living sibling, now lives in Georgia with one of his children. Most of my cousins from this side of the family now live in the South.

Our family, both of my parents, originally came from Europe and spread all across the U.S. Some of my family even spread to Australia and New Guinea. I have done my best to record as much as I could find about our ancestors.

THE BRANDTS

For my children, I must say a word or two about their father's family. Arno Brandt came from a family of 5 brothers and 3 sisters. William (Bill), Kathryn, Henry, Arno, Herman, Ann, Elise, and George (in their birth order.) The first son was born in 1894 and the last in 1911. Aunt Ann and Aunt Elsie, both of whom are in their 90s, were the only living siblings, and they live in the same nursing home. Since I finished this book they have both passed away. Uncle Bill, Henry and Aunt Ann never married.

The Brandt grandparents came from Denmark and settled in Camden, New Jersey, and, when the brothers and sisters married, they moved to various towns in Southern New Jersey and Pennsylvania. Uncle George moved to Florida and married. His daughter and granddaughter still live there. The area of Denmark they came from later became part of Germany. I believe there are some family members still living near Hamburg, Germany. Louise has assembled the Brandt family tree and history. She has made it available to the family.

Mildred Black was an only child. The Blacks were of English and Black Foot American Indian stock and came from Philadelphia. Mrs. Brandt liked to tell a story about her Grandfather Black, who was the Black Foot Indian link. Well, it seems he died at the age of 89 on his way to Poughkeepsie, New York, to marry his third wife.

Mildred married Arno in September of 1923 and they had eight children: Dorothy (Dot), Jeannette (Jean), George, Louisa (Louise), William (Bill), John, Donald, and Martha Lee. Arno died young, at age 54, from a stroke. John, Dorothy, and recently William have all passed. Dot and Donald never married. Mrs. Brandt lived to see all of her 18 grandchildren born. Most of these grandchildren are married and have children, though one grandchild died at the age of one. George Junior is the last Brandt of this large family. It seems that all of the brothers had girls. Arno was the only one to have sons. Of his sons, George was the only one to have a son. It is now up to George to continue the family name.

The Brandts are a fun family. We spend the holidays together, we travel together, and we will use any excuse to have a party. The Brandts have been a loving, kind, and supportive family to me. Nicer in-laws are hard to come by. I feel as though they are my brothers and sisters. **Post Note:** As of 2007 only Jean, George and Martha are living. Sadly all the rest of the family have passed.

FAMILY NAMES

Many names of the family have stories behind them. For example, Hattie Smith was the neighbor of Ma's mother, Virginia. Virginia named her first child Hattie Smith to honor her friend. Virginia Ruth was named for her grandmothers, but Hattie never liked the name, Virginia, so she called her daughter Ruth. Aunt Ruth went by the name V. Ruth Evans on all her legal documents. Thomas Alvin Straus was the name of the young doctor who helped deliver Hattie's third child. He promised to educate him if Hattie would name the child for him. Hattie did not want to use the name Thomas, so she said that she would call him Alvin Straus Evans, and the doctor agreed. (Years later, Ma did inquire about educating her son, but by then the doctor had married, had his own children, and declined to fulfill his promise.)

Some of the odd names that run though the family were old English and county names, such as, Medford, Ellsworth, Ethridge, Emory, and Arintha. Rozzie was, I believe, a nickname of a friend, but the child was given the nickname to serve as a full name. Dow was named for a famous Methodist minister of the 1800s. I was named for the famous movie star, Myrna Loy. She was very popular when I was born in 1937, and my mother liked her, so I was named for her and Aunt Ruth. Nicole, my daughter was named for her father and me, Nicolas and Ruth, our middle names. The names, George, Nicholas, and Ruth run all through the family.

AIRPLANES and FLYING

When Dad was a boy he spent a lot of time building model airplanes. Dad was born on February 4, 1916. Airplanes were a new thing when he was young in the early part of the twentieth century. Dad was just 11 when Charles Lindbergh flew across the Atlantic Ocean. Airplanes were just being developed for the First World War. Boys were intrigued with the flying machines; they were able to identify the many planes of the First World War. They made models of many kinds. Dad built the planes from balsa wood and rice paper and painted the models with airplane dope paint. There were no kits when he was young so he had to build planes from plans. Some of the planes had gasoline motors in them and he flew them on a tether. He kept this interest in model planes all his life and, as an adult, he built the planes with motors that had remote controls, so they could fly like real planes. He spent many a weekend flying his planes with other model builders. Dad designed a model plane that was large enough to be manned, but he never got to build it. He had some small instruction in drafting, and as in other things, when he liked something, he gathered more knowledge about the subject and was able to draft his planes very well.

Like his grandfather, my son George, Jr., has had a fascination with airplanes as well. He was born in the time of rocket ships going to the moon. George did something his grandfather never got to do, fly a plane. He took flying lessons and is very near qualifying for his license. It is a very rigorous process of qualifying and testing for piloting as well as expensive. He is hoping to complete this process in the future. I also hope he is able to do so, because it is quite an accomplishment.

THE FAMILY BUSINESS

The family banded together in 1960 to form our corporation. It is now known to the Delaware Valley as Alva Vacuum Cleaner and Janitorial Supply Center. Over the years of Alva, Mother, Dad, Alvin, his family, George and myself and our family lived very sparsely and spent long, long hours to begin a small service business that started in Dad's basement. It has grown into a large, well-known family livelihood. At one time, we had four locations and supported more than twenty employees.

The history of the business includes starting in a very small, old remodeled hamburger stand, rapidly outgrowing this location, moving to a much larger building, remodeling this store and growing by leaps and bounds. Then after many years of business, there were Mother and Dad's retirement and the tragic fire that destroyed the entire building we had worked so hard to purchase and revamp. A young boy, in a building adjoining our location, was left alone, and he played with a lighter and set his apartment on fire, which spread to the ceiling of the building. The fire ran over the ceilings and caused a fire in the entire complex of apartments and shops. Even though nobody was injured, the entire building was destroyed. The whole building had to be demolished and rebuilt. We rebuilt the structure and, after a few years, Alvin and George divided the ownership of the building and the business. We took full control of the business. Then came the time when we left the location we had been in for almost forty years to a smaller space. The business has changed to more of a commercial janitorial supply center with less emphasis on retail sales of vacuum cleaners, which didn't need as much square footage as it did for so many years.

The business is in its third generation as George, Jr., is now the manager and idea person for our now commercial business. Nearly a century has passed and now George is the fourth generation in the retail business world, starting with Ma's grocery store in Baltimore in the early 1900s. Ma was there when

Al's started. Al's Vacuum Cleaner Shop was the original name that started in Dad's basement shop. Ma had no idea how far and long the small venture would go. She often answered the phone and, in her charming way, she took the calls for her men and their new business.

Our daughter Nicole took a different route and began in high school to work in the pharmaceutical business. She started at the bottom for a large pharmacy chain as a technician, filling prescriptions. She now works for a large commercial pharmacy that supplies a nursing home chain, mental hospitals and prisons. She manages the thirty people in data processing and those who keep over ten thousand patients' records in this department. She hopes to finish her education and become a pharmacist working in research.

We are proud of both our children in their chosen lives and hope they achieve the best things in life.

ABOUT THE AUTHOR

To touch on other parts of my life that have happened after Ma's passing is an ongoing work of surprises. I sometimes think if she were able to be here to see all that has gone on in my life, wouldn't she be happy to know that I have accomplished so many things? She was my best cheerleader. She thought that I could do just about anything I put my mind to. Ma was always on my side. When times were rough, I always had thoughts of her cheering me on. My cousin Peg was another person who had no criticism of me. She thought that anything I did was great. I do miss them both a lot. Aunt Ruth was my "sister" and gave me guidance into my teenage life and my young adulthood. We shared a lot of close times and I also learned positive lessons from her. You need people like this in your life to keep you going because there sure are enough people out there to tell you what you are doing wrong!

My friend of almost 40 years, Jane Tedesco, has also been a positive force in my life. She and I have raised our children together and gone though the rough periods of their growth, as well as our own, together. Jane has always given me encouragement and support. I thank her a lot. My other close friends and acquaintances whom I have gathered along the years have all given me knowledge and strength to expand my thinking. They have given me the encouragement to broaden my attempts into things I never imagined I would have tried, or whom I never would have been when I was growing up a shy, country girl.

Ma never knew that I had two beautiful children who have grown into wonderful adults. She never knew that I finally got to go to college to study my childhood dreams of design. Ma would have been proud of the storytelling skills that I perfected in my forties, as I became involved in Community Theater. From that involvement, I was motivated to study and did my apprenticeship in the theatre for children, which allowed me to become a professional clown. I created many characters over my more than fifteen-year business as a children's entertainer. Along with clown magic, face painting, puppetry, and balloon sculpture, I developed a few characters that told stories as part of the act. I give Ma the credit for developing my ear for the art of storytelling. She was so good at it that we never tired of the same stories told over and over. I was eventually able to teach the art of clowning and children's entertaining in local high school adult education.

I played a large role in the development of our family business in its early history. I would take the children, as toddlers, to work with me and, as they grew, for many years they came to the business from school because that is where I was. I ran an in-house advertising agency for the company, using all forms of media. I edited a company newsletter and ran all our social events such as Christmas parties, picnics, and day excursions for many years. I was also on the floor as part of the sales staff and, for 25 years, did all of the window and store displays for all the stores we had. I used my design skills to locate and design the satellite locations we had in our years in business. I also designed our main store and then redesigned it after the fire. In fact, I managed the whole project from beginning to end. Each day, I was on the construction site to see that the job was being done to meet our specifications. With our latest move, I once more organized the new location, designed it, and moved us again.

Besides using the skills Ma and Mother gave me to do many kinds of needlework and tending the home, children, business and organizational work, I have led a full life of using my skills to widen my own life as well as those of others. I still cook for my family and friends, and now I have learned to use a computer. This skill has led to my writing down thoughts and ideas to help carry on the traditions of a country family. I learned the lessons well from my family and hope that I have passed some of them on to the next generation of children. I see that my children have different abilities and interests than I do. Their world was much larger and wider than mine was as a child, so their ideas and influences were different. They do like a lot of the things I do and many that I do not. Their lives will, of course, be different than mine, but I hope that some of Ma's traditions will pass on to them, such as the skill of care taking, independence, cooking and entertaining. Nicole, I think, got Ma's patience, and George got her endurance.

LOOKING BACK

Alvin was married in 1962 a year before me, so Ma knew his wife Mary Wegman. Ma got to see their first three children, Laura, Edward, and Alice born, but did not live long enough to see Sharon and Elaine born. George and Nicole, our two children, were born around the same time as these two cousins, so she never got to know them either. I am sure she would have loved them. She was so good with children and had such a way with them that the children sure missed out on a person they would not have forgotten had their time here on earth crossed. Unfortunately, it was not meant to be. Of course she would now be a great-great grandmother, as Alvin is a grandfather and wouldn't she have loved that. All of Alvin's children are married and all but one have children, for a total of eight grandchildren. In reality, she would be a great-great-great grandmother because her stepchildren have great-great grandchildren.

CHAPTER NINE

The Way It Used To Be

DANGER, DANGER, DANGER

Some of the dangerous things we were exposed to could have been very hazardous, but we survived. I remember taking my brother into the basement and having him stick his finger in the open plug of an extension cord, telling him to do so to get a tickle. I had done it, so I showed him. It's a wonder that we were not hurt or electrocuted. Dad always had a roll of asbestos insulation paper around the basement and we played with it, too. We would use it as paper and cut things out of it. Imagine that, it is a wonder that we didn't get ill from such a thing. Another dangerous item Dad had around was mercury. He had a small vial of it (why, I have no idea). He would spill it out onto the table and ask us if we could pick it up. Of course, you can't pick it up with your fingers; if you touched it, it divided into more shiny, silver droplets that shimmered around on a surface. If people had any idea how dangerous this stuff was, we would have never been allowed to play with it.

Each September when we were young, we would get new school shoes and in the spring we would get new dress shoes. We didn't wear shoes often in the summertime. Well, the biggest treat in the store was to put your new shoes on and put your feet in the bottom of a machine that X-rayed them. You would push a button at the top of the machine and look in a little window to see the bones in your toes inside the outline of your new shoes to see if there was enough room for your feet to grow. We would push the button over and over to see the X-ray pictures. The shoe store was in town, so if we were around town and went by the store, we would run in and look at our feet any old time. Little did we know. Little did anyone know. The machine was very popular, but didn't stay around too long, thank goodness.

I remember Dad siphoning gas out of the car with a hose that was put down into the tank and sucking on that hose until the gasoline came out. The gas was leaded. So was all the paint that was layered though the years on all the woodwork and walls in the house. Lye was kept on a shelf for Ma's soap and we had access to it. DDT was sprayed in the summer to kill the mosquitoes, and we would run in the mist as the trucks drove by. Dad smoked unfiltered Camel cigarettes, three packs a day, and he always had a cigarette in his mouth or hand. I breathed cigarette smoke for 25 years, until I left home, and yet with all these dangers we experienced, we suffered no ill effects!

THE RADIO DAYS

Before television, there was the radio. Most homes had one large console in the living room and maybe a small one in the kitchen. The radio programs in the daytime consisted of news and music, but the afternoons were filled with the soap operas. They were called this because the large soap companies sponsored these stories. I remember my friend Lee's grandmother was hard of hearing and every afternoon the whole neighborhood could listen to the soaps because Nana blasted her radio as she listened intently to her melodramas. Nana loved to talk back to the shows. I was a great fan of the evening program "The Shadow" mystery drama, and then there was "Fibber Mc Gee and Molly," a comedy show about a couple and the many neighborhood characters. Molly was afraid of Mc Gee opening his closet, but every once in a while he would forget that it was dangerous to open the closet door. Molly never could warn him in time and you would hear such a racket that you could just imagine everything falling out of the closet. They kept you in suspense each week, waiting for him to open the darn thing. Somehow, the writers managed to make it a surprise each time it finally happened. Then there were Fred Allen, Jack Benny, Amos and Andy, also the Great Grillersleeve. The Lux Theater with their dramas also acted out on the radio. Young actors, who in time became famous movie stars, dramatized many of the famous plays. When I was eleven to about fifteen my favorite were the New York Yankee Baseball games. I listened faithfully, kept score, and knew all the aspects of the game. I remember one year the Yanks were, of course, in the World Series. I was listening to the last game that would finally make them the World Champs again. Aunt Linda was visiting and she was outside in the garden with Ma and Aunt Ruth. I would periodically run out on the back porch and update them with the news of how the game was going. I wanted to share the excitement. Now I must tell you that neither of the women knew anything about baseball, but they would cheer my team on as I kept them informed. Finally, I ran out on the porch jumping up and down, calling to the women, "The bases are loaded, the bases are loaded and they have no outs!" Aunt Linda waved and I ran back in to find out the latest. In the meantime, Ma asked Aunt Linda what I had said and she responded, "Myrna said the bases were loaded, but I don't know what with!"

THE OLD BALL GAME

One of the best times Alvin and I had as children was when, at the ages of 12 and 14 we traveled to North Philadelphia by public transportation to Shibe Stadium. We saw a double-header baseball game between the New York Yankees and the Philadelphia Athletics (the A's). We sat behind the first base line and were able to see our favorite baseball stars. This was the time of Casey Stangel, Joe Di Maggio, Phil Rizzuto, Hank Bauer, and Yogi Berra. We bought pennants and orange drinks in cone-shaped containers. We punched the bottom of the containers out, and they conveniently became megaphones. We screamed so loud and so long that we lost our voices and neither one of us could talk for a couple of days. Somewhere in my attic, I have a piece of a seat removed from Shibe Park Stadium before it was torn down.

FAT SANDWICHES

The little sandwiches for which I work so hard to find good combinations, take the time to cut off the crusts, and make just so, are a far cry from the silly sandwich Mother used to make me as a kid. Dad didn't like the thought of it, and would tell Mother not to let me have them. She would sneak a slice of her treat sometimes for the two of us when he wasn't around to see. She made lard sandwiches. Yes, lard. She would take a plain old slice of white bread and spread it with lard and sprinkle it with sugar, and I thought it was the best ever. Maybe the fact that it was a secret between Mother and me is what made it taste so good. I have never had one since I was a child, and I don't think I have ever bought any lard in the whole time that I have had my own home. I do know that I loved to dip white bread in the fat of hot gravy, or make a sandwich of buttered bread and cold pork with lots of fat on it. I haven't done that in years and years either, but the fat sandwiches did taste good, even if I can't recommend it as a healthy food.

MORE FAT

Ma saved all the grease from cooking meat. She collected it and kept in an old pot in the basement. When there was enough fat, it was melted and a caustic soda was added to the pot to make lye soap. The soap was poured into a pan and cooled. Ma cut the soap into chunks. When we got our first electric automatic washing machine, a Bendix, Ma grated the soap to make homemade soap for the washer. The soap was a light brown color and made fabrics very clean and bright, even though it was hard on the skin.

SHOPS AND SHOPPING

Many times, Ma recalled shopkeepers and vendors she dealt with through her life. Even when I was a young child, a produce huckster stopped by the house periodically with fresh fruit and vegetables in the back of his truck. Milk, bread, pastries, and grain for the chickens were delivered to the door. Another huckster peddled household goods and clothing in his truck. Ma talked about having some of her dresses made by a dressmaker. So much of the shopping in the country those days was done in the home. When Ma lived in the city, individual proprietors who owned shops of one or two produces were the norm. There were the green grocers, the butchers, the bakery, as well as the trades; they were all individual shops. A peddler would travel with a grinding wheel to sharpen knives and scissors. Someone would repair pots and pans; a man would even bring a pony to a corner and take pictures of your child on the animals' back. Ma made most of her things, such as household decorations, clothing, and food, but she still shopped for things to do her own work.

When I was a child, it was another world to go to the city and shop in the large department stores. The floors and floors of merchandise made it look like they had compressed all the little shops into one large building. Each department was vast and offered a large selection of items. Both Mother and I worked in these large stores. Some large stores are still in Philly, but they are not as diverse as they were years ago.

As a child, I remember a local grocery store Ma would send me to for odds and ends. Also in the next town, there was an old General Store run by two elderly brothers. I can see the old gray wooden floors and merchandise packed from the floor to the ceiling. Dad used to say that he would go in for a plumbing joint or heating duct and ask one of the brothers for those particular items. The old gentleman would disappear to the basement, and be gone for ten or fifteen minutes while Dad browsed and found something he might fancy. Then the old man would appear with the requested item and ask for some nominal price. On the occasion of someone taking me along, I was only interested in the games, comic books, and candy. The sheer variety of items, some that I didn't recognize, was a fascination. Sometimes Aunt Ruth and Al's destination on a Saturday evening was to "Naffie's." It was entertaining to see all the old things they had in stock, and they often would purchase something they had not seen for years just for fun. The couple would be delighted to bring home their found treasures. There was always entertainment from the old men who gathered around the potbelly stove and swapped stories.

The hardware store in town had a bit of everything and Dad spent a lot of time there. He was always working on project for the house, and very often the hardware delivery truck was dropping off lumber, sand, cement, nails, coils of wire, paint, cinder blocks, plumbing supplies, and on and on the list went. You could buy just one brass cup hook or a handful of nails, a sheet of sandpaper, or just one or two bolts. Unfortunately, those days are gone and now you need to purchase everything in multi-packs. I enjoy thinking about the adventures in the general, hardware, the five and ten, and country grocery stores, and it was fun to have the vendors pay a visit to the house. Ma would have a nice chat with the men, and he was just another person to visit and interrupt her busy day. As time passes, we now have the mega-stores that require much time, energy and frustration trying to find that little item that you could put your finger on in those interesting shops. I still enjoy a thrift store, a consignment shop, or an antique store to rummage though and the messier and the more cluttered the better. I think back with fond memories of old time shops and shopping.

ICE CREAM

Ice cream was very scarce when I was a child. Ma and her children also didn't have it very often. Ma made snow cream in the winter sometimes. I remember her making something in the freezer with evaporated milk. After it was frozen, Ma would beat it in her electric mixer and refreeze it. It was cold and sort of sweet, but I never thought it was anything to get excited about.

Ice cream didn't come on the mass market, as it is today, until the home freezer was popular. I do remember special occasions when the family would go to the local sweet shop or a small grocery store where you could purchase hand-dipped ice cream. The confection was scooped up with a metal scoop and placed in a rectangular, white cardboard container. The ice cream was covered with a piece of waxed paper and placed in a white paper bag to rush home so that everyone could share it. Fudgesicle, creamsicle, ice cream sandwiches, and ice cream cones were available to purchase from the store or from the ice cream man who came around in a white truck. I don't recall the cost of the ice cream; I think it was about five cents but no more than ten. Whatever the cost was, it was not in the family budget for us to afford them very often.

We never churned ice cream when we were kids; that was something I introduced to the family to entertain the children. I never really enjoyed milk or ice cream as a child and still don't. I found out that I was lactose intolerant. No wonder!

The fondest memory I have of ice cream was when I was about 9 and Alvin was 7. Dad was an electrician and working in refrigeration, and a gentleman from Cape May Court House, New Jersey, approached Dad to repair his frozen custard machine. Cape May Court House was on the main road to the Jersey shores, at the very tip of the state. This man had a summer business in the seashore town and sold his cold treat to the many travelers.

One early summer day, Dad packed his toolbox and other items that he thought he might need, and the three of us piled into his old truck to head for the shore. On the long trip, after almost 90 miles, Dad was pulled over by a state policeman. Dad got out of the truck, leaving us to wonder what he had done wrong. We didn't have much experience with the police, except to wave hello to our town police. It seems that a truck was supposed to have the name of the owner painted on the side of the door. After Dad returned to the truck, we were again on the road to our shore destination.

When we arrived, Dad went right to work to see what was needed to put the machine back to work. In the meantime, Alvin and I played in the yard to the roadside stand. There were beehives in the yard and we stayed clear of them. It wasn't long until the equipment had to be tried out to see if the job had been done right. A batch of cream, eggs, and honey from the bees was churned up. The man pulled the large paddle out and gave it to us to remove the fresh mixture from it. Then we were given a large bowl of the golden, rich, and sweet frozen custard. The eggs and honey gave it its color. Today's frozen ice cream is made with milk and is sweet, but it is neither very rich nor flavorful. I never have tasted as fine a frozen treat as I had that day. I don't know if anyone makes this delight today. However, I never will forget our trip to the bottom of the state, when we ate a wonderful cold delight on that warm summer day.

CHAPTER TEN

Holidays And Events

I have collected over 150 teddy bears since my children were no longer interested in their bears. One Christmas, I used their bears and other toys to make a holiday display in my foyer. People began to think that I collected bears so they gave me some of their children's bears, which turned into them giving me new bears. I began buying and making bears myself until today I have a house full of bears. They are all sizes and made of all kinds of materials. Each Christmas, we bring them all out of the attic with their own furniture, linens, china, and Christmas tree. They find their place all over the foyer and living room. Because their number keeps growing, they are finding places in other rooms of the house as well.

My oldest bear is two years younger than I am. Ma made it for my second Christmas. He is about 20 inches tall and Ma made it from her mother's old black sealskin coat. The bear's nose and paws were made from one of her mother's old leather handbags. Dad wired his ears to stand up. He also made his eyes with small flashlight light bulbs connected to a battery; the eyes lit up when you pushed his nose. He was presented to me with a large red bow around his neck. Of course, through years of use and storage, the fur has begun to disintegrate. His eyes no longer light. He is the only bear that is not permitted to be handled by anyone, as you might expect. He is privileged to sit anywhere he wants to, because he is the old man bear of the Brandt bear family.

A few years ago, I invited my niece Alice and her three children, Brandon, Laura, and Daniel, to visit with the bears and have some cookies. I told them a story and they were permitted to play with the bears. That started a new tradition. Now, more of the nieces' and nephews' children, and friends' children and grandchildren, are invited in January to a Teddy Bear Tea.

The children look forward to searching for a green glass pickle ornament that is hidden on the tree for them to find. This is an old German Tradition, which is rewarded with a prize. They hear a Christmas or bear story and play with the furry friends. They can select one of the bears to take to the tea table with them. Sometimes, they bring their own favorite bear to the party. We all go to the long dining room table. A tea tray is set at one end, where I sit, and the other end is a service for coffee and milk, manned by Nicole.

First Grandmoms, Great Grandmother and the children are seated at the table. If there is not enough room for the Moms, they sit behind their children. The Moms also help pass the plates of tea sandwiches, cheese and crackers, pickles, and, of course, the plates of cookies and other sweets. Each child's tea is prepared the way they request and everyone sets about to do some serious eating. One of the children calls the traditional English cucumber sandwich a pickle sandwich. It is interesting to see what the children will eat and drink. I think that if their Moms had offered them a cucumber sandwich and a cup of tea at home, they may have turned their nose up at it. But as the girls sit there in their sweet little dresses and the boys in their shirts and ties, they become ladies and gentlemen and their manners do seem to surface, sometimes much to their mothers' surprise. It is a fun party and the children look forward to coming each year. Each child is given a gift, usually something to do with bears, and they and their mothers happily return home after an afternoon at a party that they will remember. Like the Easter egg hunt, I may eventually be hosting teenagers' one year, as they don't seem to grow out of the Teddy Bear Tea.

I have given teas for friends at Christmas, and it is something the family relishes. I have made the little tea sandwiches for years and everyone loves the leftovers because they make great Sunday lunches or tasty snacks. Part of the traditional English tea fare is a seed cake. My Grandmom Meddings brought a very large, old cookbook with her from England and it had a recipe she followed to make her seed cake. I have made it and it is delicious, but again, I often have had to find shortcuts to old recipes, and I like my shortcuts as well. A tea party can be given anytime of the year for just a friend or two or a large group. Take the time to enjoy a tea party.

EASTER

We never had a particular menu for Easter when I was a kid. The meal just followed the pattern of our evening meal, though with a little more flair or special dish. We children were only interested in our Easter baskets. Mother fixed everyone a basket each year. As teenagers, and as long as we were at home, she would make everyone a nest of Easter grass in a large, flat soup bowl and fill it with our favorite sweets. Easter morning, everyone had a bowl at his or her place at the breakfast table.

Another thing I thought about was my Easter outfit. Ma usually made me a new spring outfit and we got new dress up shoes. I always loved my Easter outfit. I remember when I was about 16, and Ma and I made a princess-line dress made of dark blue linen. A lime green cording was placed in each seam. A lime green coat was made in the same style to match the dress. A blue hat, shoes and handbag with green gloves completed the outfit. I looked like something out of a magazine. This look was typical of the complete ensemble that woman wore then.

When Nicole was born, I always made her Easter outfit, as I did on other holidays, until she was in Junior High. When she was in High School, I made both her prom gowns.

I often serve lamb for Easter. When I roast a leg of lamb, I use fresh rosemary and garlic to flavor my roast. It is so good! Ma very rarely cooked lamb, because Dad did not like it. Ma came from the time when pleasing the male of the house was the thing to do.

What she made with lamb was stew. Here's another illustration of her thriftiness: she would buy the breast of lamb, which was very cheap then. The ribs were boiled, cooled and pulled apart. The membrane and fat were removed and the meat taken off the bone. The meat was returned to the liquid and vegetables were added. The dumplings were included last and served with white gravy. Years later, after Ma died, I found a recipe with lamb, vegetables, and tomato gravy, and Dad loved it. Mother learned to make it and she often did.

The tradition of Easter has changed over the years. When I was first married, George, my husband, had three nephews. We started an Easter egg hunt in the house for them, which took place before dinner with the family. As the years went by, and more and more children were born into the family, (which included two of my own) the hunt moved outdoors. We would hide dozens of eggs. One was marked with a dollar, two were marked with fifty cents, and four were marked with twenty-five cents; all the rest were ten cents.

With much searching under leaves and twigs, in flowerpots and under bushes, the hunting continued until all the eggs were found and accounted for. The children lined up in front of Uncle George or Uncle Bud as his family calls him, and got paid the worth of their find. When some of the children were in high school and had no more excuses to hunt for the eggs, insisting it was to help the young ones, the hunt stopped.

I remember the year when we hid the eggs just before the children arrived, and unfortunately, our Saint Bernard, Heidi, got out into the yard and ate some of the eggs, shell, and all. We all enjoyed the humor of her find; after all, she just wanted to be one of the kids.

A tradition I started years ago, after I was married, was to make my father-in-law's eggnog. I make a double batch topped with fresh-ground nutmeg that fills a very large bowl, and everyone drinks it all up. The generations of children keep coming, so there is no opportunity to use alcohol as my father-in-law added in the drink, but I do use rum flavoring. It is very rich, foamy and delicious.

As the family grew, I would feed everyone an Easter dinner and end it with a bunny cake. The cake is a pound cake, baked in a bunny-shaped pan, and topped with seven-minute icing covered with coconut. Green coconut was put all around the bunny and candied cherries made his eyes and nose. Sometimes I use marzipan to make carrots to put in front of the bunny. One Easter, I thought I would have about twenty guests for dinner, but thirty-eight showed up. The phone calls kept coming and the total kept climbing. I had tables set all over the house. It was the last sit-down dinner I did for the whole family. I was getting too old myself for such an ambitious event.

Now the tradition of the egg hunt has started again. The nieces and nephews bring their little ones for eggnog and the hunt. These parents are just helping the little ones, they say, as they look under leaves and twigs, in flowerpots and under bushes for colorful treasures to line up in front of Uncle George in order to collect the value of the find. After the hunt, Moms and Dads and the little ones go off to the other grandmas or to their own homes to have their own Easter dinner and the Grandmoms and Granddads stay at our home for the yearly Easter Dinner.

One time I made a list that included all the brothers, sisters, in-laws, nieces and nephews, their spouses and their children. If they all came to dinner, I would have to set tables to accommodate about sixty people. If we add cousins and spouses and their children, I would have to rent a hall!

COMPANY DINNERS

I remember that the centerpiece of Ma's company dinners was often a crown roast of pork. The center was filled with stuffing; pickled crab apples were arranged around the roast. She would serve roasted sweet potatoes, mashed, or scalloped potatoes. The butcher would include paper panties and Ma would save them and put them on the protruding rib bones of the cooked roast to make her wonderful presentation.

Sweet potatoes are a favorite food that we have always enjoyed. The season for the root is short, and they don't seem to store very well. It seems that they have a short shelf life, unlike their orange cousin, the yam. The sweet potato is often confused with the yam, but it is not even a close second in terns of flavor. Sweet potatoes have a light brown skin and have several names; Jersey Whites or Sweets are what are available to us. They have a light, yellow flesh that gets darker as it is cooked; sometimes, the meat has a greenish tinge. When you bake them, they get sweet and juicy and the juice will bubble out of them, unlike yams, which are usually dry. We usually had them baked when I was a kid, but now I make mashed or home fried sweet potatoes. My sweet potato pies are a favorite with anyone who eats them. They do not taste like the yam pies, which taste much like pumpkin pie. The color is yellow and is flavored with lemon. Look for these wonderful roots in the fall and try them because they are usually gone by Christmas.

Another highlight of Ma's meals was roast beef with twice-baked potatoes; other favorites included her scalloped tomatoes, collard greens or curly kale and pickled peaches. She often served this on New Year's Day. Sometimes, especially for Aunt Ruth, she would make cornmeal dumplings in the greens. They were dense, and I never liked them, so I have no idea how she made them. It was one of the few things I didn't like. I liked her cornbread and the spoon bread she made, it was so delectable that my family insists that I serve it each New Year's Day with the pork and sauerkraut. I was raised on white cornmeal and Ma never used any sugar in her cornbread or spoon bread. Some people put jalapeno peppers in their cornbread, and I prefer it to sugar. Sweet bread is intended for coffee in the morning; it is not to be eaten with a meal and sugary cornbread just doesn't do it for me.

Years ago, the family from Philadelphia came for dinner on New Year's Day. This included my cousins Marbell, Peg, and their brother Bill (Wib) their father, Ma's half-brother Bill, and his wife Mary. Other guests included Bill's sister, Aunt Rozzie, her husband Ernie, and their daughter Catherine.

Sometimes Uncle Arthur, Ma's stepbrother, his wife, Lottie and their daughter Charlotte would attend. Aunt Linda always came along with the family and she was always the one who said grace before dinner. I remember that Uncle Bill often complained that his sister's prayer was too long. He teased her about the contents of the grace, because she included everyone who was present and not present, the event, other events, the food, all the preparation, and on and on went the prayer. It was always a very long blessing. Sometimes Ma's other brothers or sisters from Maryland would come for the party as well.

This tradition of pork and sauerkraut served on New Year's Day that we now enjoy came from my husband George's family, and everyone loves the tradition. I added the spoon bread, and some years, I serve black-eyed peas as a Southern touch. New Year's Day was a favorite holiday when I was young because it meant the family came to visit. The celebration continues.

The conversation was very animated at family gatherings, and it often expressed admiration of Ma's creativity, which her family prized highly. After dinner was finished, we would go to the living room and gather around the piano and sing old songs and hymns. The children usually sat on pillows on the floor as the adults told their stories and jokes. The conversations focused on every topic imaginable. Everything was discussed, argued, analyzed and debated; this was our entertainment and the way that we learned the history of the family and it's ideas. When we children would get bored or tired, we would go play in our playroom and entertain ourselves.

Sometimes the family would play games. I remember one year when Uncle Ellsworth, his wife Ada, and his sister Edna came to visit. When we assembled in the living room, they began to play the game "my little teapot." Each person in turn would select an object. In order to have everyone guess the object, each person would describe it by saying, "My little tea pot," and finish the sentence. The first person to guess what was being described won and was next to play the game. Such laughing, puns, innuendoes, down right rolling on the floor, and holding your sides, accompanied with a silly little children's game. We had so much fun. People made their own entertainment. They told stories, and jokes, sang, played musical instruments, played games, discussed and argued about issues and everyday topics. It was all mixed up with food, which, as Ma said, was the poor man's entertainment. Pots of coffee were always brewing and the first thing that was offered to a guest as he or she entered the home was a cup of coffee. Alcohol was never served in our home, even though Ma drank a little blackberry wine for her heart; however, she never offered it to company. I do serve some alcohol to my guests but only to those who can be moderate. We always looked forward to the holidays because it usually meant good food, family, friends and fun.

GOOD OLD SUMMERTIME

Some of Ma's traditional summer dishes included canned salmon, fried tomatoes, corn on the cob, iced tea, corn or tomato fritters, sour potatoes, strawberry and rhubarb pie. A one-pound tin of fish would feed six people. Ma made six cups of lettuce leaves on a platter. The salmon was divided and placed in each cup. Hard-boiled egg halves, sliced onion, rings of bell peppers, slices of cucumbers, and wedges of Jersey tomatoes were arranged on each leaf. Each portion was then topped with a generous dollop of mayonnaise. Sometimes, she served potato salad or her sour potatoes with the salmon cup.

She often made her own sour potatoes in the summer. The potatoes were sliced and cooked and drained. She would put them on a platter and top them with crumbed bacon and the fat the bacon was cooked in. Celery seed was sprinkled on top and topped with vinegar. It is still a favorite dish of the family and friends. Strawberries and rhubarb are a natural combination. Stewed together as a sauce or made in a pie, this duo was a treasured dessert. We only had the fruits for a short time, from the last weeks in May until the first two weeks in June.

We always had iced tea in the summer, but on Smith's Island, the residents drink it all year long. I thought that was strange when I was young, but since then, I often serve iced tea all year long. My mother-in-law, Mildred Brandt, made an iced tea punch that is a favorite drink for the fourth of July each year.

Summer was a fun time for us kids. We ran under the hose to keep cool and splashed around in the puddles when it rained. There was a deep gully in the farmer's field across the road and it would fill with water, when we had a heavy rainfall. We would "swim" in the muddy water. What fun! We picked blackberries and mulberries, rolled down the front yard's grassy banks, lay in the grass, and marveled at the occasional propeller-driven airplane that flew high overhead. Remember, it wasn't until 1943 until it was deemed safe for President Roosevelt to fly in an airplane. Then it took him 3 days, with many stopovers, to get to Africa. So Alvin and I were still in awe of air flight. It wasn't that long before we were children that flight was possible. You can imagine Ma's amazement of such things. Now, we are part of the flight pattern for the Philadelphia International Airport and the large jets and the small planes fly over-head constantly. Often, military planes fly overheard as well, as we seem to be in the path of Dover Air force Base in Delaware and the McGuire Air Force Base in New Jersey. Quite a change in a lifetime.

We spent time looking at the clouds, trying to see pictures in them. Was it an animal or a flower or a truck? Just what could you see in those billowy clouds?

The yard was filled with interesting places. Dad built an arbor with facing benches. The wisteria grew all over it, so it was a cool and quiet place where we would sit or climb all over it. In the yard, we had twig furniture, which was fun to sit on, even if it was rather lumpy. On the back porch, there was a metal glider with metal chairs; on this porch railing, Aunt Ruth would ripen some of her tomatoes. We would take a saltshaker outside and eat red ripe tomatoes to our hearts' content. Dad built us a very high, A-frame swing set out in the yard. The ropes were very long, and we could swing really high. Dad had started to build a pond in the yard, but it never was completed; it was very large and Aunt Ruth built a rock garden around half of it. We would climb all over the rocks as if they formed our little mountain. We learned to entertain ourselves using our imagination and the things around us. We were never bored we just would look for something else to do.

We played with our toys and we loved to play with Dad's building supplies. We would take the wooden boxes that two-pound American cheese came in and make blocks with them. We would take cement, stones, sand, and water mix it all together to make concrete. We poured the concrete into the cheese boxes and let it harden. Then we were able to turn them out of the containers and use the boxes to make more blocks. We would use the blocks to build forts and other structures. We played with lumber and tried to build things with it. Alvin lugged wood up high in a tree and made a platform. It was too high for me, and I would never go up.

I learned to play jacks from a cousin in Baltimore on a visit one summer. After that I would play it by the hour. Sometimes, Aunt Ruth would play with me. Jumping rope occupied us all the time and double Dutch was the most fun. We would tie the rope to a fence, and one would turn the rope while the other jumped.

On a rainy day or during other times of the year, we would put on a show in the basement. Clothesline was strung up in the rafters and sheets became the curtains. Plays were devised but the story seems to end up with Alvin being punished for his bad behavior with me being the punisher. The family was assembled on the cellar steps as the audience. We sang and danced on the "stage" at the bottom of the steps, made of lumber Dad had stored in the basement.

RED, WHITE AND BLUE

We loved the Fourth of July because the family came to visit for a picnic. Dad built a long picnic table in the wooded area of the property and a very large stone fireplace on which to barbecue. We had flags to decorate the yard, sparkers to light and cap guns to shoot. We would make our own parade with our cousins. Ma made big hamburgers and her own rolls to go with them (early "Whoppers"). We had hot dogs, Aunt Ruth's corn, and watermelon. The relish I remember and still like is ketchup with onion chopped into it. That is all I remember of the menu.

What I do remember was being together with my cousin Peg. We were friends both as children and as teenagers. We spent many weekends as teens going roller-skating, and to the movies, and we spent hours in front of the mirror, priming, and in the bedroom gossiping. We married and had our children and drifted apart. We connected again after our children were grown and spent many hours talking, sharing, reminiscing, taking trips, going to the movies and eating. I spent a couple of summers at the Jersey Shore with her and her family for their weekly stay. We spent time by the ocean and we both enjoyed each other's company. She loved my cooking, and I enjoyed cooking for her and having her and her family at my parties. We got to spend holidays together again. I am glad we had a few years to relive our childhood memories and become friends again before she had to leave her loving family and friends too soon.

The family still celebrates the Fourth of July each year with a picnic. The menu varies, but it usually includes burgers, dogs, corn and watermelon. One of the favorites for years when our children were young was fresh churned ice cream. We had two churns and would often make two kinds of ice cream each holiday. The ice cream mixture was put in the container and salt and ice was packed around it. Then the churning began. The children would turn it awhile when it was easy, but as the cream mixture began to thicken, it became harder to turn it, and this became the job for the adults. Usually Martha and George were left to finish the batch, but everyone wanted to be the first in line to get a dish of freshly made ice cream. We never got to pack it in ice to get hard. Everyone wanted it in its soft stage. Blueberry, strawberry, cherry, peach, and rocky road were some of the favorites. Just this year, we reinstated the tradition of homemade ice cream. Like Ma's snow cream, it never tasted as good after it sat in the freezer as when it was freshly made. This year, we made just one large batch of strawberry, and there were no leftovers.

Another dish I still include in my picnic menu is baked lima beans. The casserole bakes for hours, is filled with pieces of bacon, and is scrumptious.

We look forward each Fourth to our niece Sheryl Allen's miniature cherry cheesecakes. Mother makes a wonderful five-cup salad she calls ambrosia and Nicole makes an exotic tropical fruit salad, which all make for gooey desserts.

Through the years, some of our family members have participated in our town parade, but for years, we have usually watched it, then headed home to light the BBQ to get ready for the family to gather from all over. Yard games were a tradition when everyone was younger and for many years we had a large swimming pool that the children enjoyed. Now the family just visits and swaps stories and we mainly just enjoy each other. Fireworks were watched for years from Alvin's yard as he lived near the field were they were displayed. We would go to his yard for dessert and watch the fireworks until one year the township discontinued them. They did so, because someone was very seriously injured by fireworks gone ad awry. Now, we watch the fireworks displays in surrounding towns from the top of the hill were the pears use to grow. Some of the family enjoys the spectacular lights in their own towns or, sometimes, some go to the Philadelphia Museum of Art to see the concert and the fireworks. All in all, the Fourth of July celebration continues.

THE UN-BIRTHDAY PARTIES

Once, Dorothy, George's sister, and I borrowed a page from Lewis Carroll's "Alice in Wonderland" and held a un-birthday party of our own. On an August Saturday evening, she and I would gather both sides of our family and celebrate everyone's birthday. Every month but August marked at least one person's birthday. We had games and small gifts for everyone. We even played games with the gifts. Then the birthday cake and ice cream. We laid out all kinds of toppings, fruit and whipped cream for everyone to make their own sundaes. What fun! It was a fun party for all, the children and the adults. Our parties often had 25 to 30 guests. I miss Dot and our parties, but one of these summers, I'm going to have a un-birthday party again and remember my good friend and dear sister, Dorothy Brandt.

VEGGIE DINNER

For a number of years, in the month of August, I have been going to a local farm, where I buy quantities of the fresh produce available, and I have the family and a few friends for a vegetable dinner. If the weather permits, we dine on the patio; if not, we eat in the dining room with the air conditioner going full blast. I use only the fruits and vegetables that I can find at the farms. When I invited some of my gentlemen guests, they were skeptical at first about just having veggies. They were from the meat-and-potatoes school. However, now it is a favorite party with both men and women. It is difficult to cook anything ahead as it all needs to be prepared just before eating, but I do prepare as many fruits and vegetables ahead of time so that I am ready to cook everything at the last minute. It is a tradition I enjoy each late summer. This is one of the times I can invite my friends because it is not a family holiday. A theme party in the winter, the 4th of July, the August Veggie Dinner, and Halloween are my parties for family and friends. The other holidays are usually devoted exclusively to the family.

MAKE MINE WITH MUSHROOMS AND PEPPERONI

In the early 50s, Aunt Ruth and her friend Al began to talk about tomato pie. They used to eat it in Philly when they visited Aunt Rozzie. I couldn't imagine what a tomato pie could taste like. We heard a lot about the Philly Tomato Pie, which became more popular when people began to call it Pizza Pie. Of course the wonderful food is world known and, even when I was in England, we went into a pizza shop for a takeout.

In the 1980s when our children and their cousins were young, I used to give pizza parties. I would invite everyone; we would have twenty or twenty-five people. Everyone was hungry for pizza. I went to the local Italian bakery and bought 12 to 15 16-inch shells. Now you can find them in the grocery stores. I fried Italian sausage to crumble over the top, sliced up pepperoni, grated cheeses, opened cans of pizza sauce and sliced mushrooms. I used chopped olives, onions, and set up an assembly line to make pizza to order. Half the pie was made with this one and not that, the other half, another combination. Everyone stood around talking and laughing, waiting for the pies to come out of the oven.

They all ate and ate until they were stuffed. The big bottles of assorted sodas were emptied and tons of paper plates and napkins were used on those nights. It was a fun party. Having everything prepared ahead of time made it easy to make the pizzas. It was not a lot of work, and it became a group effort to see who could request the best combination of ingredients and who could get to the next pizza first.

HALLOWEEN

This holiday is difficult to forget because it is my birthday. I got teased as a kid about it; they called me a witch. It was hard to celebrate my birthday and to trick and treat at the same time. I recall a woman in the neighborhood who turned her porch into a haunted house and had lights on and spooky noisy sounds playing as the children knocked on her door. She would dress up as a witch, and she offered us cider from a cauldron and cookies. It was fun. When we got old enough, we were allowed to go up to the main highway that ran through town, to the funeral home. They gave out candied apples each year. For years and years they gave out hundreds of candied apples. I remember seeing carloads of kids being let out to get in line for an apple. The Black Horse Pike had a lot of small businesses, and the children would go up and down both sides of the pike to collect their treats. We had our family business for years on the pike and gave out boxes and boxes of candy bars each year. When I was a child, people could give homemade treats to the kids. Ma would make donuts each year for her treat. We always hated the people who gave plain old apples! Yuck! Even when my children were young, I gave fresh bags of popcorn treats, but those days are gone. These days it is considered dangerous for children to accept anything homemade or unwrapped, because some people have become so ill that they would endanger a child's health by tampering with the food they give to them.

Just this past Halloween, I reinstated the neighbor who dressed as a witch. I too dress as a witch and invited the children in offered them a cup of warm blood (warm, spiced cranberry juice) and a pumpkin cookie wrapped individually. The kids like the idea except one little girl whose mother had to convince her that it really wasn't blood.

Sometimes for my birthday, if the weather was good, we would have a hot dog roast out on the BBQ for the two of us children as well as some of our friends. After the roast, we would go trick or treating. In those days all the children were known by the neighbors and part of the trick and treating was to see if you could guess who the tricksters were. The children thought it part of the fun to fool the neighbors and make your costume good enough to make it difficult for them to guess who you were. Today, I have no idea who most of the children are, and a lot of them don't even say thanks!

Dad built our BBQ out of the stones that came from the base of one of the largest barns in southern New Jersey. It stood on the hill in front of our home. It was a giant structure and it was abandoned. One Mischief Night, someone set it one fire. Mother had to work late in the city that night and was coming home at about 10:00 that evening. When she got off the bus, she was facing towards home on the other side of the hill. All she could see was a giant blaze that was in the area of her home, and she panicked. She and Dad, who had gone to meet her at the bus stop, rushed home to find the old barn in full blaze.

How well I remember that evening, when Ma and I were in the kitchen; I was still awake, waiting to see my Mother. The kitchen faced the North and the barn was on the south side of the house. As we looked out the kitchen window, all of a sudden the night turned into day. The yard looked like daylight only orange in color. We thought the other side of the house or the roof was on fire. We ran to the dining room that looked out on the south side of the house and saw the flames leaping into the night sky. It was overwhelming. We cried out, and Alvin and Aunt Ruth came running as Mother and Dad pulled up in the driveway. We were all relieved to find out that our home and all of us were safe. It was quite a memorable Mischief Night that year. We were very fortunate that it was not a windy night, or we might have had to fight the fire away from our home.

Besides the flat stones that we trucked to our yard to make the fireplace, we inherited the mice that lived in the barn. We were the closest building to the burned-out barn, and the dwellers took up their winter residence in our home. It was quite a job of fighting off the many field mice that boarded with us for months. Ma was beside herself with these little beasts in her home, but we won the war of the mice.

In the present time, I often give Halloween parties for family and friends. Usually a costume is requested. We have the house decorated to the hilt with spooky things. The dining room is dimly lit, and the holiday theme is carried out. I usually pass a menu with things on it like "blood of anteater and gourd gruel." "Pickled meat with fungus and smelly roots stewed in rotten fruit juices" is served as the main course. Translated, it means cranberry juice, cream of pumpkin soup, and beef burgundy with mushrooms and onions. Then the real menu is passed around later, or the item is announced as each dish is brought to the table. I use caskets, skulls, and rats, mice, spiders, bugs and other horrible things to decorate my table. The colors black, orange, and purple are used as often as possible. I have brain and hand molds to make gelatin dishes that make a wonderful presentation. We play games and have any scary thing we can come up with. One year, a ghost in a black robe appeared at the party, and nobody could figure out who it was. The ghost never spoke, floated around quietly, stayed awhile, and then disappeared. Only when we had sat down to our first course of "green moss with spider legs marinated in fermented juice" (salad with shaved onion in vinaigrette) did the creature let out a blood-curdling scream. We screamed, dropped our forks, and the ghost just passed though the room and left the house. We never knew who was under the robe. Well, some of us never knew, and I am not telling. They still talk about that event.

At my last party, we had a wiener roast with dogs, baked potatoes, brain salad, and s'mores, roasted marshmallows on a stick, hot cider, hot chocolate and gingerbread. We built a fire in the grill and cooked outside. We built a fire in our patio fireplace and gathered around it with out food, and many of the guests told ghost stories. People dressed for the weather and, happily, the weather was mild. Everyone said they had a good time. It does put your mind to work to think up fun things to do to keep the party lively, but it keeps me off the streets!

THE GHOST THAT WASN'T

One October evening about seven o'clock, when I was about 7 or 8 years old, a very loud rapping came on the side of the house. One, two, three came the rapping methodically. Everyone in the house heard the noise. We questioned each other, but we all heard the same thing.

This rapping came on the north side of the house, where the rock garden was and there was some shrubbery in the garden. This side of the house was where the chimney was. The chimney was covered with ivy that grew all the way to the roof. The ivy housed many bird nests and a village of birds that were very noisy in the morning, as they rose, and at dusk, as they settled in for the night. The heavy wires for the electricity that came into the house were also on this side.

It was dark by this time of the evening, but Dad went outside to see at what might have caused the sound. None of the things that could hit or rub up against the house seemed to be loose or able to make this racket.

The very next evening about seven o'clock, the same three loud rappings came again and again, we all heard the banging on the house. Well, Dad checked again. During the daytime hours he also checked what might be creating the noise, but nothing seemed to be responsible. Dad looked inside the house as well. We all became detectives, trying to fathom what could possibly be causing the noise. And wasn't it strange that it happened at the same time each night?

Well, by seven o'clock the third evening everyone was gathered in the living room awaiting the rapping. The living room was in the front of the house and we all agreed that the sound seemed to emanate from this location. We didn't have long to wait long, like the two previous evenings. The rappings came, one, two, three, thump, thump, thump. Dad quickly ran outside to see if someone was playing tricks on us, but he saw no one. We all were puzzled.

Now, I must say that sometimes Ma had a tendency to be of the old school and account for mysterious happenings as coming from unknown, mythical sources. We pooh-wooed that notion and continued searching to find the source of the recurring sound.

Day four. Now, we were really prepared to be frightened by this mysterious incidence. As we gathered in the living room, seven o'clock came and no rapping. Seven-fifteen, no rapping. Seven-thirty came and no rapping. With a hardy sigh, we all dispersed to continue with our evening's endeavors, and the puzzle was still unsolved.

We listened many nights after this phenomenon, straining to hear the three knocks. Dad never could find an answer and neither could anyone else. So, we were left with the mysterious visitor who came those three October evenings but never paid us a visit ever again.

TV, CONVENTIONS, AND POLITICS

When television came onto the scene at our home, I was about thirteen. TV did help everyone to broaden his or her vision of the world. We found it fascinating to watch the political conventions on TV. It was a family entertainment event. We would gather around with popcorn and snacks in hand to watch the speeches, the nominations and the balloting. We would keep score, as each state chairman rose, microphone in hand, and the camera focused on him. Each politician, with a speech prepared, praised his state and how he and his delegation were proud to be voting for a particular candidate or candidates. The speculation regarding who would be nominated sometimes when on for more than one ballot. (I use the pronouns "he and him," because in those days women didn't hold many positions or offices.) The parades around the convention floor held by the delegates backing their candidate were elaborate and loud. The marching band led the parade of cheering people marching with placards, sighs and funny hats went on for long periods of time. The candidate was picked by the delegation, not in the primaries. There was really a contest at the convention. We cheered when our candidate won or moaned when he lost. The conventions went on for days, maybe a week; it was a spectacle we could never have witnessed if it had not been for TV. The final excitement was the selection of the Vice President. Newscasters speculated, but finally the nomination would come and the election of the VP would finally be known. It was quite the grand event. We watched both political conventions every four years.

I still look forward every four years to watching the conventions. They are much more cut and dry now, because all the participants are aware of being on TV and the polls and the audiences are much more jaded and want only to be entertained and not informed. There is no suspense, because now everything is known and there is no contest because of the primaries. Even the VP is announced before hand. People don't seem to understand the importance of political life and what effect it has on them. People don't seem to be able to think in the abstract and see the overall picture. Their only concern is, "What can I get out of it?" It is a shame because, even as a child, I could understand the overall importance of our political system and I wanted to keep abreast of the everyday happenings of history.

In the 1948 election, I was about ten years old when Dad took me to see President Truman in Camden New Jersey as he campaigned. We gathered around the long flight of steps leading up to the City Hall Building. At the top of the steps, a small man with a gray topcoat and fedora hat appeared from the crowd. He stepped up on the wall of the steps and began to speak to the crowd, and when his speech was over and everyone cheered, he stepped back into the crowd and was gone. I will never forget the sight. Can you imagine this happening today? It was all so simple and plain, no frills, no screaming people or news media shouting at the candidate. No flashing lights, pushing and shoving, secret service, police, officials, media, and no circus. No, not today. My, how things have changed. Maybe that is why we could have someone who was so strong, simple, and resolute as President Truman in those days and now the candidates have to have an image. Some people choose a president on his looks and how much media he can attract, not on substance or intelligence. It is sad to watch, because, when any uneducated electorate chooses our leaders who have little qualifications, it affects us all.

Of course after the conventions, there came the election in November. On election night, after everyone had voted and returned home, Ma would have a supper laid out in buffet style. We would get our plates and move into the sunroom, where the TV was, and get comfortable. In the 50s and 60s the media didn't have the electronics they have today so the race was really a race. They would start talking about the election and how the polls were running and, at 8:00, they would start to report the balloting and how it was going. We would keep a tally of the electoral votes and how each state had polled at each report. We would refill our plates and glasses or cups throughout the evening because it was going to be a long night. No projections as to how the vote would go, just raw numbers as the districts reported. It was exciting, tense, and dramatic, and we loved it.

In spite of it all, I am still a political junkie and watch the conventions and sit up to watch the elections. It seems it is no longer a contest, and the outcome is now known before 9:00 due to projects and polls. They have taken the fun and excitement out of it. No more sitting up half the night as we sometimes did in the past, not knowing until the morning who will be the next President of the United States of America.

This 2000 election is something I hope never to see again. Maybe it showed us all how our election system has to be changed and watched. It was shocking to find out that, in places in this country, voters can still be manipulated and some people can still be intimidated and prevented from voting because of who they are and how they might vote. Quite an eye opener! I hope we have learned a lesson we can benefit from and change how things are done so that the tragedy of 2000 never happens again. Sometimes we have to go a few steps back in order to go a few more steps forward. The best thing is that every four years we get to change our minds! This time we will have to vote with both eyes open!

Even though Ma could not vote until she was 39 years old (because it wasn't until 1920 until women could legally vote in the United States) she voted every time there was an election. It didn't matter if it was for the school board or the President, Ma voted. We all voted every time. We still do. I get a call from Mother on each Election Day to get a ride to the polls. We learned to take our duty to be good citizens seriously. I have passed that lesson to my children and reminded them to change registration when they move. Even though they are not as avid political people as I am, they do stay informed and take their responsibility to heart. I am sorry more people do not. It has been a part of my life ever since I can remember. I can't think of a time that it hasn't come up in the way of discussion almost daily since I was a child. At the dinner table each evening, politics and what was going on in the world was the topic of conversation, with or without company.

CHAPTER ELEVEN

Uncle Peach And Fond Family Memories

Grandfather Evans had two bothers, Peter and Mitchell. His mother died and his father, Solomon, married Anna Eliza Bradshaw and had five more sons, George, Nicolas, John, Benjamin, and Dow. I do not know very much about all of these men, nor have I uncovered a lot about them, but the information I have is this: The brothers were all born on Smith's Island, and most lived their adult lives there. Most married and had children, but I have no information about any family that remains. Mitchell lived on the part of Smith's Island known as Tylerton or Drum's Point. Nicholas married and had two daughters, Rosemond (Rose) and Audrey. I will speak of the history of the other two brothers John and Peter, because I know more of that.

Captain John Smith (of Pocahontas fame) brought English and Welsh settlers to the shores of Virginia. In 1603, he sailed up the Saint James River and deposited them there in the wilderness. They carved out a settlement they called Jamestown and, when John Smith came back with more passengers the following year, he found that only a handful of people had survived the winter. John Smith brought many settlers to the New World for many years. He ventured more inland and up the waterways to forge new settlements. During one of these trips in 1608, he sailed up to the Chesapeake Bay and River and deposited some of his passengers on an island in the river, which was named for the Captain himself

At least that is how the story was told for many, many years. "Many a Islander went to their grave believing that story." Says Jennings Evans, a

Smith Island residence. He told me this as he reveled the real historical tale to me. There may have been a small island off the coast of Virginia named for John Smith. He does allude to in a book he wrote while at home in England, recovering from a bullet wound he received in America. This Smith Island, however, was not named for him.

It seems in 1657 a Western Shore, Marylander, solicited a representative, Colonel Stevens, of Lord Baltimore, to purchase this piece of very lucrative real estate sitting in the middle of massive beds of luscious oysters. The land was large enough and arid enough for raising cattle and for farming. This very wealthy businessman, with not a very nice reputation, named the bit of land for himself, Henry Smith.

The northern end of the Island was used for cattle raising, while the center of the land, now the main area called Ewell, was just the right rich land of farming. When the island began to attract more residents the farming area also gave way to homesteads. Some of the first families to reside on the green land were three brothers named Evans. As I spoke to Jennings he unfolded the lineage of the Solomon Evans brother, dates and all. It seems that the name Solomon repeats about three times. My Great Grandfather Solomon was the last. Jennings also was knowable of the lines of the other two brothers, he being the member of one of those. As you read on you will hear about Jenny Evans, she was a descendent of the same family.

Jennings was a fountain of information about his beloved Smith Island. The stories of the involvement of the island in the Revolution and Civil Wars and the many other bits of history were amazing. I encouraged him to please get all of this history recorded for all the lovers of history, especially American history.

The present pieces of information he gave me were that the northern part of the island is now a National Wildlife Refuge. Grandfather Evans home, of which you will find a picture in the family picture section of this book, has been purchased by an Evans and has been restored.

Jennings figured I was the decent from about the eighth generation of the Evans brothers who first came to the Chesapeake River land. I have traced the seventh generation from the last Solomon. Grandfather Evans and his siblings were descendants of one of the three families. The Evans name is Welsh. In Wales, the name Evans is a very common one.

Thomas was the oldest of the sons, having been born in 1864 in the midst of the Civil War, Abraham Lincoln was President, and the Transcontinental Railroad wasn't completed until five years later. And of course, as we remember, Victoria was still the reigning queen of England. The telegraph was invented shortly before his birth. Imagine that!

Uncle John, grandfather's half-brother, married Hattie's sister Margaret (Maggie). Maggie, like her sister, Hattie, had gone to the island to work for one of her cousins, a minister. This is how she met her brother-in-law, John. John worked in the seafood business, crabs and oysters, all his life. They married and had two sons, Granville, named for her sister Linda's husband, and John Nevitt, (Nevitt). They moved to Crisfield in 1923. Granville, who was much like his cousin Alvin, had the ability to do almost anything with his hands. He worked at many things, including boats. He built many of them. I remember visiting them in Crisfield and he had built a very large, in-ground pool on his property and had opened it to the public for a fee. It served as a community pool for many years. Granville married a woman by the name of Mary Agnes Sommers, whose family also came from the island, and they had two girls. Eileen married Edward Marshall and had two sons. Her sister, Linda Sue, married and has one daughter.

Nevitt, who studied for a number of years, became a minister in the Church of God. Reverend Evans retired after many years in the church in 1982. As a young man, he married Lois Kelly, and they had a son named John Nevitt Jr. and two daughters named Nevelyn and Nevitta, names their mother had coined in honor of their father. The daughters married, and Nevelyn has two children and Nevitta has a son. Lois died and Nevitt was married again to Leona Platt.

I remember when Aunt Maggie would take charge of Ma's kitchen to make her wonderful, always-requested applesauce cake. She would mix it up without consulting a recipe. It was always a moist, spicy, rich and delicious dessert. It had the applesauce in it, as well as raisins and nuts. It was baked in a tube pan and she would whip up a batch of seven-minute icing to top this luscious cake. She never wrote the recipe down. Aunt Theresa's daughter, Vasso, has given me her mother's recipe for applesauce cake and it is very much like Aunt Maggie's. Maggie was famous for her navy bean and ham bone soup, served with Maryland beaten biscuits. It is a lot easier to make the biscuits today because we have machines to do the work, but when Aunt Maggie make them, she really had to beat them. They still go great with a pot of beans.

Aunt Maggie and Uncle John spend months at a time with us through the years. I remember them celebrating their fiftieth wedding anniversary with us, and we had a party for them to honor the date. Aunt Maggie gave me a white pitcher and basin that Uncle John had given her as a wedding gift. I still have it. I also have a cut glass plate that was the only wedding gift Ma was able to save. These are memories that can only be appreciated by someone who has the memories of the women who treasured them. These sisters used their pitcher, basin set and the plate through their married years. I still have the use of them today. Now they are not very practical items, but are treasured mementos of loved ones passed.

Brother Peter (Cap'n Pete), who was also a Waterman, married Margaret Dize and they had many children. There were Russell, Carol, Adrian, James, and Susie all of whom did not survive their babyhood. The two daughters who did survive were Theresa (pronounced Th-res-a) and Susan. Susan lived to be an adult, and became a nurse. She nursed tuberculosis patients and, unfortunately, contracted the disease herself and died at the age of 26. When Theresa was young, about nine, her mother died and Hattie helped raise her until she was about 14, when she went to work for Emma Stevens, who had a boarding house in Crisfield. Uncle Pete married again to Margaret Brown (Maggie) and had three more children named Naomi, Ruth, and Newell. I recall Naomi and her sister Ruth visiting us when I was a child.

Theresa married a Greek man named John Legidakes who had settled in Crisfield. John was a storekeeper; his store was a luncheonette and candy store, and included shoe repair. The store was next door to Miss Emma's boarding house, which is how they met. The couple had three sons who were born there and then they all moved to Reading, Pennsylvania. They followed Theresa's cousin Roseman (Rose) and her husband Edward (Eddie) Smith. John opened his business in Reading as well. Eddie was a hairdresser and, after living in Reading for a while, he found little work. He then found a job in the very large and old department store, John Wanamaker's, in Philadelphia. They all relocated to Philly on 69th Street. John opened his shoe shop there again. Eddie worked at the department store for years and years. Incidentally, I recall when he and Aunt Rose brought me small samples of make-up, rouge, lipstick and the like from the beauty salon. I was very young, and it was quite a treat because I was not allowed to wear make-up until I was in my mid-teens. The Smiths moved back to Smith's Island to take care of Rose's father, Nicholas. Eddie opened a barbershop in Crisfield. Eddie also loved to carve ducks out of driftwood from the shores of the island. I have some of his carving on display in my dining room. Rose and Eddie never had any children but lived their lives out on the island.

Theresa's and John's three sons are Nicolas (Nick), George, and Constantine (Dean). Fifteen years after Dean's birth, a daughter was born in Philadelphia to John and Theresa; her name is Vasso. These siblings have all married and had children, and their families all live in the Philadelphia and South Jersey area with their spouses, children, and grandchildren.

What I remember of this part of the family is how, when I was very young, Uncle Pete came to visit a number of times. I can see him as a slight built man, slender and bent. They say that he was a dead ringer for his brother Tom. He was a quiet man and loved to walk in Aunt Ruth's garden and talk to her as she gardened. When I was very young, I often reversed words or misspoke. When they spoke of Uncle Pete, what I heard was Uncle Peach. So that is what I called him and always referred to him by that name. He seemed to like the reference and accepted the new name.

Although I never knew my grandfather, my experiences with his brothers John and Peter did give me an insight to him. Neither of the men was very educated and they were just simple watermen. They found joy in simple things and were comforted by their family even though they were not demonstrative. I think that is how Grandfather Evans must have been as well.

When I was a child, adults were always addressed with a title. Mrs., Miss, Mr., Uncle, Aunt, Cap'n, Sister, Brother and Buddy were all titles attached to people older than yourself as a sign of respect. Aunt Theresa, as I was taught to call her even though she was my cousin, was very close to her Aunt Hattie and kept in touch with her aunt her whole life. Aunt Theresa visited often and sometimes brought Vasso with her. Vasso and I are separated by a couple of years. I remember one summer when they visited, and Vasso and I wanted to play outside. She was not dressed to play in the yard and to get dirty and sweaty; after all, she was a city girl. Our hair was put up in braids, and Ma gave Vasso one of my sundresses to wear. I always recall that day. I thought it was such an important thing that I could have my cousin wear one of my dresses. I think I was possessive about my things. I thought that made me important, to share my dress with my cousin. This is how a child thinks. I recollect that we did run, play and enjoyed the visit.

I never forgot Aunt Theresa's awful experience of losing her son Nicolas (Nick). When he was just forty-four years old, he fell off a scaffold and was killed. She mourned for the rest of her life as one might expect when one loses a child. Ma and she were a comfort to each other because of this unfortunate part of each of their lives, losing a son. Years later, Peg told me how much Aunt Sissy[2] meant to her when she, Peg, lost her first son, Joey; Ma knew how she felt. Peg said that Aunt Sissy told her no matter how long you have a child, whether he was four months like Joey or twenty-seven years like her son Homer, when you lose him there is no pain like it. It will always be a part

---

2 Aunt Sissy" refers to Peg's father, Bill, who was Ma's half-brother, calling her "Sissy"

in your heart that could never be filled by that loss. Peg never forgot it; nor did she forget the special connection she had shared with her Aunt and what a comfort it was to have someone who understood her pain. Aunt Theresa seemed to have the same kind of relationship with her aunt. There were not a lot of other people around us, and I did not have a lot of playmates—some, but not many. Lee Koring, my best friend from the age of five, moved away when we were twelve, and I could only visit her occasionally. I didn't have many other friends so when I think of my aunts, uncles and cousins of my youth, I think of them in a special way because they seem to have brought happiness, kindness, enjoyment and a feeling of importance to me in my young life. When I think of times past, each member of the family was such a contributing force to my perception of the world. I am glad they buffered me so that when life became more complicated and difficult, I had pleasant memories of people who were dear, kind, and loving and who honored me as a sweet child. I would hope that every child would have this kind of experience to fall back on as they meet life and all it has to offer, good and bad. I do remember this part of the family with love.

Years later, after Uncle Peach, Ma and Aunt Theresa had passed on, we had a family reunion. The cousins came from near and far, along with the few aunts and uncles who were still left. They all came together at Mother and Dad's house and what a reunion we had. Cousins who did not know that they had cousins met for the first time. The Greek cousins, who had married other Greeks and Italians, were all dark-haired, dark-skinned, and dark-eyed. The children of their Welsh and Irish cousins, who had married other English, Irish, and Germans, had blond hair, light eyes and light skin. They were shocked to meet each other from their different ancestors. What they all had in common were family ties, going back to Smith's Island and the Eastern Shore of Maryland and to my Grandmother, Ma.

This was quite a mixture of people. Everyone was fascinated to meet his or her long-lost cousins. I made a large family tree. Everyone had fun seeing where they fell in the long lineage. Everyone brought enough food to feed his or her family. We put all the food on a big table and everyone sampled and shared each other's food. What a menu! It reflected the diversity of the family.

Ever since that summer afternoon, I have wanted to have another get-together of the families but have not achieved it. I think that in writing this book about them all, I am having a family reunion. Needless to say, the family I knew has grown smaller and smaller. The next couple of generations really have no connections to each other. A second reunion would look a lot different than the first. My cousins and I would be the elders and still the others' relatives would not know who we were. This is sad after coming from such a connected family. Times have changed and people don't spend months in each other's homes so the children don't learn all the connections. I have made an attempt to make a family tree here in this publication to visually show how we are all connected. I know it is hard for young people to get the connection to family relationships. We lived with the people, saw them, talked to them, heard their stories and still had a hard time connecting them all. So for people who have no idea whom they came from, I am sure it will be a maze. I hope the family tree in diagram form helps. I want it to be helpful to your family, to have a connection to the past and to see where you came from as you make your family's history. It would have been interesting to be able to trace the family back and know the connection to our ancestors in Europe and back through history. However, this amount of genealogy I have recorded is a place to start for present and future generations to continue the tree. Add to it and keep records. Talk to your parents and grandparents and keep a record of their memories and your own. Not everyone is interested in where they came from, but your children may be. I hope you write down or record your memories and pass them on to your family as I have tried to do here. Thanks for the memories.

Love,
Myrna

CHAPTER TWELVE

Pictures

As I sorted through the many albums of my mother's photographs, so many events came back to me. The large boxes of photos that were Aunt Ruth's reminded me of her fun-loving nature. There were pictures of the many trips she and Al took. Some of the trips she made by herself were to Arizona to see the painted dessert and her last trip was to the Scandinavian countries. Aunt Ruth had albums of that trip. Yes, going though the old photos brought back fond memories.

There were pictures of dogs, Niffy I and II. They were both mixed breeds, black and brown, medium sized dogs. Both were smart dogs, and I remember that many stories were told about both of them and their amazing abilities. We heard how they paid so much attention to the family and how well they behaved. The story of the chocolate was told about the first dog. When the family lived in the city, one week, every day Niffy came home with a chocolate-covered butter cream candy, which he would place on the back step. He was highly praised for his behavior and the candy was thrown away. One day, a neighbor told Ma what a well-behaved dog he was and that she had rewarded him with a chocolate. Ma told her that she hated to disappoint her, but she had had to throw the candy away. The neighbor was surprised as to why she would do such a thing. Ma told her that Niffy was taught not to eat anything from anyone but the family, so he had brought it home and put on the step and since Ma did not know where it came from, she threw it away. Well, the neighbor thought that was amazing. Ma allowed the dog to take treats from the neighbor, so he was able to have a sweet reward once in awhile.

The other dog lived when I was a young child and Uncle Homer was still living. He would put a treat on the arm of a chair and tell the dog he could have it when he had preformed a trick or when he was told to have it and not until. One night, he put the treat on the arm and forgot to give permission for Niffy to have it. The next morning, when everyone got up the treat was still on the arm of the chair; Niffy had done what he was told and never touched the treat. There were many more stories about the two dogs; these are but two

There were pictures of Spot, Ma's fox terrier. Ma and she were inseparable. Spot looked just like this famous RCA dog. She was white with one black spot over one eye and a large black spot in the middle of her back. This is how she got her name. Ma had her for many years; Spot was a devoted companion.

I found a picture of our goat, Nanny, whom we had as children. I saw pictures of my dogs, Kim, a German Shepherd who got killed on the highway when George Jr. was an infant. George Sr. then bought me a Saint Bernard puppy, and we named her Heidi. She was born in October, two weeks after George, and they grew up together. Both children loved her and she protected them. This huge dog who frightened strangers with her loud bark was really a pussycat. Heidi died the July before her fourteenth birthday. Although we still miss her, she was my dog and pal, so I remember her with great affection. The many cats in the family were immortalized as well. Everyone took pictures of all the pets we had all through my life.

Pictures recorded the many family parties. I had forgotten the luau I gave when I was first married. George built a 16-foot long picnic tabletop. Before he put the legs on it, we propped it up on cinder blocks to use it for our table. I remember going to the florist and getting tropical leaves to lay down the middle of the table on which I placed all the bowls of food. Everyone was asked to bring a pillow to sit on and so we did. We sat around the long table on pillows as we devoured a Hawaiian-style menu. We all received leis and straw hats; the women wore muumuus, and the men came in flowered shirts. Family and friends had a good time that day. Now, most of us would find it difficult to sit down on the ground, cross-legged, with or without a pillow!

We recorded the births of the babies into the family with many pictures of their growth and as they became teenagers. There are pictures of their proms, graduations, weddings, and then the birth of the next generation. Pictures do record a passage of time. I didn't remember some of the people in the photographs, and the ones who would have known who they were passed long ago. I will try to label my photos so that when I am no longer here, members of my family can look back and know who these people are in the faded photos, which were taken so many years ago. I really wanted to find the old pictures my mother had of the years past. But my pictures were over 40 years old as well. It seems as though time goes by without us realizing it. Looking at old pictures and albums was part of our family gathering. Everyone seemed to relive the memories the photos brought back. I don't often look at the old photographs anymore, but in researching pictures I want to include in this book, I was reminded of many people, what they looked like, what we all did, and how fondly my memory is of them all. I hope you enjoy looking at the family pictures. I know you may have no recollection of these people, as most of you were not born when these photos were taken. But seeing brothers and sisters and family members gathered together, I think, it showed in their faces how much they enjoyed being amongst their family.

Ma and her family 1890 to 1950s

Myrna from 1943 to Wedding June 1, 1963

Aunt Ruth from 1912 to 1962 with Al Volz

Mother 1915 to 1955 and Dad 1916 to 1955

Myrna & Alvin
1941-1958

Ruth and Linda in the Fall Garden 1959
Truck that killed Homer and Bella Aug. 1938

Ma's stepchildren, Annie, Edna, her daughter Sue & family, Ellsworth and Ada

Edith, Medford, Rozzie and Ernie, Harold and Hazel,
Bill and Mary

Will and Lucy Ford. Son Lewis, wife Ruth, Son Lewis Jr.

Family Gathering 1923-1950

Home Sweet Home when purchased 1936
Winter in the 1950s

Smith Island Boats, Crab Shanty, Church, and Evans Homestead

Nevitt and Lois, Annie's husband Dan
Catherine and Myrna

Virginia McDaniel Beauchamp Blake with daughter, Rozzie 1920s

THE FAMILY TREE

A grafted family tree I prepared became unmanageable to print when the tree becomes so large. I decided to at least write down the names and connection, as best as I could gather, as clear as possible. That way the people I speak about in the book can because clearer to the reader. This description should tell who everyone is and how all of them are connected. There are some blank spaces left in the family line and I tried to get as much information as possible but I was not always successful.

The Three Sisters
Mary, Virginia and Lucy
"The McDaniel's"

1st. **Mary** married **Daniel Blake (Dan)** *2nd.* Children: **Fred, Aretha (Rethy)** and **Daniel Arthur (Arthur)**

Fred married **Sedona (Donie)** *3rd* Grandchildren **Lewis.**
Lewis married **Lillian (Lill)** *4th* Great—Grandchildren: **Jay and Jack**

Aretha died as a young woman

Arthur married **Lottie** *3rd*. Grandchildren **Charlotte.**
Charlotte married **Edward Stadler** *4th*.Great-Grandchildren: **Richard (Richie)** and **Donald (Donnie)**

1st **Virginia** married **George Beauchamp** *2nd* Children: **Hattie, Margaret (Maggie), Linda, George Harold, (Harold).**

Hattie married **Ellsworth Thomas Evans** *3rd*.Grandchildren:**Virigrin Ruth (Ruth), William Homer (Homer** and **Bill)** and **Alvin.**
Alvin married **Marjorie nee Meddings** *4th* Great Grandchildren: **Myrna Ruth** and **Alvin Strauss Jr**.
Myrna married **George N. Brandt** *5th* Great—Great grandchildren: **George Nicolas Jr.** and **Nicole Ruth**
Nicole married **Anthony Weal**. *6th* Great-Great Great Grandchildren **Dante Nicolas** and **Kayla Ruth**.

Alvin married **Mary Wegman** *5th*. Great—Grandchildren: **Laura, Edward, Alice, Sharon** and **Elaine Hope**.
Alvin divorced and remarried **Joan (Joanie)** No children

Laura married **Brian Kaighn**,
Edward married **Dawn** *6th*. Great—Great Grandchild: **Angela,**
Alice married **Thomas (Tom) Buscio.** *6th*. Great—Great Grandchildren: **Brandon, Laura, and Daniel.**
Sharon married **Ronald (Ron) Brannon** and daughter **Rachael** *6th*. Great—Great Grandchildren **Ronald (Ronnie)** and **Roberta**
Elaine's son *6th*. Great—Great Grandchildren **Andrew** and she married **Kenneth (Ken) Buiner**

Maggie married **John Evans** *3rd*. Grandchildren: Grandville and **John Nevitt**.

Grandville married **Mary Agnes** *4th*. Great-Grandchildren: **Eileen** and **Linda Sue.**

Eileen married **Edward Marshall** *5th* Great—Great Grandchildren: **Brain** mad **Bruce**
Linda Sue married **Calvin Lutz** *5th* Great-Great Grandchild: **Jillian**

Nevitt married **Lois** *4th*. Great—Grandchildren: **Nevelyn, John** and **Nevitta**

Nevelyn married **James Elliott** *5th* Great-Great Grandchildren: **Lois** and **Michael**

Lois married **Richard Burkett** *6th* Great—Great Great Grandchildren: **Erin, Christina** and **David**

Erin married Anthony Van Grdeveuitz *7th* Great—Great—Great—Great Grandchildren: **Aiden**, **Evan** & **Madison** (twins,) and **Brendan**

John married and had no children
Nevitta married **William Ruddy** *5th*. Great-Great Grandchild: **William (Bill)**

Linda married **Grandville Dougherty** *3rd*. Grand children **Grandville** and **Edward**

Grandville married **Faith** *4th*. Great—Grandchildren four children

Edward married **Mary** *4th* Great Grandchildren five children of whom I am sure they are married and have *5th* Great—Great Grandchildren and *6th* Great—Great—Great—Grandchildren.

Harold married **Rose** *3rd* Grandchildren **Marian** and **Virginia.** *4th* Great—Grandchildren both daughters married and had children but I have no record about that part of the family.

Harold married **Hazel** and had no children

1st. **Virginia** married **Dan Blake** *2nd*. Children **Rozzie, Medford and William Etheridge, (Bill).**

Rozzie married George Dize *3rd.* Grandchildren: **Catherine**. Rozzie divorced George and married **Ernie Herzog** they had no children

Catherine married and had no children

Medford married **Edith** and had no children

Etheridge married **Mary Hall** *3rd*. Grandchildren: **Marbelle, Margaret (Peggy)** and **William (WIB or Bill))**

Marbelle married Tomas Roach 4th Great—Grandchildren: **Donna, Patricia Ann (Patty)** and **Barbara**

Donna married *5th* Great-Great-Grandchildren: two daughters

Barbara married Tim *5th* Great-Great-Grandchildren: **Timothy, Amber,** and **Matthew**

Peggy married **Joseph Mc Fadyen** *4th* Great-Grandchildren **Joseph, David** and **Mary Elizabeth (Beth** & **Missy)**

Joseph died at four months

David married **Amal** *5th* Great—Great—Grandchild: **Colin**

Missy married **Keith Pusey** *5Th* Great—Great Grandchild: **Kyle**

Bill married **Cathy** *4th* Great—Grandchildren: **Mark, Angela, Dawn** and **Catherine.**

Mark died as a young man

Angela married **Wayne Atkinson** *5th* Great-Great Grandchild: **Kenneth**

Catherine had *5th* Great-Great-Grandchild: **Danielle**

1st **Lucy** married **Will Ford** *2nd*. Children: **Wallace, Lewis**

Lewis married **Ruth** *3rd*Grandchild: **Lewis** Jr.

The Evans Family

1st. **Solomon Evans** married **Ruth Marshall** *2nd*. Children: **Ellsworth Thomas (Cap'n Tom), Peter (Cap'n Pete)**, **Mitchell**. 2nd. wife, **Anne Lisa** Children: **George, Nicholas, John, Benjamin** and **Dow**.

Thomas married **Kitty Guy** *3rd*. Grandchildren**: Emory, Annie, Edna** and **Ellsworth.**

Emery married and had *4th* Great—Grandchildren and moved to the Eastern Shore Maryland and we lost tract of them.

Annie married **Dan Sommers** *4th* Great-Grandchildren **Eloise, Lucille, Eugene and Ruth**

Eloise married **Ewell Crockett** *5th* Great-Great Grandchildren: **Connie, Ewell (Sunny)** and **Daniel (Danny)**

Lucille married **Donald Middleton** *5th*. Great—Great Grandchild: **Joan**

Joan married **John Krouse** *6th* Great-Great Great—Grandchildren **Donald (Don) and Joy.**

Don married **Lynn** *7th* Great-Great-Great Great Grandchildren: **David** and **Ryan**

Joy married **Michel Tidwell** *7th* Great Great-Great-Great Grandchildren: **Drew** and **Brett**

Eugene married *5th* Great-Great Grandchildren: **Debbie** and **Eddie**

Ruth married **Edward (Eddie) Smith** *5th* Great-Great Grandchildren:

Ellsworth married **Ada Middleton** *3rd* Grandchild: **`Elmer Francis**

Elmer married **Annie Rose**. *4th* Great—Grandchildren**: Mary Ada** and two Sons

Mary Ada married **Dwight Marshall** *5th* Great-Great Grandchild: One son

Edna married a **Sommers** *4th* Great—Grandchild **Susan**

Susan married *5th* Great—Great—Grandchild one daughter

Peter married Margaret *3rd*. Grandchildren **Ruth, Naomi, and Newell**
2nd wife Margaret Dize *3rd* Grandchildren: **Theresa, Susan (Susie), James, Russell, Adrian** and two others. Most died in childhood

Ruth married **William Cordero** *4th* Great-Grandchildren **Brenda** and **Wayne.**

Wayne married. *5th*. Great—Great-Grandchildren: **Clementine** and one son

Naomi married **Mr. Zimmerman 4th** Great-Grandchildren: **Joyce Ann**

Joyce Ann **married** Jim Germack *5th*. Great-Great Grandchildren; **Jim** and **Susan**

Theresa married **John Legidakes** *4th*. Great-Grandchildren: **Nicolas, George Constantine (Dean),** and **Vasso**

Nick married **Kay Paris** *5th* Great—Great-Grandchildren: **Estelle, John Elaine, Stephanie**

Estelle married **Robert Raysik** *6th* Great-Great-Great Grandchildren **Lynnette** and **Alexis**

John married **Lucille** *6th* Great-Great-Great Grandchildren: **Christopher** and **Jason**

Elaine married **Bernie Mastrogustino** *6th* Great-Great Great-Grandchildren: **Vanessa** and **Melrania**

Stephanie married **John Orsino** *6th* Great-Great-Great Grandchild: **John**

George married **Helen Sheertz** *5th* Great-Great-Great Grandchildren: **Nicholas (Nick)**

Dean married **Irene Murset** *5th* Great-Great-Great Grandchildren: **Dean jr., Claire** and **Leo**

Vasso married **Joseph (Joe) Stenta** *5th* Great-Great-Great Grandchildren: **Theresa** and **Cynthia**

Theresa married **Richard Dougherty** *6th* Great-Great Great-Grandchildren **Brian, Erica** (twins) and **Mecanzie.**

Cynthia married Joseph Porini *6th* Great-Great-Great Grandchild: **Zachary**

John married **Margaret** (see **Maggie Beauchamp)**

Nicholas married *3rd* Grandchildren: **Roseman** and **Audrey**

Roaseman married **Edward (Eddie) Smith** and they had no children

Audrey No information

NOW ENJOY

PART TWO

FAMILY RECIPES & HOW I ENTERTAIN

INTRODUCTION

The following are recipes from the family. Ma's recipes are as I remember them and still use. There are recipes in this collection that were given to me by family members and friends. The other recipes are from me and they come from many sources. I have gotten these recipes from books, magazines, newspapers, food labels and some are just my own concoctions. I don't mean to plagiarize but I really don't recall where they all have come from. I have just used them for many years. I don't know if my file will ever be finished, as I keep on adding to my collection. Here, however, is the most up-to-date list I have at this time in history. Enjoy.

USING THE RECIPES

To cut the fat in your diet, substitute a cooking spray for oil or butter in many of these recipes. You may need to adjust the herbs, spices or salt to compensate for the loss of the fat flavor. The three main flavorings in a recipe are fat, sugar and salt; when you eliminate any, you need to compensate in some other way.

I like to use a lot of garlic, spices, butter instead of margarine, olive oil, very little bell pepper, and other things that may not be your favorites. So add, subtract, or change the recipe to suit your taste. In baking, it is important that the proportions are accurate, but other cooking to adjust the proportions is fine. Sometimes, just substituting an ingredient for something you don't have or don't like is fine. Check out *Tips & Information* to see my opinion of herbs and spice and how I use them.

NOTE: When a recipe or a title of a section is referred to in a recipe, it is done in *Italics.* This will let you know that you can find the recipe.

FAMILY RECIPES

ODD DISHES

The potato always raised eyebrows as to what it was doing in a chocolate cake. Even more questions have been asked about some other odd recipes. Ma and I have made mayonnaise cake, sauerkraut cake, tomato cake, carrot pie, onion pie, banana sandwich, pot liquor, and tomato, watermelon or cantaloupe preserves. The recipe for zucchini muffins and the constant preference for ketchup on buckwheat cakes spark questions. You will find all of these things in my recipes. Before you turn up your nose at the oddity, read the ingredients and take a chance. Nobody has died eating my food yet! The potato, mayonnaise, and sauerkraut add moisture to the cakes. The tomato soup adds more spice and richness to the cake. The carrots in the pie are treated much like pumpkin, but the pie is lighter and sweeter.

For some fun taste sensations, try putting salt on a melon, any melon, especially if it is not very sweet. If you really want to go crazy, add some black pepper also. I don't like pepper on watermelon for some reason, but I love it on other melons. Do you really want to try something way out? Next time you make a nice fresh glass of lemonade, sprinkle the top of the glass with some cayenne pepper. Don't dismiss it—just give a try. Start with a small glass and a light sprinkle, and see what you think; you might be pleasantly surprised. If not, you haven't wasted much. Put a leaf or two of lettuce on your next peanut butter sandwich. A splash of vinegar on cabbage or other cooked greens is very tasty, and the Italians love to use a good balsamic vinegar as a dip for their fresh strawberries. Ma used to say, "Nothing bets a trial but a failure."

I have just recently found an old recipe for a German onion pie. It is sort of like a quiche but not quite; it makes a wonderful first course. We loved banana sandwiches as kids; they are just rich and wonderful. Pot liquor is the water that greens are cooked in. They tell me that pot liquor was given to me as a baby in my bottle. It is served like soup and is strong and very flavorful.

Aunt Ruth grew little, yellow, plum-shaped tomatoes and Ma preserved them with a bit of thinly sliced lemon. The melon preserves were a summer treat too. The skin of the watermelon and cantaloupe was removed and the rind and part of the flesh of the fruits was preserved. Yum! I have discussed the ketchup on the buckwheat cake; you just have to taste it to appreciate it. After all, ketchup is quite sweet, and the spices complement the hearty flavor of the buckwheat. Using food differently than is expected is adventurous and creative. I say try them before you make a decision.

My Cookbook Library

I have quite a large library of cookbooks. I have borrowed from these books for my repertoire of recipes throughout these many years. They have helped me experiment and increase my use of unusual or just different flavors and food combinations. I always use my books when designing a menu for a special occasion. They help me with preparations and cooking times.

I used many of these books to help me put my recipes down on paper. They helped me with proportions and with writing the directions.

Very old cookbooks, some dating back to the early 1900s, have influenced me. Other books are ethnic recipes. Coming from country cooking, learned from my family, I used restaurants and cookbooks to help me experience other cuisine from other parts of the world.

When Julia Child came to television in the 1960s, I followed her and her direction faithfully. Now the television is loaded with cooking gurus of every description. There are Yan Can Cook and The Frugal Gourmet, the Galloping Gourmet as well as many others; all made their impact. I, of course, bought their books. We can thank PBS for starting this programming but now the screen is full of cooking shows. Now, there is a cooking channel were people cook all day long. Today we have Martha Stewart and Emeril, just to name a couple, who are our big TV stars. I too have bought their books and have used their recipes to enhance and influence my cooking.

I have also gotten recipes from magazines, newspapers, labels on products, pamphlets from food councils, women's organizations' cookbooks and, of course, the web. You will see a bit of each of these sources in many of my recipes. Thanks to them all for the good influence

APPETIZERS

For many years, I had an open house on Christmas Eve. I invited family and friends to have their evening meal at our home. It allowed them to take a break from the hustle and bustle of this hectic time. They could rest, visit, and enjoy a hot meal to fortify themselves for the rest of this traditional, late night marathon of tree trimming, gift-wrapping and preparation for Santa. Very often, many of us worked until the early morning hours. I often had an appetizer buffet, both hot and cold, as well as a substantial meal for those who wanted a full meal. Some of these recipes were found yearly on the buffet.

Dips are something that came along in the 1960s. I am not sure but I think they are something I brought to the family's diet. I sometimes don't like to serve dips because, unfortunately, I don't like to see double dipping in my food. I guess it is a leftover from Ma's idea about handling food. I have learned to put a spoon in the dip bowl, hoping everyone will take the hint to put a portion on their plates and dip their chips or veggies in their own helping!

Beef, Cheese Ball

Servings: 2 balls

This is a twist on a standard.

1-2 oz. (1cup)	Chipped beef, finely snipped
1-8 oz.	Cream cheese, softened
¼ cup	Parmesan cheese, grated
¼ cup	Olives, stuffed, chopped
2 tsp.	Horseradish
2 cups	Potato chips, crushed

Mix together all ingredients except chips and shape into 2 balls. Roll on crushed chips. Chill about 1 hour.

Brie in Pastry

Servings: 12

Wonderful for a buffet or cheese tray.

1 package	Phyllo dough, frozen
1 lb. Wheel	Brie cheese
¼ cup	Almonds sliced, toasted
¼ cup	Butter, melted

Thaw dough. Using about 12 leaves, layer dough while buttering each layer. Cut cheese in half horizontally and layer the almonds. Put the cheese back together and place in the center of dough. Fold dough around cheese, cutting away excess. Place seam down on baking sheet and bake in pre-heated oven at 400° for 20 minutes. Let stand about 10 minutes before serving. Serve with crackers or toasted French bread slices and fruit.

Caponata

Servings: 6-8

This is one of my favorites. I first had this when an Italian friend brought it to work on chunks of bread.

1	Eggplant unpeeled, cut into 1-inch chunks
2	Onions, thinly sliced
½	Green pepper, seeded cut into strips
½	Red pepper, seeded cut into strips
2 ribs	Celery, chopped
1 can, or 2 cups	Italian plum tomatoes
8 Tbsp.	Olive oil
2 cloves	Garlic, chopped
1 tsp. Or to taste	Salt
To taste	Fresh ground black pepper
2 Tbsp.	Capers with juice
1 dz.	Black Italian olives, chopped or whole
2 Tbsp.	Parsley, chopped
1 Tbsp.	Sugar
2-3 Tbsp., or to taste	Wine vinegar
	Fresh lemon juice
½ cup	Pine nuts, toasted
½ tsp. dried **or**	
3-4 fresh	Basil leaves, chopped

Prepare vegetables and force tomatoes through a sieve. In large heavy pan, heat 2 tablespoons of oil, add eggplant, and cook until it is soft and lightly browned. Remove to bowl. Heat more oil add onion and peppers, stir until coated and shiny, and cook gently about 5 minutes. Heat more oil, add the celery and garlic, stir until mixed with the oil, then cook gently 3 minutes longer. Add tomatoes, the browned eggplant, other cooked vegetables and salt and pepper to taste. Cook, stirring frequently, until vegetables are tender and liquid has cooked down somewhat, about 20 minutes. Add capers, olives, basil pine nuts and parsley. Mix sugar and vinegar; add to mixture and taste.

Adjust seasoning if necessary. Cover and simmer 20 to 25 minutes longer until flavors are blended. Cool, then cover and refrigerate. This dish tastes better with age. Will keep in refrigerator for several weeks. Splash with fresh lemon juice before serving. **NOTE:** Use as a condiment or on Italian bread or in a roll. Great for lunch.

Cheese and Bacon Rollups

Servings: 16

This recipe came from a friend, Betty Ostlie, and it is something that is gobbled up very quickly.

1 loaf	White bread, sliced, crusts removed bread, crusts removed
1 medium jar	Cheese spread
1lb.	Bacon

Spread the cheese on the bread and roll up. Wrap a slice of bacon around the roll. Place on a baking sheet with a lip. You can place the rolls close together. Bake at 350°for 20-25 minutes or until the bacon is done and the bread is lightly brown. Remove from the pan and place on a warm serving dish. I like to use a warming tray to keep them warm. Simple and yummy! No counting fat grams!

Cheese Ball

Servings: 8-10

An old standby.

4 oz.	Blue cheese, crumbled
4 oz.	Cheddar cheese, finely grated
3 oz.	Cream cheese, softened
2 Tbsp.	Parsley, chopped
½ tsp.	Onion, grated
½ cup	Chopped nuts

Mix ingredients together except nuts, and shape into a ball. Wrap, refrigerate until firm. Reshape ball and roll in chopped nuts.

Crab Dip

Servings: 2 cups

A simple recipe just right to whet the appetite for a wonderful meal.

½ cup	Sour cream
1 Tbsp.	Onion, grated
1 cup	Mayonnaise
1 tsp.	Lemon juice
8 oz.	Crab meat
2-3 drops	Hot sauce

Mix together and chill for several hours. Serve with chips or raw vegetables.

Crab-Flavored Balls

Servings: 50 balls

These are not cakes. Because the base of this is a white sauce and includes crabmeat, I call it "crab flavored".

1 lb.	Crabmeat
3 Tbsp.	Butter
2 Tbsp.	Onion, grated
3 Tbsp.	Flour
½ tsp.	Salt
Dash	Black pepper
2-3 drops	Hot sauce
1 Tbsp.	Dried parsley
½ cup	Corn flake, crushed. Can substitute flavored breadcrumbs
1 cup	Milk
3 Tbsp.	Butter

Melt butter, cook onion for 1 minute over medium heat. Add flour and stir to keep smooth. Add milk slowly, stir with a whisk to keep smooth. Add spices. Remove from heat and add crabmeat. Cool. Roll into small balls and roll in crumbs. Place on baking sheet that has been sprayed with baking spray. Place balls on pan. Bake at 350° for 15 minutes. Serve with cocktail or tartar sauce using cocktail picks or forks for dipping. **NOTE:** Can be divided for a smaller amount.

Dips

Servings: 2-3 cups

Use the label.

1 box	Soup mix
As called for	Sour cream
As called for	Mayonnaise
	Spinach
	Pumpernickel bread
	Asst'd raw vegetables
	Chips

I use the recipe on the packages of Lipton onion soup mix and Knorr's vegetable soup mix for their excellent recipes. The onion soup with sour cream was one of the first dips that became popular. The vegetable soup makes two kinds: 1) a vegetable dip with sour cream and mayonnaise, and 2) the spinach dip for dipping pumpernickel bread, which is excellent. These three recipes are standard dips found at a lot of parties. Use vegetables like mushrooms, peppers, cucumber, carrot, celery, broccoli and cauliflower to make a veggie dish to go with the dips. If you can find jicama, add that; snow peas are nice also. Assorted chips include: corn, blue corn, potato and other vegetable chips. Enjoy!

Fried Ravioli

Servings: 8

A nice addition to a hot appetizer buffet.

1 bag	Frozen ravioli cheese or meat
	Oil
	Pasta sauce

In a hot frying pan, add about ½ inch of cooking oil. Slowly slip 4 or 5 ravioli into hot oil and brown on both sides. Drain on paper towels. Keep hot on a heating tray. Serve with a bowl of hot pasta sauce and cocktail fork or toothpicks.

Guacamole

Servings:

Serve with corn chips or add to a taco salad.

2 ripe	Avocados peeled, mashed
4 Tbsp. mild or hot	Salsa
1 Tbsp.	Lime juice
Pinch	Cumin
A few grinds	Black pepper
1 Tbsp.	Cilanrano. fresh is best (optional)

Mix everything together and chill covered. Best made just before serving to keep avocado from turning dark. **NOTE:** Some say that returning the pit to the guacamole keeps it from getting dark also. Of course, remove the pit before serving.

Kielbasa in Spicy Sauce

Servings: 8-10

Try this for your appetizer table.

1 lb.	Kielbasa, sliced ½ inch thick
½ cup	Red currant jelly
1 Tbsp.	Vinegar
½ tsp.	Mustard, dry
1/8 tsp.	Cloves, ground
1/8 tsp.	Cinnamon

Cook all ingredients, except kielbasa, in saucepan over low heat, stirring until jelly melts. Add kielbasa and heat. Serve in a container that you can keep warm. Have toothpicks or hors d'oeuvres forks handy.

Lebanon Baloney Stack

Servings: 8-12 wedges

Betty Ostlie shared this recipe with me years ago. A tangy bit my guests like a lot.

½ lb.	Lebanon baloney lunchmeat, sliced
3 oz. Package	Cream cheese, softened
About 1 Tbsp.	Horseradish

Mix the cream cheese and horseradish together to your taste. Spread some of the cheese on a slice of baloney and top with another slice. Keep spreading cheese on each slice of lunchmeat until you have a stack about 2 inches high. Top with one more slice of baloney. Refrigerate for about 3 hours or until it is firm. Cut into wedges and serve with toothpicks.

Quick Crab Spread

Servings: 10

This recipe is so simple but very popular with everyone.

8 oz.	Cream cheese
1 6-8 oz. Can	Crab meat, drained
1 cup	Cocktail sauce
A few leaves	Lettuce

Arrange lettuce on a serving plate. Place block of cream cheese in center of lettuce. Put crabmeat over cream cheese. Pour *Cocktail Sauce* over crabmeat. Arrange crackers around the cheese and serve. **NOTE:** I like to use Triscuit crackers with this dish. **NOTE:** To use shrimp, I prepared it this way. Soften cream cheese. Spread in a layer in serving dish. Top with cocktail sauce. Cut 1 lb. of cooked shrimp in half horizontally, and arrange over cocktail sauce. Chill and serve with crackers.

Sausage Cheese Balls

Servings: 8 1/2 dozen

George Jr. is a big fan of these. The recipe makes plenty, so make them for a crowd.

2 cups	Baking mix (ex. Bisquick)
1 lb.	Italian sausage, skin removed
4 cups	Cheddar cheese, grated (1/2 lb.)
½ tsp.	Rosemary, crushed
½ tsp.	Paprika
1 tsp.	Grated onion

Pre-heat oven to 350°. Mix everything together and shape into 1-inch balls. Place on a jellyroll pan, ungreased, and bake until brown about 25 minutes.

Shrimp Dip

Servings: 2 cups

I have made this dip for more than 30 years, and it is always a hit.

1-3 oz. package	Cream cheese, softened
1 cup	Sour cream
2 tsp.	Lemon juice
1 package	Italian salad dressing (dry)
1-6 oz. Can	Shrimp, finely chopped

Blend cream cheese with remainder of ingredients. Chill at least 1 hour before serving. Serve with crackers, chips, or toast points.

Swedish Meatballs

Servings:

Just right to include in a buffet of appetizers.

2 lbs.	Ground beef
2 cups	Breadcrumbs
2 cups	Milk
2	Eggs
1 small	Onion, grated
1 tsp.	Salt
¼ tsp.	Black pepper
¼ tsp.	Nutmeg, freshly ground
2-4 Tbsp.	Oil
	Flour

Soak crumbs in milk and add all ingredients except oil and flour. Milk well. Shape into small balls, roll in flour, and brown in hot oil. Cover and simmer for 30 minutes. **NOTE:** Can be served in a brown gravy as an appetizer or use this recipe for a main course and serve with gravy over rice.

SOUP, SOUP, BEAUTIFUL SOUP

A favorite dish through the years has been soup. Ma made Friday night soups to use up scraps and leftovers, but she made others from scratch as well. Bean soup was a favorite. Dad said he could have eaten beans every day. Aunt Maggie was known for her navy bean and ham soup, served with *Maryland beaten biscuits. Split pea soup with a ham* bone was something Ma often made. Black-eyed peas, of course, were an old standby. I have added many kinds of soup to my repertoire. Every kind of soup has been included in my menus, from cold soups, such as *vichyssoise* and *gazpacho* to hot soups like gumbo or *Scotch Broth.* I especially like to serve cold fruit soup as a first course of a summer meal. They are all good and filling. Most of the time, a pot of soup is the whole meal; a salad and a fresh baked loaf of bread complete a satisfying meal. I have included them all, and many more, in my recipes.

For various organizations, I worked on putting together Soup Suppers. We would serve everyone a salad and roll, then supply the people with disposable bowls so they could sample as many soups as they liked. We had crock-pots lined up on a buffet table for everyone to help himself or herself. The members supplied a variety of homemade soups and desserts to finish this Saturday night supper. It was a good fundraiser and very popular. It's also a good idea for a party.

COLD SOUPS

Borsht, Cold

Servings: 6

I had eaten this soup but never made it. When I finally tried it, I found it very easy and very nice. This is my recipe for this fresh flavored soup.

6	Beets, fresh peeled, cut into chunks
1	Onion, peeled, cut into chunks
2 ½ qt.	Water
1 tsp.	Salt
1/3 cup	Lemon juice
3 Tbsp.	Sugar
To taste	Black pepper
Dash	Allspice
	Sour cream for decoration

Boil beets and onion in water with salt for about 1 hour. Add lemon juice and sugar, and cook for 30 minutes more. Add allspice at end. Adjust flavor by adding more lemon juice or more sugar according to taste and to the sweetness of the beets. If you want a clear broth, strain and chill the juice. Use the beets for a salad. I like to use about ¼ of the beets in the soup. Strain and grate the cooked beets, by hand or in a food processor. Return the grated beets to the broth and continue as above. To serve, the soups should be very cold. Place in individual bowl, and top with a dollop of sour cream. **NOTE:** Use rubber gloves to work with raw beets to keep your hands from being stained red. **NOTE:** See beet recipes in this book to use unused beets.

Carrot Soup

Servings: 4

This soup can be served hot or cold (I preferred it cold.)

2 Tbsp.	Butter
1	Onion, sliced thinly
1 lb.	Carrots, sliced thinly
1	Bay leaf
2 Tbsp.	Parsley, chopped
3 Tbsp.	Rice
1 tsp.	Paprika
1 tsp.	Cumin
½ tsp.	Coriander
	Freshly ground black pepper
½ tsp.	Salt
7 to 8 cups	Vegetable stock
½ cup	Sour cream
1 Tbsp.	Chives, chopped

Melt butter in soup pot. Add all vegetables, rice, bay leaf and parsley. Stir frequently for about 5 minutes to soften vegetables. Add the spices, salt and pepper to taste. Cook for an additional 5 minutes. Add broth and cook for 25 minutes partially covered. Let cool. Remove bay leaf. Blend in blender or food processor until smooth. If you want a really smooth soup, strain though sieve. Refrigerate. Serve cold with a dollop of sour cream topped with a sprinkle of chives. To serve hot, just reheat and serve as suggested.

Gazpacho

Servings: 8

Because this is George's favorite, I make a gallon at a time. Dot said it was most like the kind she had in Spain.

½	Cucumber peeled, diced
4	Tomato, peeled, chopped
1/3 cup	Onion, finely chopped,
3 cloves	Garlic, finely minced
½ cup	Green pepper, chopped
¼ cup	Oil
¼ cup	Wine vinegar
2 cups	Mixed vegetable or tomato juice
1 tsp.	Salt
¼ tsp.	Black pepper

Combine all ingredients in a large bowl. Cover well and chill for at least 4 hours. Serve cold. This soup really tastes best the next day. **NOTE:** To peel tomatoes, see *Tips on Food*. **NOTE:** For an extra kick, add 2 tablespoons finely chopped cilanrano.

Melon Soup

Servings: 8

In the summertime, this makes a wonderful first course for any meal!

1 (about 2 1/2 lb.)	Honeydew melon (Can substitute with Persian casaba or cantaloupe)
1	Lime (zest and juice)
½ cup	Sour cream or unflavored yogurt
Dash	Salt

Peel melon and remove seeds. Cut into pieces, saving a few for garnish, and blend rest in blender or food processor. Stir in lime zest and juice, and a dash of salt. Cover and refrigerate. To serve, make sure soup is icy cold. Pour into individual bowls and top with a dollop of sour cream and a few small pieces of melon. **NOTE:** I have made a batch of honeydew and a batch of cantaloupe and poured the two at the same time into each serving bowl. It is a lovely presentation and tastes good!

Vichyssoise

Servings: 6

A lovely soup for the first course.

4	Leeks or 1 ½ cup onions
3 cups	Potatoes, pared, sliced
3 cups	Water
4 cubes	Chicken broth (bouillon)
3 Tbsp.	Butter
1 cup	Cream
1 cup	Milk
1 tsp.	Salt
¼ tsp.	Pepper
2 Tbsp.	Chives

Cut the leeks in half lengthwise. Wash very well, changing the water often. Cut leeks into small pieces using all of the white part as well and about 3 inches of the green tops. Cook with potatoes in boiling water, covered, until very tender. Process vegetables and liquid in blender or food processor, returning to the top of a double boiler. Add chicken broth, butter, cream, milk, salt, and pepper, mix well. Reheat over hot water. Serve hot or very cold, topped with chives.

MEAT SOUPS

Bean Soup

Servings: 8

This is a basic recipe for cooking beans.

1 lb.	Dried beans
¼ cup	Olive oil
2 medium	Onions, chopped coarse
2	Carrots, pared and chopped coarse
3 ribs	Celery, chopped coarse
1 tsp.	Salt
½ tsp.	Freshly ground black pepper
	Options
1 Tbsp.	Garlic, chopped
2	Bay leaves
2 Tbsp.	Parsley
1	Ham bone
1 can	Whole tomatoes

The trick I found about cooking beans is to start out this way. Rinse and sort beans. Place them in a large soup pot and cover them with cool water. Bring the beans to a boil and boil for 2 minutes. Cover and turn heat off. Let them sit in water for 1 hour. Drain and rinse beans in cool water. Heat oil in pot. Sauté onions stirring frequently until just golden, about 4 minutes. Stir in celery, carrots and spices. Add pre-cooked beans, ham bone if using, and cover with fresh water. Bring to a boil. Reduce heat to a simmer. Cook for 1 ½ to 2 hours until beans are tender. At this time, add the salt and tomatoes if using. Do not add these items until the beans are tender because they prevent the beans from doing so. Cook for 20 minutes more. Adjust seasoning. Serve hot. **NOTE:** Pre-cooking is only necessary with hard beans such as limas, navy, pinto, etc. Slit peas, lentils and black-eyed peas do not need this process.

Beef, Barley, and Vegetable Soup

Servings: 12-15

This takes some time, but is good and gets better each time it is heated.

1 large	Soup bone, have cracked
3 lbs.	Beef. chuck cut into 1 inch cubes
2 Tbsp.	Vegetable oil
1 small	Onion, sliced
1	Carrots, sliced
1 rib	Celery, roughly chopped
6 qt.	Water
1 tsp.	Salt
1 cup	Barley
2 cups	Carrots, diced
2 cups	Cabbage, shredded
2 cups	Celery, diced
2 medium	Onions, diced
2 cups	Potato, cubed
3 cups	Tomatoes
1 cup	Rutabaga, cubed
1 small can	Corn, with liquid
1 10-oz. Pkg., frozen	Green beans
1 can	Kidney beans without sugar include liquid
3 small	Zucchini, sliced
1 cup, frozen	Peas
1 10-oz. box, frozen	Spinach
1	Bouquet garni
3 cloves	Garlic, minced

Bake bones in 300° oven for about 1 hour or until marrow is cooked. In large soup pot, brown meat in oil, add carrot, onion, celery and garlic. Cook until onions are soft, but not brown. Add salt, baked bones and water. Cook for 2 hours. Add barley cook for 1 hour more. Add beans, bouquet garni, and vegetables, except peas and spinach. Cook for 1 additional hour. Add peas and spinach. Cook for 15-20 minutes more or until peas are tender. Remove bones and bouquet garni and cool. Remove fat from top. To serve, reheat and sprinkle top of each bowl with grated cheese. A hot loaf of garlic bread is great with this dish. **NOTE:** To get most of the fat from the soup, refrigerate. When completely cold the fat can be lifted off very easily.

Beef, Mushroom, and Barley Soup

Servings: 6

This soup is good in the winter when you need something to warm you up!

1 lb.	Beef, chuck, cut into 1-inch pieces
¼ cup	Barley
1 large	Onions, chopped
1 large	Carrot, sliced
1 large rib	Celery, chopped fine
¼ cup	Parsley fresh, chopped
8-10 oz.	Mushroom, coarsely chopped
2 Tbsp.	Vegetable oil
2 ½ cups	broth or water

Brown meat in oil. When brown on all sides, add onion, carrot, and cook for 5 minutes. Add barley and broth or water and simmer for 1 hour. Add celery, parsley and mushrooms and cook for 15 to 20 minutes more or until the barley is tender. Serve hot.

Beef Tea

Servings: 1 cup

This is what Ma used for her aging family to restore their strength when they were ill.

1 lb.	Beef steak lean, ground
1 cup	Water
½ tsp.	Salt

Place meat with water in the top of a double boiler. Simmer over very low heat for about 3 ½ hours. Add salt, remove all fat and strain. It may be diluted with some boiling water.

Chicken Soup

Servings: 6-8

This is a standby. A basic mild soup that can be served any time.

2 to 3 lb.	Fryer chicken
1 tsp.	Salt
Pinch	Pepper
1	Onion, chopped
2 ribs	Celery, chopped
2	Carrots, chopped
1 48-oz. Can	Chicken broth
1 Tbsp.	Vegetable oil
½ cup	Rice OR
6-8 oz.	Egg noodles OR
¼ cup	Barley

Heat oil in large pot and sauté onions until soft. Add celery, carrots, chicken and salt. Add chicken broth using water to have liquid cover chicken. Bring to a boil, cover and simmer for 1-½ hours. Remove chicken and vegetables to cool. Skim fat from broth. Bring broth to a boil, add rice or noodles. Cook rice for 25 minutes, noodles 15 minutes. If using barley, add with chicken and vegetables. When chicken is cool, pull meat from bones and cut into pieces. Chop vegetables into smaller pieces. Add to the broth and heat for 5 minutes more. **NOTE:** I often return only a small amount of the meat to the soup, using the rest for a salad.

Gumbo

Servings: 15

Another New Orleans recipe.

3 ½-4 lb.	Chicken, cut up
1 ½ lbs.	Andouille sausage
1 cup	Flour
1 cup	Oil
4 cups	Onions, chopped
2 cups	Celery, chopped
2 cups	Green pepper, chopped
4-5 cloves	Garlic, chopped
8 cups	Chicken broth
	Salt
2 cups	Green onion, chopped
	File
About 8 cups	Rice, cooked
4-6 cups	Okra, optional

Season chicken with salt and pepper and brown in oil. Add sausage and brown. Remove meat from pot. Make a roux with equal part of oil and flour and cook till it becomes a dark color, being careful to stir and watch so it does not burn. Add onions, celery, green pepper, and later garlic to roux and stir continuously until vegetables reach desired tenderness. Return meat to pot and cook with vegetables, continuing to stir frequently. Gradually stir in broth and bring to boil. Reduce to simmer and cook for an hour or more. Season to taste. Approximately 10 minutes before serving, add green onions. **Options:** Gumbo may be served over warm cooked rice. File may be added to each bowl at time of serving. Do not add to pot if gumbo will be reheated. **NOTE:** If you want to use okra in gumbo, add to trinity, sauté, and cook together with roux. **NOTE:** Trinity refers to the three vegetables used in Cajun cooking, onions, celery and pepper. **NOTE:** File is a spice available in specialty stores or mail order from New Orleans shops.

Scotch Broth

Servings: 8

I like to make this soup after I have enjoyed a leg of lamb. I use the bone from the roast with some meat left on it to make this hearty dish.

1	Lamb bone from a leg roast with some meat left on it or the bone left from a boned roast.
2	Carrots
2 (large)	Onions
½ cup	Barley
2 Tbsp.	Parsley
2 ribs	Celery
To taste	Salt
To taste	Black pepper

Place lamb bone in large pot. Roughly chop vegetables and add. Then add about 1 tsp. of salt. Add water to cover bone and vegetables, bring to a boil. Add barley, cover, and simmer for about one hour. Taste and adjust seasoning. Continue to cook until barley is tender. Skim any excess fat. As with most soups and stews, the flavor is better Addional leftover meat, chopped, can be added right at the end, long enough to hat, for when served the next day.

Soup Augdemono (Greek Chicken soup)

Servings: 8

One of my special soups I use with a Greek meal or with any meal. The soup is just plain, good, and easy to make. The lemon gives this soup an extra kick. Give it a try and see what you think!

8 cups	Chicken broth
2/3 cups	Rice
5 yolks and 1 white	Eggs, beaten
1/3 cup	Lemon juice

Heat broth and add rice, cover and cook until the rice is just done, about 20 minutes. Beat 1 cup of broth into the eggs, beating constantly. Slowly add the lemon juice to mixture, then slowly add mixture to broth, stirring constantly. Bring soup almost to a boil but *do not boil.* Add salt and pepper to taste. Serve. NOTE: Be careful when reheating this soup. Again bring just to the boil but do not boil or the soup will curial.

Spinach, Meatball Soup

Servings: 8

My friend Madalyn Hempsey (Madge) supplied me with a complete Italian menu. I share it with you.

1 ½ lb.	Ground beef
½ cup	Breadcrumbs, seasoned
1 or 2	Eggs
1 Tbsp.	Parsley, chopped
½ tsp.	Basil
1-2 cloves	Garlic, minced fine
½ tsp.	Salt
Dash	Black pepper
¼ cup	Grated Locatti cheese
2 10-oz. Boxes	Leaf or chopped frozen spinach
1 large and 2 small cans	Chicken broth (can use low salt)
2 Tbsp.	Olive oil
2 oz.	Small pasta (optional)

Mix meat, breadcrumbs, egg, parsley, basil, garlic, salt, and cheese together. Roll into quarter size balls. Heat oil in soup pot, brown the meatballs, add broth, bring to a boil. Add spinach to broth and heat until the soup is very hot. Do not cook too long as the spinach can get soggy. If you want to add pasta, it is suggested to cook it separately. This way the chicken broth is not used up cooking the pasta. Just put the pasta in at the last minute. Serve immediately with additional grated cheese. **NOTE:** Madge suggests serving a loaf of Italian bread, a simple salad of lettuce, tomato and onion with a light dressing of olive oil, and a smidgen of white wine vinegar and a tiny bit of water, sprinkled over salad, and tossed lightly. Sautéed pepper and eggs will make this menu a full meal. Yummy!

Turkey Soup

Servings: 8

What to do with the bones?

1	Turkey carcass
1 large	Onion, chopped
2	Carrots, chopped
2 ribs	Celery chopped
	Water
2 tsp.	Salt
½ lb.	Pasta bow ties, other small pasta, noodles
	OR
1 cup	Rice

Place carcass in large pot with onion, carrots, celery, salt and pepper. Add water to cover. Cook for about 1 hour until meat falls off bones. Remove meat and bones from liquid and cool. Remove all meat from bones and cut into bite size pieces, return to pot. Bring to a boil and add pasta or rice. Cook until pasta or rice is done. Add any other leftover meat or gravy and heat. Adjust seasoning, serve hot.

Vegetable Beef Soup

Servings: 10

Ma's Friday night soup started with what was in the fridge and then she added more to make a large pot of soup. This recipe can start with leftovers or not.

1 ½ lbs.	Beef, chuck
2 Tbsp.	Olive oil
4 qt.	Water
½ medium head	Cabbage, shredded
2	Onions, chopped
4	Carrots, cut into pieces
3 ribs	Celery, chopped
1 large can	Tomatoes
½ 9-oz. Pkg. frozen	Green beans
½ 10-oz. Pkg. frozen	Lima beans
½ 10-oz. Pkg. frozen	Peas
8-oz. Can	Corn
1 large	Potato, pared and cut in cubes
2 Tbsp.	Parsley
1 ½ tsp.	Salt
¼ tsp.	Pepper

Brown the beef in oil and add salt. Cover with water and simmer for 1 hour. Add cabbage, onions, carrots, celery and tomatoes. Cook for 30 minutes. Add other ingredients and simmer 2 hours. Add any leftovers at this point and cook for ½ hour more. Cool, skim fat. Reheat to serve or refrigerate to serve at another time. **NOTE:** A 20-oz. bag of mixed or soup vegetable can be substituted for green beans, lima beans, peas and corn. **NOTE:** The fat is easiest to remove when soup is cold. The fat just lifts off the broth.

Zucchini Soup

Servings: 8

George loves this! Great soup to use the zucchini from an abundant garden supply.

1 lb.	Italian hot or sweet sausage, casing removed
2 cups	Celery, sliced at a angle
2 lbs.	Zucchini sliced into ½-inch slices
1 cup	Onion, chopped
2 28-oz. Cans	Tomatoes
2 tsp.	Salt
1 tsp.	Basil
1 tsp.	Oregano
2-3.	Garlic cloves, minced
2	Green pepper, cut into ½-inch pieces
	Parmesan cheese

Brown sausage in a large soup pot. Drain off fat. Add celery, cook for 10 minutes. Stirring occasionally. Add all remaining ingredients except green pepper. Simmer covered for 20 minutes. Add peppers and cook for an additional 10 minutes. Serve topped with grated Parmesan cheese and hot garlic bread.

SEAFOOD SOUPS

Fish Chowder

Servings: 4

Had this in Maine the first time. I came home and had to create my own recipe. Here it is.

4 Tbsp.	Butter
1 ½ cups	Onions, chopped fine
2 cups	Potato, cubed
1 cup	Water
2 cup	Milk or evaporated milk
1 lb.	Cod, haddock, or any solid white flesh fish, cut into large chunks

Melt butter in large pot and cook onion until soft. Add potatoes, salt, and pepper to taste and water. Cover for 5 minutes. Add fish. Cook for 5 minutes more. Add milk. Cook on low, but **do not boil**, until fish and potatoes are fork tender. **NOTE:** The New Englanders use bacon to sauté the onions in their chowders, fish and clam. Use the bacon fat in place of butter and the crumbled bacon to top the bowl of chowder for an authentic touch.

Oyster Stew

Servings: 2

Ma always made her stew this way.

1 pint	Oysters and liquor
2 cups	Milk, scalded
1 Tbsp.	Butter
	Salt
	Black pepper

Heat the oysters in their liquor about 5 minutes or less, until the edges curl. Skim off the top foam. Combine oysters and liquor with the scalded milk, add the butter and the seasoning to taste. Serve immediately. I love OTC crackers with all chowder. **NOTE:** See *Tips About Food* to scald milk.

Quick Clam Chowder

Servings: 4

Another soup made with milk, seafood, and potatoes.

3 Tbsp.	Butter
1	Onion, chopped fine
2 8-oz. Cans	Clams, chopped
1 small bottle	Clam juice
2 (medium)	Potatoes, small cubes
1 can	Evaporated milk
2 cups or to taste	Milk
1 tsp.	Salt
	Black pepper, to taste

Sauté onions in butter. Do not brown. Add potatoes, salt, pepper and clam juice. Cook until potatoes are tender. Add clams and heat. Add evaporated milk. Heat. Add milk to taste. Serve hot, but do not boil after adding milk.

VEGETABLE SOUPS

Butternut Squash Soup

Servings: 6

The use of a winter vegetable that is so satisfying.

4 cups	Milk
½ (small)	Onion, chopped roughly
½	Bay leaf
2 cups	Butternut squash cooked, mashed and blended
3 Tbsp.	Butter
3 Tbsp.	Flour
1 tsp.	Salt
Dash	Cayenne pepper
½ tsp.	Seasoned salt
Few grinds	Fresh black pepper

Scald milk* with onion and bay leaf. Let stand while processing squash. Melt butter, blend in flour, salt, cayenne, seasoned salt. Add to squash. Strain milk. Gradually add milk to squash mixture, stirring constantly. Put soup though a fine sieve to ensure a smooth, not grainy, texture. Return to pot and simmer for 5 minutes; serve very hot. **NOTE:** Other winter squash can be used, and the flavor will change as each has its own distinct flavor. **NOTE:** *See *Tips About Food* to scald milk.

Cream of Asparagus Soup

Servings: 6

We love this wonderful soup any time of the year. The asparagus is most plentiful in the spring, so that is when I make it most often.

1 lb.	Asparagus
1 can	Evaporated milk
2 Tbsp.	Butter
2 Tbsp.	Flour
1 tsp.	Salt
1/8 tsp.	Black pepper
3-4 cups	Water (can substitute chicken broth)

Wash asparagus, break off tips, cook in water, and then set tips aside. Cook rest of asparagus in same water until tender. Drain, saving water, put asparagus in blender, blend until smooth and add to saved water. Melt butter in pan, and add flour, salt and pepper, stirring constantly. Cook for about 1 minute, but do not brown. Add milk to flour mixture slowly, then the asparagus mixture. Heat but DO NOT BOIL. Add asparagus tips and heat for 3-4 minutes. Serve. **NOTE:** For an extra kick add a slice of Swiss cheese in each bowl.

Cream of Mushroom Soup

Servings: 6

We didn't have mushrooms too often when I was a child, because they were too expensive. But I sure did learn to love them when I grew up. And of course, they are now plentiful and not very expensive. There are also so many varieties available now that I like to experiment. This is a very rich and very good soup.

1 ½ lb.	Mushroom (include 1 Portabella)
2 Tbsp.	Butter
1 Tbsp.	Onion, chopped fine
2 cubes	Chicken bouillon
2 cups	Boiling water
A few grinds	Fresh black pepper
3 Tbsp.	Flour
2 cups	Evaporated milk
1 tsp.	Salt

Clean all the mushrooms by wiping them with a soft cloth. Chop fine. Sauté mushrooms and onions in 1 Tbsp. butter and cover for 5 minutes. Add bouillon cubes to boiling water then to the mushrooms and simmer uncovered for 10 minutes. In large pot, melt another tablespoon of butter and add flour, stirring for 1 minute until smooth. Slowly add milk, salt and pepper and cook over low flame until thickened. Add mushroom mixture and heat. DO NOT BOIL. Serve hot. **NOTE:** use milk to achieve desired constancy.

French Onion Soup

Servings: 6

A soup that the family loves. I usually make a large pot by tripling the recipe.

4 cups	Onions, yellow, thinly sliced
¼ cup	Butter
¼ tsp.	Black pepper
2 cups	Beef stock
6 slices	Italian bread, toasted
6 slices	Mozzarella cheese

In a soup pot sauté onions in butter until the onions are a dark brown, being careful not to burn. Add stock and pepper, cook for 30 minutes over low heat. To serve, pour hot soup into a microwave-safe or ovenproof bowl, float bread on soup top with cheese and put in oven until cheese melts. Serve immediately. **NOTE:** When making large pots of soup, 3 pounds of onions equal 10 cups sliced. **NOTE:** I sometimes use six pounds of onions to make a very large pot of onion soup. Browning this many onions on a moderate heat takes a long time and you have to stir frequently to make sure the butter and onions do not burn.

Minestrone

Servings: 8

This hearty soup is so good, that it sticks to the ribs.

4 Tbsp.	Olive oil
2	Onions, chopped
3 cloves	Garlic, crushed
2 medium	Potatoes, diced
4	Carrots, sliced
4 ribs	Celery, sliced
½ small head	Savoy cabbage, shredded
1 large can	Tomato, whole, chopped
10-12 cups or 2 large cans	Chicken stock
1	Bouquet garni
2 cans	Kidney beans without sugar
1 can	Chickpeas
	Salt and pepper to taste
4 oz.	Pasta, small (like elbows or shells)
1 ½ cups	Peas
½ cup	Parmesan cheese

Sauté the onions and garlic in the oil until the onions are soft. Stir in the potatoes, carrots and celery, and fry for 5 minutes. Add cabbage and tomatoes. Cook for 5 minutes. Add chicken broth, bouquet garn, beans, and salt and pepper. Bring to a boil, reduce heat to a simmer, cover and cook for 35 minutes. Uncover, remove bouquet garn, and add pasta. Cook for 10 minutes, add peas, and cook for 5 minutes more or until the pasta is done. Serve, topping each bowl with the cheese. Add a loaf of crusty bread and plenty of butter, and you will be in for a wonderful meal!

Miso Soup

Servings: 4-6

This soup has a delicate Asian flavor.

4 cups	Dashi stock*
½ cup	Miso paste*
½ lb.	Tofu, cut into small cubes
2-3	Scallions, chopped with some of the green

Prepare Dashi according to directions on package. Bring to a simmer and stir in the miso. Add tofu and bring to a simmer again. Pour into bowls, and top with scallions. **NOTE:** *These items can be found in any Asian grocery store. Dashi is a Japanese fish broth. Miso is a bean curd paste.

Mushroom/ Chicken Soup

Servings: 10

A light soup.

5-6 oz.	Button mushrooms
5-6 oz.	Portabella mushroom
6 Tbsp.	Butter
1 large	Onion, finely chopped
¼ cup	Flour
2 ½ quarts	Chicken broth

Cut off stems of mushrooms. Chop some of the mushrooms thinly across the capes; set aside. Chop the stems and the rest of the mushrooms very finely. Sauté the finely chopped mushrooms and onion in butter, cover, and cook until soft. Add the flour and stir well, adding 2 cups of the broth slowly. Bring to a boil and add the rest of the broth seasoning with salt and pepper to taste; simmer 10-15 minutes. Add the rest of the mushrooms, and simmer for 5 minutes more. Adjust seasoning. Serve.

Onion Soup

Marjorie Evans
Servings: 6

This is Mother's recipe for this rich soup. It's nice because you make it in a crock-pot.

4 Tbsp.	Butter
6	Yellow onions, sliced
2 cans concentrate	Beef broth
1 ½ soup cans	Water
½ soup can	Sherry wine
6 slices	French bread, about 1-inch thick
6 slices	Mozzarella cheese

In a skillet, melt butter and sauté onions until lightly browned. Pour them into a crock-pot slow cooker along with the beef broth, water and sherry. Cook on low for 4 to 6 hours. Before serving, put the hot soup into heatproof bowls. Top with a slice of bread and a slice of cheese. Put under broiler or in microwave to melt cheese. Serve.

Portuguese Greens Soup

Servings: 10

This is wonderful soup I found when I was putting together a Portuguese menu with my friend Lee Neves, who comes from this country.

2-3 Tbsp.	Extra virgin olive oil
1 ½ cups	Onions, chopped
3-4 cloves	Garlic, finely chopped
3 ½ lb. (about 7, large).	Potatoes peeled & cut into small pieces
1 lg. can	Chicken broth
1 link (8 oz.)	Chorizo mild sausage
½ lb.	Kale, turnip green or collard greens, stems removed, leaves cut in very thin slices
To taste	Freshly ground pepper
	Salt, only if needed

Heat oil in a large soup pot. Add onion and garlic. Cook, stirring occasionally until translucent. Add potatoes and chicken broth. Bring to a boil, and reduce heat to medium. Cook until potatoes are very soft, about 15-20 minutes. Turn heat off and blend the potato mixture with an immersion blender or place in blender or food processor and blend until smooth. Return to heat, bring to boil, add greens and cook on low for about 10-12 minutes. Cut sausage in half lengthwise then cut each piece into thin slices, sauté in a frying pan, and add to soup. Let sausage sit in the soup for a few minutes to impart flavor. Make sure the soup is very hot before serving. **NOTE:** Chorizo sausage is a smoked Portuguese sausage available in specialty grocery stores.

Split Pea Dal (Soup)

Servings: 12

This soup is the center of an Indian meal.

1 lb.	Split peas, dried (green or yellow)
	Water
1 (large)	Onion
2	Carrots
4 Tbsp.	Oil
2 cloves	Garlic, chopped fine
1 tsp.	Ginger, ground
1 tsp.	Cumin
1 tsp.	Turmeric powder
2 tsp.	Cilantro
1 tsp.	Fresh ground black pepper
2 tsp.	Salt
2-3 large	Potatoes, cubed
3 cups	Rice, cooked

Cook peas with onion and carrots in water to cover 1 inch higher than vegetables. Cover and cook until done, about 1 hour, adding more water to keep from sticking. Cool enough to process until smooth in food processor or blender. Cook potatoes in peas with salt, adding more water if necessary. Heat oil in frying pan and add garlic and spices cooking them less than a minute but **DO NOT** burn. (If you burn the spices, start again with fresh oil, garlic and spices.) Add cooked spices to pea soup and heat a few minutes to blend flavors. Serve with cooked rice. **NOTE:** I like to serve a fresh chutney, plain yogurt or *Cucumber Raita*, flat bread cut in wedges to scoop up the food, raisins, nuts, coconut, and a curried vegetable or meat. A nice East Indian meal is complete with *farina* or rice pudding and a cup of green tea. **NOTE:** To make a split pea soup with or without a ham bone, use just the peas, carrot, onion and salt. Follow the cooking and pureeing instructions.

SANDWICHES

Sandwiches that have been favorites through the years are given here, along with my plans for a tea party. I hope you will try some of these hearty delights if you have not done so already.

A TEA PARTY

TEA SANDWICHES

Ingredients:

Bread
Butter, room temperature
Assorted fillings

BREADS

White, firm, sandwich slices. Whole wheat, rye, date and nut, raisin, fruit breads.

Try some of these combinations:

Egg salad with curry powder or bacon
Tuna salad with celery, onions or capers
Ham salad with sweet pickles or celery
Chicken salad with cashew nuts, raisins, peanuts, grapes or celery
Salmon salad with cucumber
Assorted flavor cream cheese
Cucumber with cream cheese
Watercress with cream cheese
Mushrooms chopped fine, sauté in butter and a bit of white wine, chill.
Cheese (American, Swiss, Gouda, Munster, etc.) with different styles of
mustard
Roast beef with horseradish sauce
Ham with mayonnaise
Turkey with cranberry jelly
Avocado, cucumber, sprouts, mayonnaise on whole wheat bread

Other combinations:

Date and nut bread with cream cheese
Raisin bread with cream cheese or peanut butter
Tea biscuits with strawberries preserves and clotted cream[3]

This is how I make tea sandwiches:

Remove all crusts from bread by stacking several slices and, with a serrated-edge knife, slice down through all slices close to the crust. Keep bread covered with plastic while you are fixing sandwiches so that the bread does not dry out. When all slices are prepared, spread each piece of bread with butter. Place filling between two slices of buttered bread using additional flavoring like mustard or mayonnaise, if desired. Stack sandwiches in plastic bags and seal. Refrigerate for at least 4 hours. Just before serving slice sandwiches into 4 triangles or squares. Arrange on sandwich plates or platters. You can decorate some of the sandwiches with small slices of tomatoes, pickles, olives, sprigs of parsley, dill, or any small items you have available. Use small dabs of cream cheese to affix decorations to sandwiches. To keep sandwiches fresh, lay dampened paper towels over them. To store, add a covering of plastic wrap over towels and sandwiches.

What to put on a tea table:

A combination of savories and sweets is the tradition. Savories such as finger sandwiches, cheese and crackers, pickles and olives are basics. If you wish to expand the menu, add a dish of fresh vegetables and a dip, nuts, and/or meat stick and maybe a dish of deviled eggs. The sweets can be any combination of things you have available and enjoy. Cookies, teacakes, pound cake, seed cake, petit fours, miniature tarts, miniature Danish or sticky buns are a few suggestions. Assorted varieties of candies add a nice touch.

---

3 Clotted cream is a thick cream found in specialty delis. This sandwich is a typical treat found in English tearooms

Don't forget the tea. I like to set a tray of cream, sugar and lemon slices, a pot of hot tea concentrate and a pot of hot water in front of me. You can use granulated sugar or sugar cubes, cream, half-and-half, or milk (the English use milk.) About six or eight teabags added to a teapot make a nice strong pot of tea. The hot water allows you to serve the strength of the tea to each person's preference. The English usually put the milk in their cup first, then the tea and sugar. Why? I have no idea. I just remember my grandfather insisting on his tea fixed this way and, other English people to whom I have spoken agree that is the way that tea is served. It's a tradition, I suppose. If you want to serve coffee in addition to tea, I usually ask a guest to help by pouring the coffee. I set a tray for cream, sugar and a coffeepot for that purpose. With this menu, you now have a high tea. A simple tea is just something easy, like bread and butter, and a sweet or two with tea.

How to arrange the table:

If everyone is sitting at one table, have all the food arranged on that table. Sit at one end of the table, and serve each person individually, as they prefer their tea. If coffee is served, have someone sit at the other end of the table to serve anyone who prefers it to tea. A salad-size plate for each person should be set at each place or in a stack for a buffet, plus a teaspoon and napkin for each. If you are serving a large group, you can set the table in the same manner or have the food at one table and the drinks poured at another. People can help themselves to the food and sit and stand as you have space to accommodate them.

When to have a tea party:

The usual time is 4:00, but anytime in the late afternoon is fine. When high tea is served, it really is a meal. Dinner can be postponed until later in the evening. If you serve just a simple tea with a few sweets, the tea becomes a late afternoon snack.

The most important thing about a tea party:

The most important thing is to have a good time! Enjoy your company with nice conversation, a relaxed atmosphere, pleasant music, and an attractively arranged table with your best dishes, linens and nicest manners. Enjoy the afternoon.

P.S. Teas are loved by women, but not exclusively. My men enjoy tea parties, as many men do.

Bacon, Lettuce and Tomato

Servings: 1

Referred to as "BLT" and enjoyed by everyone.

3-4 slices	Bacon cooked, crisp
1-2 leaves	Lettuce
2-3 slices	Tomato
2 slices	White bread toasted
1 Tbsp.	Mayonnaise
	Salt, to taste
	Freshly ground black pepper

Spread mayonnaise on toast, arrange BLT on bread, flavoring generously with salt and pepper. Top with second slice of bread, cut in half, and enjoy.

Banana Sandwich

Servings: 1

We ate these sandwiches all the time as children. I still like them very much.

1 small	Banana
1-2 leaves	Lettuce
2 slices	White bread, toasted
	Salt, to taste
	Mayonnaise, to taste

Spread toast with mayonnaise. Slice banana lengthwise and arrange on toast. Sprinkle lightly with salt and add lettuce. Top with other slice of toast. **NOTE:** We usually ate this on saltine crackers. In times past the cracker came in four crackers attached to each other so it made a bread size cracker. Today, they come in single crackers, which makes it more difficult to use. But if you have time, make this sandwich with crackers; you don't need to add the salt.

Cold Meat

Servings: 1

I love cold lamb and pork sandwiches.

3-4 thin slices	Lamb (substitute pork or beef, if desired)
2 slices	Bread
	Salt, to taste
	Pepper, to taste
	Butter

Butter the bread generously, top with meat, and flavor with salt and pepper, top with the other slice of bread. **NOTE:** To make HOT SANDWICHES, heat gravy from roast. While gravy is very hot, slip sliced meat into it, bring back to boil, then, turn gravy off and let the meat sit in the gravy until heated well. Put meat on bread. Reheat gravy; pour over open-face sandwich.

Grilled Cheese

Servings: 1

A basic idea for a quick meal. Add a bowl of tomato soup and a salad and dinner's on.

2 slices	Bread
2 slices	Tomato (optional)
3 slices	Bacon, cooked crisp (optional)
	Butter
	Cheddar cheese

Heat a frying pan to get hot, then turn down the flame to medium. Butter the bread and place butter side down in pan, top with cheese, and if desired, tomato and/or bacon. Butter other slice and place on top butter to the outside. Slowly brown bread then turn to brown other side. Cheese should melt when ready to eat. Try not to burn bread, and watch heat. Have soup heating. Serve.

Healthy Veggie Sandwich

Servings: 1

I found this in one of the many diet books I have read. I like it very much.

3 slices	Avocado
3 slices	Cucumber, cut lengthwise
2 slices	Tomato
2 slices	Whole wheat bread
To taste	Salt
To taste	Black pepper
	Alfalfa sprouts
	Mayonnaise

Cover each slice of bread with mayonnaise. Layer each of the vegetables on bread. Flavor with salt and pepper, top with second slice, cut in half and enjoy,

Hoagie

Servings: 1

I have made a party around a six-foot version of this sandwich!

1 10-inch	Italian roll
2-3 oz.	Ham, lunchmeat
½ oz.	Capacole lunch meat
2 oz.	Provolone cheese, sliced
½ oz.	Salami
1	Tomato, sliced
2	Lettuce leaves
4 slices	Salad onion
	Hot peppers
	Oregano, dried
	Salt
	Black pepper
	Olive oil

Slice roll lengthwise, and drizzle oil over the two pieces. Put layers of ham, capracole and cheese over two slices. Top with onion and tomato slices. Sprinkle with salt, pepper, and oregano and put as many slices of hot peppers as desired. Lay lettuce over sandwich. Put a layer of salami over entire sandwich and, with a long knife, press down into the middle of the sandwich lengthwise as you close it. Tightly wrap sandwich in wax paper or plastic wrap, and let it sit for 10 minutes. Open and enjoy!

Muffuletta Sandwich

Serving: 4

This is the New Orleans version of a hoagie. You need to prepare the olive salad a day or two beforehand so the flavors blend with each other.

	Olive salad
6 oz.	Green olives, stuffed, sliced
3 oz.	Black olives, sliced
3 oz.	Black olives, in oil, sliced
3 oz.	Green olives, in oil, sliced
1 rib	Celery, cut diagonal
1/2 cup	Onion, diced
3 cloves	Garlic, minced
½ tsp.	Basil, dried
About 1 cup	Olive oil
6 Tbsp.	Wine vinegar
	Black pepper
3-4 drops	Hot sauce
	Fillings
1	Round loaf of Italian bread, about 9 or 10 inches in diameter
4 oz.	Roast beef lunchmeat
4 oz.	Ham lunchmeat
2 oz.	Salami
4 oz.	Mortadella
2 oz.	Provolone cheese

OLIVE SALAD: Several days before use, blanch celery, and onion until just soft. Drain, cool and put in a quart jar with olives. Cover vegetables with oil. Add basil, garlic, vinegar, pepper and hot sauce. **To make sandwich:** Cut bread into two slices, horizontally, with a serrated knife. On the bottom slice, sprinkle some of the juice from the olive salad. Next, layer the lunchmeats and cheese, making sure to cover all the bread. With a slotted spoon, put a thick layer (about ½ inch) of the olives on the meat and cheese. Sprinkle some to the juice on the top slice, and cover the sandwich. Press down so that the olives stick to top slice of bread. Wrap whole loaf of bread in plastic wrap and let sit for 15 to 20 minutes or longer. Open plastic, cut into four wedges. and enjoy a sandwich that is not to be believed!

Onion Sandwich

Servings: 1

One of my childhood sandwiches.

2 slices	Bread, white
	Butter
	Slices of salad onion
	Salt and pepper, to taste
	Ketchup

Butter bread. Slice the onion very thin and make a nice thick layer to cover bread. Salt and pepper, then top with ketchup, and cover with other slice of bread. This is an onion sandwich!

Peanut Butter Spread

Servings: 2

As children, Alvin and I whipped up this special spread. We made it all the time and I still do.

1 Tbsp.	Peanut butter smooth or chunky
1 Tbsp.	Butter
1 Tbsp.	Honey

Whip these together and spread on crackers or bread. Nice anytime.

Sandwich Loaf

Servings:

I remember Ma making this for an evening party for friends.

1-1 ½ lbs. loaf.	Bread, unsliced
1 stick	Butter, softened
1 ½ cups	Chicken salad
1 ½ cups	Egg salad
1 ½ cups	Ham salad
2-8 oz. packages	Cream cheese, softened
2 Tbsp.	Milk

Remove all crust from bread. Slice bread into four slices lengthwise. A serrated edge knife is easiest. Butter the inside of slices, both sides. On bottom slice spread a layer of salad, top with next slice of bread and continue until the 3 salads are on a slice, top with last slice. Cover with plastic wrap and refrigerate for at least one hour until the bread and salads are cold and firm. Remove from refrigerator and trim away any loose bread or salad. Mix milk with cream cheese until the cheese is spreadable. Ice the loaf with the cream cheese. Decorate cream cheese with olives, whole chive leaves, pimentos, small tomatoes, cucumbers or any other item you like to make the loaf attractive. You can use dried parsley or paprika to dust the cheese as well. Refrigerate again until the cheese is firm. To serve, carefully slice the loaf into slices. Each slice can be cut in half or in thirds to make finger sandwiches. Good for lunch, dinner or an evening party. **NOTE:** You can use any three salad combination you wish. These were the ones Ma used.

Tomato Sandwich

Servings: 1

This is a must in the summer, and you will need more than one.

1	Tomato, sliced
	Mayonnaise, to taste
	Salt, to taste
	Fresh ground black pepper, to taste
2 slices	White bread, toasted

Spread both slices of bread with mayonnaise. Pile tomato on bread, and add salt and a good amount of pepper. Top with other slice of bread, cut into two and get ready to make more. **NOTE:** Really only make this sandwich with garden fresh tomatoes. It is a waste of time to use winter tomatoes.

SALADS

When I was a kid, salad meant a bowl of fresh greens and other raw vegetables with a dressing. When I visited Smith's Island and a salad was part of the meal, what they were referring to was potato salad. Now the salad has many definitions and is used in all parts of the meal, including being the meal itself. I have included some of the ones that we have enjoyed though the years.

VEGETABLE SALADS

Bean Salad

Servings: 14 cups

This is my version of the traditional 3-bean salad.

1 can	Green beans, cut
1 can	Wax beans, cut
1 can	Kidney beans
1 can	Lima beans
1 can	Carrots, sliced
1 can	Chick peas
½ cup	Celery, chopped
¼ cup	Red pepper, chopped fine
½ cup	Oil
½ cup	Vinegar, apple or red wine
¼ cup	Sugar
2 cloves	Garlic, crushed
½ tsp.	Salt
A few grinds	Fresh black pepper
	Salad onion slices, to taste

Drain all canned vegetables and mix in a large bowl. Add other ingredients and mix well. Refrigerate overnight, stirring occasionally. This salad will last for several weeks if kept cold.

Carrot and Raisin Salad

Servings: 4

A much-requested recipe and an old-time favorite.

4 large	Carrots, peeled and grated
¼ cup	Raisins
1 large rib	Celery, finely chopped
½-2/3 cup	Mayonnaise
Pinch	Salt

Mix together and chill for 3-4 hours or overnight. The raisins need time to plump. **NOTE:** Adjust the mayonnaise to suit your taste.

Carrot and Pineapple Gelatin Salad

Servings: 3 cup

Tastes great with cold meat or with a baked ham. Got this one from my Jell-o cookbook

1 3-oz. Box	Lemon gelatin
½ tsp.	Salt
1 ½ cups	Boiling water
1 8-oz. Can	Pineapple tidbits
1 Tbsp.	Lemon juice
1 cup	Carrots, grated

Dissolve gelatin and salt in boiling water. Add pineapple and lemon juice. Chill until thick. Fold in the carrots. Pour into a 1 qt. mold. Chill until firm. Unmold. **NOTE:** Can be doubled for a larger group.

Coleslaw

Servings: 4

Everyone has their own combination. Ma made hers simple. This is how I make her recipe.

4 cups	Cabbage, finely shredded
1-2 Tbsp.	Onion, grated
¼ cup	Carrots, grated
½ cup	Mayonnaise
½ to ¾ tsp.	Salt
Dash	Black pepper
1 tsp.	Sugar
1 Tbsp.	Wine vinegar

Mix mayonnaise and the following ingredients together. Pour over vegetables. Stir well and chill for at least 2 hours. To serve, sprinkle with paprika for color.

Garlic Beets

Servings: 6

For the garlic lovers!

2 1-lb. Cans	Beets cut, or
2 lb.	Fresh beets, cooked and cut
6-8 cloves	Garlic, minced fine
½ cup	Olive oil
½ cup	Wine vinegar

Drain beets and combine ingredients, seasoning with salt and a generous amount of fresh ground pepper. Marinate overnight for the best results.

Green Bean Salad

Servings: 2-4

Ma would make this with leftover green beans.

1 to 2 cups	Green beans, cooked, cold, chopped
½ cup	Onion, finely minced
½ cup	Mayonnaise
¼ cup	Celery, finely chopped

Mix all ingredients together. Chill. **NOTE:** Adjust amounts to suit amount of leftover beans.

Japanese Cucumber Relish

Servings: 4

A nice relish for any meal, but a must when serving a Japanese menu.

2 (medium)	Cucumbers (I like to use the European style)
1 Tbsp.	Salt
¼-1/3 cup	Rice wine vinegar
¼ cup	Sugar
¾-1 tsp.	Ginger root, grated

To prepare cucumbers, peel and cut in half lengthwise. Slice very thin, at an angle. Place cucumber in a colander and sprinkle with salt. Let stand for 30 minutes. Rinse and dry. Place cucumbers in a clean tea towel and twist to thoroughly dry. Place the rest of the ingredients in a bowl and mix. Add cucumbers and chill.

Marinated Carrots

Servings: 6 cups

Nice salad to perk up a meal.

2 lb.	Carrots, sliced thinly
1	Onions, chopped fine
1	Red bell pepper, chopped fine
3 ribs	Celery, chopped fine
1 can concentrated	Tomato soup, undiluted
1 cup	Sugar
¼ cup	Oil
¾ cup	Vinegar
1 tsp.	Salt
1 tsp.	Black pepper
1 tsp.	Worcestershire sauce
1 Tbsp. dry or regular	Mustard

Cook carrots until tender but still crisp; drain, and cool. Add onion, pepper, and celery. In saucepan, mix soup, sugar, oil, vinegar, mustard, salt, pepper, and Worcestershire sauce, and bring to a boil. Pour over vegetables and marinate overnight or for 12 hours. Serve cold or at room temperature. **NOTE:** If you can fine multicolored carrots they make a delightful appearance in a lovely white or clear bowl.

Orange and Onion Salad

Servings: 4

I use this recipe in the winter when the tomatoes are not very good.

2 large	Oranges, peeled and sliced thin
1 large	Salad onion, sliced thin
1 large	Cucumber, sliced thin
½ cup	Vegetable oil
¼ cup	Orange juice
1/8 tsp.	Mint leaves
	Salt, to taste
	Black pepper, to taste
	Red tip lettuce leaves

Marinate orange, onion, and cucumber in oil, orange juice and seasonings for 15 minutes. Serve over lettuce leaves.

Perfection Salad

Servings: 6-8

A nice cold salad for any meal.

1 cup	Boiling water
1 3-oz. box	Lemon gelatin
2 Tbsp.	Lemon juice
1 tsp.	Salt
1 cup	Cold water
1 cup	Celery, finely chopped
1 cup	Cabbage, finely shredded
¼ cup	Red pepper, chopped
½ cup	Carrot, grated

Pour boiling water over gelatin in bowl, stirring very well to dissolve gelatin. Stir in lemon juice, salt and cold water. Chill until slightly thickened. Stir in rest of ingredients, pour into mold and chill until firm. Unmold on a platter with lettuce leaves as decoration.

Pickled Beets

Servings: 8

Ma served these very often.

2 lb.	Beets cooked or canned, sliced
1	Onion, sliced thin
1 Tbsp.	Sugar
	Salt and pepper
	Apple cider vinegar

Drain beets, saving liquid. Put beets in a bowl, using liquid to fill the bowl halfway, fill the rest with vinegar. Add onion, sugar and season with salt and pepper. Best if it is marinated for 4 or more hours. **NOTE:** Try adding 3 or 4 whole cloves for a spicier taste.

Potato Salad

Servings: 6

My recipe.

6-8	Potato, all purpose
1 tsp.	Salt
½ cup	Mayonnaise
1-2 Tbsp.	Wine vinegar
2 Tbsp.	Olive oil
½ cup	Celery, chopped fine
¼ cup	Onion, chopped fine
2	Eggs (optional)

Peel potatoes and cut into large chunks. Cover with water, add salt and eggs, if used, to hard boil. Cook until tender, but not falling apart. Drain and rinse in cold water to stop cooking and cool. Peel eggs, chop and add to potatoes, celery and onions. Mix mayonnaise, vinegar, oil, salt and pepper to taste. Pour mixture over potatoes mixture. Mix carefully so the potatoes do not become mashed. Taste and adjust seasoning. **NOTE:** Always add salt to water when cooking potatoes. Adding salt after does not achieve the best flavor.

Sour Potatoes

Servings: 8

Ma's recipe that some call "German potato salad", but I call it "just plain good!"

2 ½ lbs.	Potatoes, peeled and sliced ¼ inch thick
6 slices	Bacon
2-3 Tbsp., to taste	Apple cider vinegar
1 tsp.	Salt
	Black pepper, to taste
	Celery seed

Boil potatoes with salt until just tender, drain, and put on a warm platter. While potatoes are cooking, fry bacon until crisp, drain and save fat. Pour hot fat over cooked potatoes, sprinkle with crumbled bacon, black pepper and celery seeds. Sprinkle 2 tablespoons vinegar over whole platter. Keep warm for 5 minutes, taste and add more vinegar if needed. Serve warm.

Waldorf Salad

Servings: 6

A nice fresh salad you can make any time of the year, but good in the winter when fresh vegetables aren't always the best and are expensive.

4 Gala or Winesap	Apples, pared and cut in chunks
1 large rib	Celery, diced small
¼ cup	Raisins
¼ cup	Walnuts
½ cup	Mayonnaise
Pinch	Salt

Mix all ingredients together and chill for 3-4 hours or overnight. Serve on a lettuce leaf. **NOTE:** You can leave the skins on the apple if you prefer, but the skins should not be tough or bitter.

Watercress Salad

Servings: 4-6

This was a salad I always loved, and Ma fixed it so simply that anyone can make it.

1 bunch	Watercress
1-2 Tbsp.	Sugar
1-2 Tbsp.	Vinegar

Wash the vegetables and cut off about an inch of the stems. Tear the greens up and place on salad plates. Sprinkle each plate with the sugar, vinegar, salt and pepper and let sit a few minutes before serving. Adjust the flavors to suit your taste. So wonderful! Watercress has such a definite flavor, almost spicy, that once you use it, you will be on the lookout for it!

Watercress and Walnut Salad

Servings: 4

I had this salad at a restaurant and was so impressed, that I wrote down the ingredients so I would not forget. Then, of course, I went home and duplicated it. See what you think!

4 cups	Baby field salad greens
¾ cup	Red grapes
4-6 very thin slices	Onion
½ cup	Walnuts, roasted
2-3 oz.	Blue cheese, crumbled
½ bunch	Watercress
	DRESSING
½ cup	Olive oil
3 Tbsp.	Balsamic vinegar
1 tsp.	Ginger root, grated

Roasting the walnuts is the most important part of this recipe. Put them in a shallow pan and roast them in a 350° oven until you begin to smell them, or about 10 minutes. Shake the nuts a couple of times so they will not burn. If they burn, throw them away and start again. Divide all ingredients onto 4 salad plates. Make a base of the greens. Add the grapes, onion slices and walnuts. Sprinkle cheese over everything. Place a few sprigs of watercress upright in the center of the salad. Mix dressing ingredients together and shake in a jar, and sprinkle dressing over salad. So very good!

Wilted Spinach Salad

Servings: 2

This salad is nice beginning course to any meal.

1 10-oz. Bag	Fresh spinach
4 slices	Bacon, cooked crisp and crumbled, save fat
3 Tbsp.	Water
3 Tbsp.	Wine vinegar
1 ½ Tbsp.	Onion, finely chopped
1 Tbsp.	Sugar
	Black pepper, to taste

Wash spinach, removing thick stems. Dry well. Sauté onion in bacon fat, then add rest of ingredients and heat until liquid comes to a boil. Just before serving, pour boiling dressing over spinach leaves. Sprinkle with crumbled bacon, toss lightly and serve immediately.

FRUIT SALADS

Cranberry Gelatin Mold

Servings: 4-5

I like to use this as a side dish for a lunch or as a relish for dinner.

1 3-oz. Box	Cranberry gelatin
1 cup	Boiling water
¾ cup	Cranberry juice
1	Apple, crisp, peeled, chopped
1 rib	Celery, chopped
¼ cup	Walnuts, chopped

Dissolve gelatin in boiling water. Add cranberry juice. Chill until thick, stir in other ingredients. Chill until firm. Serve on lettuce leaf with cream cheese balls. **NOTE:** Cream cheese balls: 1 8-oz.package of cream cheese. Roll into 1-inch balls, and roll in chopped walnuts. Chill.

Exotic Fruit Salad

Servings: 8

Another taste of Philippine cuisine. Given to me by Nicole, this recipe is delicious.

1 large can	Tropical fruit salad, drained
1 large can	Pineapple chunks, drained
1 can	Lychee, drained
1 jar	Nata de Coco, drained
1 can	Nestle Cream
1 can	Condensed milk (not evaporated)

Combine all ingredients into a large bowl. Chill for at least 4 hours. **NOTE:** Nata de Coco, Nestle cream, and Lychee can be found at any Asian grocery store.

Fruit Salad

Servings: 8-12

Ma made this as the different fruits came in season. Now you can get most fruits all year long. Be creative and choose your favorite ones to combine into a salad.

2	Apples
2	Pears
2	Oranges
1	Grapefruit
1 cup	Grapes cut in half
½	Cantaloupe
½	Honeydew melon
1 ½ cups	Watermelon
½	Pineapple

I have given an idea of what I might put in a salad. Peel, pare, remove seeds and cut the fruit into chunks. Cut the fruit in bite-size pieces so when you chew the fruit you taste each of the flavors. Mango and other tropical fruit give a nice flavor. Dried fruit and coconut are something Ma often added. When you have assembled all your fruit, pour a ½ to 1cup of fruit juice (orange, cranberry, pineapple, and apple to name a few) over the fruit and stir. Cover and chill. Serve a generous portion to everyone. **NOTE:** Do not use banana in salad as it will turn dark and sour very quickly. If you really want to use banana, add at the last minute just to the portion being used.

Mother's Ambrosia

Servings: 8

Mother gets many requests for this salad.

1 can	Pineapple, crushed
2 8-oz. cans	Mandarin oranges
1 cup	Coconut
1 16-oz. container	Sour cream
2 cups	Marshmallows, miniature or large, cut into quarters

Drain fruit, saving some juice to thin sour cream. Mix all ingredients in a large bowl. Use juice to get the right consistently. Refrigerate for at least 4 hours before serving**. NOTE:** I use pineapple chunks. Five Cup Salad: This is the original name of this recipe. Five ingredients 1 cup each.

MAIN DISH SALAD

Chef's Salad

Servings: 4

In the summer I often make this nice salad. When the children were young, I would make it as a quick dinner so they could get back to the pool.

4-5 cups	Assorted salad greens, torn into bite size pieces
2	Tomatoes, cut into wedges
1	Cucumber, peeled cut thin
8 oz.	Ham lunchmeat, sliced julienne
4-6 oz.	Turkey lunchmeat, sliced julienne
2-4 oz.	Cheddar cheese, cut into small cubes
2 oz.	Swiss cheese, sliced julienne
	Black olives, to taste
2-3	Eggs hard boiled, wedges
1 cup	Croutons
	Salad dressing of choice
	Onion slices as desired

Toss everything together and serve with everyone's favorite dressing. **NOTE:** A nice, crisp loaf of bread, butter and a pitcher of ice tea makes the meal. **NOTE:** See *Food Tips* for cutting julienne.

Chicken Salad

Servings: 6

Ma made chicken many ways. I always loved chicken salad. Although I have eaten it a lot of places, homemade is best.

3 cups	Chicken, cooked, diced, all white meat or use the whole chicken
1 cup	Celery, chopped fine
¼ cup	Onion, chopped fine *OR*
1Tbsp	Grated onion
½ tsp	Salt
¼ tsp.	Fresh-ground black pepper
1/3 to ½ cup	Mayonnaise

Mix all ingredients together and chill. Serve as a sandwich filling or on lettuce leaves and garish with tomato wedges, cucumber slices, hard-boiled egg wedges. **NOTE:** I sometimes add ½ cup of cut white grapes,1 Tbsp. rinsed capers, and ½ cup pineapple tidbits. To use in tea sandwiches, cut the chicken and vegetables into very small pieces. **NOTE:** For a spicy touch, add ¼ teaspoon of curry powder to recipe.

Cobb Salad

Servings: 8

I like this salad, which I take to covered dish lunches or serve it for family and friends.

4	Chicken, breasts broiled or grilled, sliced (or use half a turkey breast)
1	Head of red or green-tipped lettuce or romaine, torn
3	Tomatoes, cut into wedges
3	Eggs, hard-boiled, cut into wedges
1	Avocado, peeled and sliced
15-20	Black olives in oil
½ lb.	Bacon, cooked crisp and crumbed
2-3 oz.	Blue cheese, crumbled

Dressing

½ cup	Olive oil
2 Tbsp.	Wine vinegar
½ tsp.	Mint leaves
	Salt to taste
A few grinds	Black pepper

Prepare dressing. Set aside. Arrange lettuce leaves on a large platter. Then, using all other ingredients, make a pleasant pattern. Sprinkle blue cheese and bacon over the whole salad. Shake dressing and drizzle over the top of the salad just before serving. A loaf of crusty bread with butter is a nice accompaniment.

Greek Salad

Servings: 4

This is a favorite of my niece, Laura. I always served it to her when she would make her yearly Christmas visit.

2 heads	Romaine lettuce
½	Red bell pepper, sliced in thin strips
1	Cucumber, peeled and sliced thin
2	Tomatoes, cut into wedges
8-oz.	Feta cheese, cut into large cubes
1 can	Anchovies, drained
Use amount to taste	Greek black olives
2-3	Eggs hard boiled, cut into wedges
	Croutons
	Red onion slices, to taste

Strip leaves of the romaine from the stems and tear into bite size pieces. Discard the stems. Place in a large salad bowl. Top with other vegetables, cheese, and olives. Mix *Greek Style Salad Dressing* and shake well, or mix with a wire whisk, pour over salad and toss. Serve with anchovies and croutons to be used at the table as desired.

Pasta and Seafood Salad

Servings: 6-10

Use for a main course or as a side dish.

1 lb.	Pasta, shell or other similar kind
1 lb.	Shrimp, cooked, peeled
½ cup	Mayonnaise
½ to ¾ cup	Celery, chopped fine
¼ cup	Red pepper, chopped very fine (optional)

Cook pasta per package directions. Drain and rinse in cold water until cool. Drain very well. Chop shrimp and add to pasta. Add rest of ingredients, mix well. Use amount of mayonnaise to taste. Chill. **NOTE:** Substitute other seafood for shrimp, or use a combination. Crab, imitation crab, scallops, lobster are wonderful additions.

Pasta Salad with Tuna

Servings: 10

Nicole's pasta salad with a flair.

1 lb.	Spiral pasta, cooked and drained
1 cup	Mayonnaise
1 8-oz can	Pineapple crushed, drained well
1 12-oz can	Tuna fish, drained
1 Tbsp.	Sweet pickle relish
	Pepper, to taste
	Salt, to taste
	Cayenne pepper, to taste

Combine all ingredients in a large bowl. Add more mayonnaise to taste. Refrigerate for at least 1 hour. Serve cold. **NOTE:** Nicole sometimes likes to use mandarin oranges in place of pineapples.

Seafood Vegetable Salad

Servings: 2

George asked me to make this, and it turned out very well. I share it with you. Check note for variations.

¾ lb.	Imitation crabmeat, thawed
1 Tbsp.	Olive oil
1 Tbsp.	Butter
¼ cup	Onion, chopped
3-4 cloves	Garlic, minced
About ½ cup	White wine
4 cups	Greens, torn
1	Tomato, cut into wedges
½	Cucumber, peeled and sliced
2 slices	Red onion
	Salad dressing

Sauté onion and garlic in oil and butter until soft. Add crabmeat and sauté for a minute or two. Add the white wine and simmer until it is absorbed. While the crab is cooking, divide the greens between 2 plates. Arrange tomatoes, cucumber and onion slices. Top with crabmeat and use your favorite dressing. **NOTE:** This recipe can be varied many ways. Use other seafoods like, shrimp, scallops, crabmeat, and solid white fish. You can add or subtract the vegetables Add croutons, chickpeas or other beans. I like a oil, vinegar and garlic dressing. Different vinegar like rice wine, balsamic, herb flavored or white wine changes the flavor. Make your own combination to meet your taste.

Tabbouleh

Servings: 4

I found this recipe many years ago. It is a vegetarian dish and a delicious addition to a menu.

¾ cup fine or medium	Bulgur (cracked) wheat
4 Tbsp.	Fresh lemon juice
4	Scallions, chopped
2 cups	Parsley, flat leaf, chopped
1 cup	Mint leaves, finely chopped
3 small	Tomatoes, diced
½ cup	Olive oil, extra-virgin
1 head	Romaine lettuce
1(small)	Cucumbers, diced (optional)

Put the bulgur in a bowl and cover with water. Let stand for 30 minutes or until the liquid is absorbed and the grains are tender. Drain and press out any excess liquid. Return to bowl and toss with ½ the lemon juice, scallions, tomatoes, parsley, and mint, let sit for 30 minutes to finish softening. In a small bowl, mix the rest of the lemon juice, olive oil, salt and pepper. Pour over bulgur and vegetables. Serve on a bed of romaine. Stir in cucumber if used. **NOTE:** The tradition is to use the romaine leaves to scoop up the salad.

Tuna Molded Salad

Friends of the Haddon Fortnightly
Servings: 6

Nice for a luncheon, but I have served this for brunch as well.

1 can	Tomato soup, concentrated
1 can	Water
1 8-oz. Package	Cream cheese
2 envelopes	Gelatin (unflavored)
½ cup	Water
1 6 ½ oz. Can	Tuna fish, solid white, flaked
1 cup	Celery, chopped
¼ cup	Onion, chopped fine
½ cup	Mayonnaise

Heat soup with 1 can of cold water. Stir in cream cheese and beat until smooth. Add gelatin, which has been dissolved in ½ cup of water. When cool, but not set, add tuna, celery, onion and mayonnaise. Pour into mold and let set. To serve, unmold onto a platter. Decorate with lettuce leaves, tomato wedges, hard-boiled eggs slices and serve with plain or a flavored mayonnaise. **NOTE:** I usually use a fish mold, but you could use a bowl if a mold is not available.

SALAD DRESSINGS

Greek Style Salad Vinaigrette

Servings: 6

Great on any green salad, but this is what I use on my Greek style salad.

½ cup	Virgin olive oil
3 Tbsp.	Lemon juice
½ tsp.	Dried mint leaves
½ tsp.	Salt
A few grinds	Black pepper
	Oil drain from a can of anchovies
1/8 tsp.	Dried basil

Wisk oil into all the other ingredients. Or use a small food processor to blend ingredients. Use right away or store in refrigerator until needed. Stir or shake before use.

Instant French dressing

This is so easy when you are in the mood for French and there is none in sight.

1 part	Mayonnaise
1 part	Ketchup
½ part	Sweet pickle relish

Stir mayonnaise and ketchup together and you have French. For Thousand Island dressing add relish. I make both, and they are good!

Vinaigrette

Servings: ½ cup

This is a delicious dressing to serve over any green or tossed salad.

2 cloves	Garlic
2 Tbsp.	White wine vinegar
6 Tbsp.	Extra virgin olive oil
½ tsp.	Coarse salt
A few grinds	Fresh black pepper

In a small food processor or a blender, add garlic and vinegar, processing until garlic is blended with the vinegar. Add oil, salt and pepper. Process until emulsified. Pour over salad or into a container; cover and refrigerate until needed.

BREADS

Dad always insisted that the evening meal include starch and bread of some type. It was simply a part of Ma's preparation of dinner to consider what bread she would prepare: raised, baking powder, or corn. When she didn't make something from scratch, a loaf of store bread was on the table. *Pancakes, waffles, French bread*, and *dumplings* were all a simple part of preparing a meal. With instant food these days, these recipes are a treat some people reserve for the weekends or a holiday.

Buckwheat Cakes

Servings: 6-8

I love these wonderful, hearty breakfast cakes. Serve with butter and ketchup or syrup.

2 cups	Buckwheat flour
2 tsp.	Baking powder
½ tsp.	Baking Soda
1/2 tsp.	Salt
2 to 2 1/2cups	Milk
¼ cup	Butter, melted
2	Eggs, beaten
¼ cup	Sugar

Combine dry ingredients; mix well. Combine milk, eggs and butter and stir into dry ingredients until smooth. Let this batter sit for 15 minutes before using. Preheat frying pan at 3350°. Use about ¼ cup of batter in a hot, oiled skillet turning cake when the top of cake is covered with bubbles. **NOTE:** I like to use buttermilk when possible. Substitute buttermilk for milk and increase amount by ½ cup. Increase baking soda by 1tsp.

Corn Bread

Servings: 6-8

Ma baked her corn bread in a big, black, cast iron frying pan. It gave the cornbread a wonderful crust.

2 cups	Cornmeal, white, stone-ground
4 tsp.	Baking powder
1 tsp.	Salt
1	Egg
1 ½ cups	Milk
2 Tbsp.	Oil

Preheat oven to 450°. Put oil in 8" or 9" cast iron or round baking pan. Heat in oven until hot. Combine dry ingredients. Combine milk and egg, and add to dry mixture. Stir until smooth. Pour into hot pan. Bake for 20 to 25 minutes. Serve hot, cut into wedges with butter.

Dumplings

Servings: 4

Use with chicken, beef or lamb stew.

1 cup	Flour
½ tsp.	Salt
2 tsp.	Baking powder
½ cup	Milk
1 Tbsp.	Fresh parsley, chopped fine

Mix ingredients into a paste. Drop from spoon into boiling meat broth. Cook with lid off for 10 minutes. Cover pot, and cook for 10 more minutes. Remove lid, lift dumpling out of gravy immediately and serve with stew. **NOTE:** I double this recipe because we really like dumplings. Cook exactly as instructed for light fluffy dumplings.

Garlic Bread

Servings: 4

A wonderful addition to any meal, and people love garlic. For those who don't, omit the garlic and use other favors.

1 loaf	French bread
1/3 to1 stick	Butter, melted
2 cloves	Garlic minced, or ½ tsp. garlic powder
1 Tbsp.	Parsley, minced (or 1 tsp. Dried)
	Paprika

Cut bread in half lengthwise. Sauté garlic in some of the melted butter to soften but not brown. Add garlic to he rest of the butter. Brush the butter over the entire inside of the bread. Sprinkle with parsley and paprika. Put the bread back together, and wrap in aluminum foil. Bake at 350° for ten minutes or until the bread is crisp and the flavor is heated through the bread. You can cut the bread in large diagonal slices before or after baking. **NOTE:** If you don't want garlic, just use the butter and parsley. You can add other spices such as a dash of curry, some basil, or any flavor you like to give a zing to the bread. When making a few loaves for a group, I usually make one without garlic, just in case.

Irish Soda Bread

Servings: 6

Make it with or without the raisins. I serve it with corned beef and cabbage on St. Patrick's Day.

6 Tbsp.	Shortening
2 cups	Biscuit mix
1 Tbsp.	Sugar
½ cup	Raisins (can use currants)
1 Tbsp.	Caraway seeds
¾ cups	Milk

Heat oven to 375°. Cut shortening into biscuit mix with 2 knives or pastry blender until it looks like coarse corn meal. Stir in sugar, raisins, and caraway seeds with a fork slowly stir in milk until blended. Form into a ball and place in a 9-inch greased pie pan. Bake 30 minutes or until a cake tester, inserted in center, comes out clean. Serve hot in wedges with a lot of butter.

Maryland Beaten Biscuits

Servings: 18 biscuits

This is the old way Aunt Maggie made this country biscuits. I have given up-dated directions in case you don't have the time or the wooden potato masher. By the way, I have my Great-Grandmother's wooden potato masher that Aunt Maggie used!

¾ tsp.	Sugar
½ tsp.	Salt
3 cups	Flour, sifted
1/3 cup	Cold shortening
½ cup	Milk

Sift sugar, salt and flour together, blend in shortening, and add just enough milk to make very stiff dough. Beat with a wooden potato masher for 30 minutes or until dough blisters. Roll to ½-inch thickness. Cut with a small biscuit cutter, prick with a fork, bake at 350° for 30 minutes. The biscuits should be a very pale ivory color. **NOTE:** To make these biscuits easier, put the dough though a meat grinder several times or use a food processor until the dough blisters.

Pancakes

Servings: 12 cakes

I use this recipe for pancakes and as a base for fruit or vegetable fritters.

1 ½ cups	Flour
½ tsp.	Salt
½ tsp.	Baking Soda
1 tsp.	Sugar
1	Egg
1 ½ cups	Milk, soured*
3 Tbsp.	Butter, melted

Sift dry ingredients together. Beat egg, sour milk and melted butter together. Add liquid mixture gradually to dry mixture, stirring constantly to keep it smooth. Drop the batter by ¼ cup ladle onto a hot greased griddle or frying pan. Cook until top is full of tiny bubbles and the underside is brown. Turn and brown other side. Serve with butter and syrup. **NOTE:** *See *Food Tips* for soured milk.

Potato Bread

Servings: 2 1-lb. loaves

I could make a meal on Ma's bread with butter. When she baked potato bread, you could "swallow your tongue," to quote an old saying.

3	Potatoes
1 package	Yeast
2 Tbsp.	Shortening
2 Tbsp.	Sugar
6 to 6 ½ cups	Flour

Boil potatoes until tender, mash in liquid. Heat 2 cups to lukewarm. Sprinkle yeast on ¼ cup of liquid. Let yeast set for 5 minutes. To remaining liquid, add shortening, sugar and salt. Add dissolved yeast and half the flour. Beat and add the other half of flour gradually. Knead on floured board for about 10 minutes, until elastic. Place in bowl, cover, and let rise until doubled. Divide into 2 parts, shape into loaves and place in greased loaf pans, to rise again until doubled. Bake at 375° for 45 minutes or until bread separates from side of pan. **NOTE:** Can be made into rolls. After dough first rises, shape dough into rolls and place on a baking sheet or in a cake pan if you want your roll to touch. Let rise to double and bake at 400° for 20 minutes. **NOTE:** To up date this recipe, use a dough hook in your mixer to knead the dough.

Pumpkin Raisin Muffins

Servings: 2-2½ dozen

Everyone loves these year round.

1 30-oz. Can	Libby's Pumpkin Pie Mix
2 boxes	Nut bread mix
1	Egg, beaten
1 cup	Raisins, golden
2 tsp.	Sugar
1 tsp.	Cinnamon

Combine pumpkin pie mix, nut bread mix, egg and raisins, thoroughly, stirring until just moistened. Spoon into lightly greased muffin cups, filling about 2/3 full. Sprinkle tops of each muffin with mixture of sugar and cinnamon. Bake at 400° for 15-20 minutes. Serve warm.

Raised Donuts

Servings: 2 dozen

A fall favorite in my childhood house.

1 ¼ cups	Milk, scalded*
¼ cup	Shortening
½ tsp.	Salt
1 packet	Yeast
5 cups	Flour, sifted
3	Eggs
¾ cup + 2 Tbsp.	Sugar
1 ½ tsp.	Cinnamon
¼ tsp.	Nutmeg
¼ tsp.	Cinnamon
	Oil

Combine milk, shortening and salt as soon as milk is heated. Cool to lukewarm. Add yeast to milk. Let sit for 5 minutes. Add 2 ½ cups of flour, beating until smooth. Cover and let rise until bubbly. Mix eggs, ¾ cup sugar and spices; add to mixture; mix well. Add enough flour to make a dough that can be kneaded. Knead until smooth. Cover and let rise until doubled in bulk. Roll out ½-inch thick. Cut with a donut cutter. Let donuts rise on baking sheet until doubled in bulk. Fry a few at a time in hot deep oil (375°) for 3 minutes or until lightly browned, turning once. Drain on brown paper. Roll in 2 Tbs. Sugar and ¼ tsp. cinnamon mixture while still warm. **NOTE:** Can be rolled in 10X sugar instead. *Donuts, filled :* Cut dough with cutter without hole. Donut can be filled with a custard or jelly after fried, then rolled in sugar. **NOTE:** *See *Tips About Food* for scalded milk.

Spoon Bread

Serving: 6

Ma only used white stone ground corn meal in all her recipes. I do too.

1 cup	Cornmeal, white, stone ground Shorting or butter
2 Tbsp	Butter
3 cups	Milk, separated
1	Egg, well-beaten
¾ tsp.	Salt
1 Tbsp.	Baking powder

Preheat oven to 450°. Combine cornmeal, shortening and 2 cups of milk in saucepan. Heat over medium heat bringing mixture just to a boil, stirring constantly. In a bowl, combine egg, salt and 1 cup of milk. Add to the cooked cornmeal, mixing well. Stir in baking powder. Pour into greased 2-quart baking dish. Bake 25 to 30 minutes or until firm in the center. Serve hot with lots of butter.

Yorkshire Pudding

Servings: 6

Yorkshire pudding is something Mother likes and I like to serve. Ma made it sometimes as a treat for her. This recipe is usually cooked in the drippings of a roasted beef.

1 cup	Flour
¼ tsp.	Salt
3	Eggs
1 cup	Milk

Mix flour and salt together. Beat eggs until light and add flour, mixing well. Add milk gradually and beat 2 minutes with electric mixer. Prepare pudding in time to pour into pan 30 minutes before beef has finished roasting. Put aside in pan. Pour off all fat except ¼ cup and pour in pudding. Bake at 400° for 30 minutes. Cut into squares and serve at once. **NOTE:** Pudding may be baked separately in pan heated very hot and well greased with beef drippings. Also can be baked in hot muffin tin with a tablespoon of hot beef dripping in the bottom of each well, then pour in pudding bake until pudding is fluffy and brown. This is another dish that, it will not wait for you, you need to wait for it. Be ready to serve Yorkshire pudding as soon as it is finished.

Zucchini Walnut Muffins

Servings: 24 muffins

This recipe won me a Blue Ribbon in 1998 at the New Jersey Federated Woman's Club's yearly convention.

2 cups	Zucchini, grated, unpeeled
1 cup	Raisins (half white, half dark)
3 cups	Flour
1 tsp.	Baking Soda
1 tsp.	Salt
¾ tsp.	Baking Powder
1 tbsp.	Cinnamon
4	Eggs
2 cups	Sugar
1 cup	Vegetable Oil
2 tsp.	Lemon rind, grated
1 cup	Walnuts, chopped

Prepare grated zucchini and set aside. Rinse raisins, drain, and mix with 2 tablespoons of the flour. Sift flour with baking soda, salt, baking powder and cinnamon. Beat eggs and gradually beat in the sugar, then the oil. With rubber spatula, blend in dry ingredients alternately with grated zucchini. When thoroughly mixed, stir in raisins, lemon peel and nuts. Divide batter into 24 cups of muffin pans lined with muffin papers. Bake at 350° for 20 minutes or until top springs back when lightly touched. Cool in pan for 5 minutes, then remove to wire racks to cool. **NOTE:** For an extra treat serve with Orange Butter. Add 1 Tablespoon orange rind to a stick of softens butter.

MEAT

In the 19th and 20th centuries, animal products were thought to be imperative to one's health. We ate a variety of meats in our diet even if it was not prime. Ma was very clever in her handling of proteins, and I followed in her footsteps. Now, of course, we realize that animal protein should be a much smaller portion of our diet, but I have included many old-time ways of handling them. On the occasion of including meats in your plans, you might try one of these.

BEEF

Beef Stroganoff

Servings: 4

This is a favorite recipe that even the children liked when they were young!

1 tsp.	Salt
3 Tbsp.	Flour
¼ tsp.	Pepper
1 lb.	Beef steak, about ¼-inch thick
4 Tbsp.	Butter
1-2 cloves	Garlic
½ cup	Onions, minced
10-12 oz.	Mushroom, fresh, sliced
2 medium	Tomatoes, skin removed and chopped
1 cup	Water
1 ½ cups	Sour cream
1-2 Tbsp.	Fresh parsley, snipped for topping

Combine flour, salt and pepper. Dip meat into flour mixture and pat well so flour will stick to meat. Cut meat into 1-inch strips. In hot butter, using a deep frying pan, sauté meat, turning until brown. Add onions. garlic and sauté until golden. Add water, scraping brown bits from the bottom of pan. Add mushrooms and tomatoes and simmer over low heat, uncovered, until meat is tender, for about 20 minutes. Just before serving, add sour cream, reheat but DO NOT BOIL. Sprinkle with parsley. Serve with rice, boiled noodles, or mashed potatoes.

Beef Wellington

Servings: 8

An elegant main course for a special meal.

8, 1-inch thick	Filet mignon
1 Tbsp.	Oil
1 package	Phyllo dough, frozen
½ lb.	Chicken liver
2 Tbsp.	Shallots, finely minced
2 Tbsp.	Parsley, finely chopped
1 stick	Butter, melted
½ tsp.	Salt

Thaw dough. Use oil to lightly brown filets. Drain on absorbent towel and chill. Sauté chicken liver and shallots in same pan until firm. Cool, blend into smooth paste. Mix chicken liver, salt, and parsley spread over the top of each fillet. Use about 12 to 14 layers of dough, brush with melted butter on each layer to make a stack of dough. Cut into 6-8 inch squares. Place filet with topping down, on dough. Wrap dough around filet; seal edge by moistening with water. Place stem side down on baking sheet. Place in a 400° pre-heated oven; bake until the pastry is brown. If the filet needs more cooking, place a piece of foil over pastry for an additional 5 minutes.

Brisket of beef

Servings: 8-12

I saw this recipe on TV many years ago and tried it. Loved it!

1 whole	Brisket
1 bottle	Chile sauce
1 can, with sugar	Cola
1 envelope, dry	Onion soup

Mix ingredients and pour over brisket. Cover with foil or lid and bake at 350° for 3 to 5 hours, or until tender. Take meat out of gravy, cool, refrigerate meat and gravy. The next day, remove fat from gravy and meat. Slice meat. Pour gravy over meat and reheat.

Hungarian Goulash

Servings: 4

A hardy dish for any time of the year.

3 Tbsp.	Butter
3 cups	Onions, thinly cut
1 ½ tsp.	Salt
1 ½ tsp.	Paprika
1 ½ lbs.	Beef, chuck, cut into 1-inch cubes
5 tsp.	Paprika
3 cups	Water

Sauté onions with salt until golden in a medium pot. Mix in well 1½ tsp. of paprika, add meat and simmer, and cover for 1 hour. Add other paprika and enough water to cover meat. Simmer, and cover 1 hour until meat is very tender. Add more water if you want more gravy. Serve with buttered noodles, rice or mashed potatoes.

Meat or Chicken Croquettes

Servings: 4

Something Ma often did with leftovers to stretch the meat.

4 Tbsp.	Butter
4 Tbsp.	Flour
1 cup	Milk
2 cups	Cooked meat, chicken or turkey, finely ground
½ tsp.	Salt
1/8 tsp.	Black pepper
1 tsp.	Parsley
Pinch	Nutmeg
	Breadcrumbs, fine, dry
1	Egg
2 Tbsp.	Water
2 Tbsp.	Oil

Melt butter, add flour, stirring constantly, and cook for 1 minute. *Do not* brown. Add milk slowly, stirring constantly until thick. Add meat, seasonings and parsley. Chill thoroughly. Form into cylinders. Dip into breadcrumbs, then into egg mixed with water, then into breadcrumb again. Fry in oil in frying pan. **NOTE:** You can add 1 Tbsp. of grated onion for a nice flavor, if you wish. **NOTE:** Try mixing leftover meats and poultry for an interesting flavor.

Meatballs

Servings: 4

Good to use with spaghetti or with a brown gravy to top noodles or rice.

1 lb.	Ground beef
½ cup	Breadcrumbs
2 cloves	Garlic, chopped fine
2 Tbsp.	Parsley, chopped
¼ cup	Parmesan cheese
1	Egg
½ tsp.	Salt
Few grates	Fresh black pepper
1 Tbsp.	Onion, grated
2 Tbsp.	Olive oil

Combine all ingredients, except oil and mix well. Shape into balls and brown in oil on all sides. Add to sauce or gravy to finish cooking before serving. **NOTE:** For a new dish, we like a Veggie Sauce: Use a couple of sliced onions and red pepper, sautéed with the meatballs before adding the sauce. Adding a ½ pound of sliced mushrooms is very nice as well.

Meatloaf

Servings: 6-8

I have made meatloaf for years and never liked it, until I came upon this way of making it. Now it is one of my favorite dishes. Anyone who has had it loves it. See if you are one of them.

1 Tbsp.	Olive oil
1 large	Onion, chopped
1 Tbsp.	Rosemary, dried, crushed
1 Tsp.	Sage powder
1 heaping Tbsp.	Dijon mustard
1 lb.	Pork*, grounded
1 lb.	Turkey*, grounded
3	Eggs
1 cup	Breadcrumbs, dry
1 cup	Heavy cream or evaporated milk, undiluted
1 ½ tsp.	Salt
To taste	Fresh ground black pepper
1-2 cloves	Garlic

Heat oil, and add onion, garlic, herbs, and sauté until onion is clear, add mustard and heat. Remove from pan to a large bowl. After onion has cooled, add the rest of ingredients and mix well. In a shallow baking dish, make a loaf shape of the mixture. Bake at 350° for 1 hour. Slice and enjoy. I like cranberry sauce, applesauce or other fruit relish with this dish. Ketchup is also good. **NOTE:** * You can use other combinations of meat, such as beef chicken or veal, but I like this combination best. **NOTE:** Leftovers, make great sandwiches. Choose a hearty bread to compliment the flavors of the meat.

Sauerbraten

Serving: 8

I make this occasionally. George enjoys it. Serve it with *Red Cabbage* and some buttered noodles.

Marinade

1 ½ cups	Wine vinegar
2 Tbsp.	Sugar
½ tsp.	Peppercorns
3-4	Bay leaves
2-3	Onions, sliced
10	Cloves, whole
2 tsp.	Salt
1 cup	Water
4 lbs.	Beef, rump roast

2 Tbsp.	Flour
1 ½ tsp.	Salt
A few grinds	Black pepper
1	Onion, sliced
6	Cloves, whole
¼ cup	Peppercorns
2 Tbsp.	Flour
¼ cup	Oil
½ cup	Gingersnaps, rolled into crumbs
½ cup	Sour cream

You need a few days to marinate the beef before cooking so plan ahead. Combine marinade ingredients in a bowl large enough to hold roast. Place meat in marinade, cover and refrigerate. Marinate for 2 to 3 days, turning meat each day. You can marinate the meat up to 4 days. On the day you want to cook the roast: Remove meat, reserving marinade. Dry meat well on paper towels. Combine flour, salt and pepper and coat meat all over. Brown roast in hot oil in a heavy ovenproof pot. Add about 1 cup of reserved marinade 1 onion sliced, cloves, and peppercorn. Simmer, covered, about 3½ hours or until meat is tender. Add about ¼ marinade at a time, if needed. Remove meat and slice. Place on a platter, keep warm. To make gravy, strain pan drippings. Let sit for a few minutes for the fat to rise to the top. Pour off fat, leaving about 1/3 of the dripping. Return to pot and dissolve gingersnaps, adding 2 cups of reserved marinade. (Use water if necessary.) Bring to a boil, cook until thickened. Stir in sour cream and heat but do not boil. Adjust seasoning. Spoon some gravy over the meat and serve the rest in a gravy boat.

Roast beef
This is the way I cook roast beef, very simply.

1/2 pound per person Rump roast of beef

Put fat side of roast up, on a rack in a roasting pan. Do not add salt or water. Roast at 350° For 20-25 minutes per pound (160° internal temperature for a medium-done roast). Let sit for 15-20 minutes before slicing. Slice against the grain, lightly salting the sliced meat before serving. Make gravy with dripping. **GRAVY:** Use stained juices, adding some water if you wish to pour over meat. For a thicken gravy, add water to dripping in roasting pan stirring to get meat scrapes from bottom as you heat liquid. Make a mixture of ½ cup of cold water and 2 Tbsp. flour and add slowly until thick enough. Make more water and flour if not thick enough. Season with salt and pepper to taste. **NOTE:** For a different flavor, add slice onion to roast about 1 hour before end of baking. Another way is to add slices of garlic inserted into slits made in meat. You can also use your favorite herb to lie on roast while baking.

LAMB

Lamb Stew

Servings: 6

Ma used the breast of lamb to make her stew, but I use lamb chunks. This is just a country stew recipe that I still enjoy these many years later.

1 ½ lb.	Lamb stewing meat
2 Tbsp.	Oil
1	Onion, roughly chopped
1	Carrot, chopped
1 rib	Celery, chopped
1 tsp.	Salt
¼ tsp.	Freshly ground black pepper
6	Potatoes, cut in half
½ lb. (small)	Onions
6	Carrots, cut into large chunks
1-2 recipes	Dumpling recipe

Brown large chunks of lamb in hot oil. Remove meat and set aside. Add chopped onion, carrot and celery to oil and lightly brown. Add browned meat, salt and pepper, stirring to coat meat and vegetables. Add enough water to cover meat and vegetables well. Cover and reduce heat to medium; cook for about 45 minutes. Adjust seasoning. Add other vegetables and more liquid if necessary to cover vegetables. Bring liquid to a rolling boil and drop dumplings into the liquid; cook for 10 minutes, reduce heat to medium, and cover. Cook for 10 more minutes. Remove dumpling to warn platter. Keep warm. Remove large pieces of vegetables if tender to platter. Add meat to platter. Using a potato masher or an imerseable blender into liquid and blend the chopped vegetable pieces into the gravy. Taste for flavoring. Serve gravy with vegetables and meat. **NOTE:** The dumplings usually thicken the liquid as they cook. If gravy is not as thick as you like you can make a combination of 1 Tbsp. flour to ¼ cup of water, shaking to blend well. Slowly add flour mixture to the boiling gravy until it is the thickness you like.

Roasted Leg of Lamb

Servings: 8-10

Many of the family love lamb. When serving lamb to a large group, I often serve an alternative meat for those who do not.

5-6 lbs.	Leg of lamb
4 cloves	Garlic, sliced
3-4 fresh sprigs	Rosemary (or 1-2 Tbsp. dried)

Cut small slits in the roast and insert pieces of the garlic all over the roast. Place on a rack in a roasting pan. Lay the springs of rosemary over the roast or sprinkle the dried over the roast. Put lamb in a pre-heated oven at 325° and roast without basting for 25 minutes per pound. I like to use a thermometer to make sure that the meat is cooked just right. I also like the meat to be a little pink. The internal temperature should reach 150-155°. Remove the roast at about 5° less than desired, and it will cook as it rests for 15-20 minutes. Remove the rosemary twist before serving. **NOTE:** Lamb is more difficult to carve than beef. Ask the butcher for a boneless roast for easy carving. But ask for the bones because that is what I make *Scotch Broth* from. **NOTE:** Don't forget to serve mint jelly with the fragrant lamb.

PORK

Baked Pork Roll

Servings: 6-8

This always pleased George, Sr.; his mother, Mildred Brandt, made it this way.

1-2 lbs.	Pork roll
1 can	Pineapple, crushed

Place pork roll in a baking dish and cover with pineapple. Bake at 350° for 45 minutes. Slice and serve.

Crown Roast of Pork

Servings: 12-18

This is so impressive to serve to a large group. I like to stuff it, but you can serve it with a steamed head of cauliflower in the middle. This was one of Ma's extra special meals.

1	Crown roast of pork
1 recipe	Bread stuffing

Request your butcher to make you a crown roast. Ask for the trimmings to be ground. Allow one rib per person. A crown roast requires two rib roasts, so the roast is quite large. Remove the ground meat from the packaged roast. I turn the meat into sausage by seasoning it with a teaspoon and a half of salt, some freshly ground pepper, two tablespoons of sage and a pinch of red pepper flakes, (optional). Mix well, then use half to brown in a frying pan. Refrigerate or freeze the rest (can be made into patties). Add the sausage to a recipe of *Bread Stuffing*. Stuff filling into center of roast, which has been placed in a baking pan on a rack. Bake at 350° for 15-20 minutes per pound with an internal temperature of 185°. Remove to a warm platter. Decorate the ends of the ribs with paper panties (butcher can supply), and crabapple or pickled apple slices, and parsley. Watch your guests' eyes when you present this impressive dish!

Pork and Sauerkraut

Servings: 8

A New Year's Day tradition.

6-8 lbs. (about 8 ribs)	Center cut pork loin
2 2-lb. Bags	Sauerkraut
1	Apple, quartered
1	Onion, quartered
	Pepper
1 tsp.	Salt

Place roast in pan on the ribs rub salt into roast, bake at 325° for 20-25 minutes per pound. Cook for about 2 hours, then remove meat from pan; set aside. Add sauerkraut, apple and onion to pan and drippings. Return roast to pan and return to oven; continue cooking for the rest of the time. Internal temperature should reach 150°. Let set for 15-20 minutes until the internal temperature reaches 160°. Serve. **NOTE:** I usually serve this with mashed potatoes with or without garlic and applesauce. To top the tradition, add a dish of *Spoon Bread* with lots of butter. Yum! **NOTE:** Another flavor to add to the sauerkraut is stir in 1 tablespoon of caraway seeds.

Scrapple

Servings: About 10-12 lb.

Something Ma made that everyone enjoyed each year.

3-4 lbs.	Pork roast, inexpensive cut
1 whole	Pork liver
3-4 lbs.	Chicken, fryer
About 1 lb.	Chicken giblets
	Cornmeal, white
	Salt
	Pepper
	Sage

This recipe is a general way to prepare scrapple because of the nature of the dish. Put pork, pork liver, chicken, chicken giblets, even a piece of beef if desired, in a large pot and cover with water, about 5 quarts or more. Bring to a boil, reduce heat, cover and cook for about 2 hours or until the meat falls from the bones. Remove all meat from liquid, then cool enough to handle, remove all meat from bones and cut into pieces small enough to go into a meat grinder. Discard bones, fat and skin. Grind all meat, saving any juice that comes from grinding. Grind any cooked meat you have as scraps. Skim as much fat from liquid in pot as possible. Put meat and juices back into liquid and bring to a boil. Season with salt, pepper and 2 to 3 tablespoons of sage, according to taste. *Very slowly*, as the liquid boils, pour the cornmeal into the pot, stirring constantly, with a large spoon. The amount of corn meal depends on the quantity of meat and liquid. The scrapple will thicken as you stir the cornmeal in. When it is very thick and difficult to stir, like a mush, stop adding meal. Cook carefully, because it will scorch, for an additional 5 minutes. Pour scrapple into a greased oblong pan or pans and let cool. When cool, refrigerate. Slice and fry in hot fat or oil until crisp and brown on both sides. **NOTE:** Use within one week or scrapple will spoil. This dish does not freeze well, the texture changes. Great recipe for a large group, such as a large brunch or supper. You could be generous and give some as gifts, **NOTE:** After Ma had a freezer; she would save the giblets from her chicken and use them in the scrapple. Mother made scrapple also and would save giblets, wings and backs to add to her pot of meat. I enjoy scrapple hot or cold on hearty bread with a generous amount of ketchup.

POULTRY

Since we had a yard full of chickens, it only would follow that we ate chicken very often. I have included some of the ways that Ma prepared chicken and a few other poultry dishes. Black duck was thought to be a delicacy that was brought from the Island. As time passed, people were not allowed to hunt them, save once in a while when Ma and Aunt Ruth would return from Maryland with their treasure. I never cared for the very dark meat of the bird, but I did learn to like Long Island duckling. I have included the recipe for how I prepare it.

Thirty-Minute Dinner

Servings: 4

Something I use a lot.

4	Chicken, boneless, skinless breast halves
4 Tbsp.	Parmesan cheese
¼ cup	Breadcrumbs
1 tsp.	Salt
¼ tsp.	Pepper
1 head	Broccoli
1 cup	Rice
2 cups	Water
1 tsp.	Salt
1 Tbsp.	Oil
1	Egg, beaten
1 Tbsp.	Parsley, chopped fine

Put rice water and salt in microwave bowl. Cover, microwave for 5 minutes on high, then on about level 7 for 15 minutes. (Check you microwave cookbook for rice recipe.) Prepare broccoli and steam with a bit of salt in water for about 15 minutes or until broccoli is as tender as you like. Mix breadcrumbs, cheese, salt and pepper together. Dip chicken breast into egg and then into breadcrumb mixture. Spread oil over the bottom of a microwave dish. Place chicken in dish. Microwave for 4 minutes, then turn chicken over, cook for 3-5 minutes. Top chicken with chopped parsley. Dinner is ready. Enjoy. **NOTE:** If you want a salad, that takes a few more minutes, prepare while everything is cooking.

Chicken Cacciatori

Servings: 6

Of course this is served with pasta. To make it a complete Italian meal, add a salad, a loaf of bread, and a nice bottle of red wine and voila! You are in business.

2 lbs.	Frying chicken, cut into serving
¼ cup	Oil
2 (medium)	Onions, chopped
1	Red pepper, chopped 1 inch pieces
1	Green pepper, chopped 1 inch pieces
3-4 cloves	Garlic, minced
1 1-lb. Can	Tomato
1 12-oz. Can	Tomato puree
1 ½ tsp.	Salt
1/8 tsp.	Black pepper
½ lb.	Mushroom, chopped or 1 8-oz. can

Brown chicken in hot oil. Add onion, peppers, garlic and mushrooms and brown lightly. Add remaining ingredients and simmer 30-40 minutes until chicken is tender. Serve over pasta with grated cheese.

Chicken Cordon Bleu

Servings: 6-8

My family likes this dish very much, and it is a good company meal because you can make it ahead of time

8	Chicken, boneless, skinless breast halves
4 slices	Gruyere cheese, can use Swiss*
4 slices	Ham*
¼ cup	Flour with ¼ top. salt and a pinch of pepper
1	Egg, beaten + 1 Tbsp. Water (egg wash)
½ cup	Breadcrumbs
2 Tbsp.	Oil
2 Tbsp.	Butter

Place each breast between two pieces of wax paper and pound to get the breast flat and even in thickness. If breasts are very thick, you can butterfly** them. Cut the ham and cheese in half and put one of each of them at the edge of the chicken. Roll the chicken up to cover the ham and cheese; secure with a toothpick. Roll the chicken in the seasoned flour, then dip in egg wash, then roll in breadcrumbs. Press the crumbs into the chicken. Heat the oil and butter in a frying pan and slowly brown the chicken. When browned on all sides and firm to the touch, put on a baking sheet and place in a warm oven until ready to serve. Remove toothpicks before serving. **NOTE:** *Have ham and cheese sliced thick for lunchmeat. **NOTE**: **To butterfly chicken, lay your hand on top of breast and with a sharp knife carefully slice horizontally, almost completely through. Open the meat out and pound to make it even. **NOTE:** Can be assembled before hand and cooked at the last minute. Don't keep chicken in oven too long or it will dry out. Don't cover or the crust will lose its crispiness.

Chicken Stew

Servings: 8

We ate a lot of chicken and this is one way Ma often served it.

4 lb.	Chicken, cut into serving pieces
Vegetables for flavor	
1 cup	Chopped onion
1 cup	Chopped carrots
1 cup	Chopped celery
1 tsp.	Salt
6	Peppercorns

Vegetables for stew

8 medium	Potatoes
8 (whole)	Carrots
3	Onions, cut in half
4 ribs	Celery, cut in large pieces

Heat oil. Sauté chicken pieces on all sides until brown; remove from pot. Sauté flavoring vegetables in same pot. Return chicken and add water to cover chicken. Add salt and peppercorns. Bring to a boil, then reduce to a simmer. Cover and cook until chicken is tender, about 1 ½ to 2 hours. When chicken is tender remove chicken to a heated platter and keep warm. Add stew vegetables and simmer until tender, about 25 minutes. Remove vegetables and keep hot with chicken. To make gravy, reduce liquid to about 2 cups. Strain liquid and return to pot. For each cup of liquid, use 1 teaspoon of flour with a little bit of cold water to make a liquid. Slowly pour flour into the boiling liquid and stir until it thickens. Pour over chicken and vegetables, serve. **NOTE:** For chicken and dumplings, make a dumpling recipe. Remove chicken and vegetables, keeping warm. Strain liquid, return to pot, adding more liquid to make about 2-3 quarts or more and bring to a boil. Drop dumplings in and cook 10 minutes. Cover pot and cook for 10 minutes more. Remove dumplings and add to chicken and vegetables to warm. If the liquid is not thickened to your taste, make gravy as before. Serve.

Fried Chicken

Servings: 4

Mrs. Scott was my children's Nanny. She showed me this simple and delicious dish, real southern fried chicken.

About ½ cup	Milk, or buttermilk
1 cup	Flour
1 ½ tsp.	Salt
Generous amount	Freshly ground black pepper
1	Chicken fryer, cut into serving pieces
½ cup or more	Oil

Dip chicken pieces into milk, then into flour into which salt and pepper have been blended. Heat oil in large deep frying pan. Fry chicken a few pieces at a time; *do not crowd chicken.* Cook on high heat for about 5 minutes, browning all the pieces then reduce the heat to medium and cook, partly covered about 25 minutes for larger pieces shorter time for smaller pieces. When pierced, juices should run clear. If needed, remove cover and cook on high for a few minutes to crisp crust. Drain on paper towels.

Italian Chicken

Serves: 8-10

This recipe I used for one of my Italian style meals. You prepare it the day before and pop it in the oven for an hour and half before you want to serve it. It is moist, tender and delicious. Bon appetite!

1 7-lb.	Roasting chicken, butterflied*
6-7 (large)	Shallots
6-8 (large cloves)	Garlic
1/3 cup	Extra virgin olive oil

Add later

1/3 cup	Extra virgin olive oil
1/3 cup	Good balsamic vinegar
1 (large)	Lemon, juiced
1 tsp.	Basil
1 tsp.	Rosemary
½ tsp.	Chives, dried or 1 Tbsp. (fresh)
¼ tsp.	Ground sage

Preheat oven to 350°. In a shallow baking dish, place shallots and garlic that has been peeled. Add 1/3 cup of oil and toss to cover vegetables. Bake for 30 minutes or until the shallots are golden. In a blender or food processor, place the contents of the baking dish as well as the rest of the oil, vinegar, lemon juice, and herbs. Blend until smooth. Rub ½ of the marinate over both sides of the chicken, cover and refrigerate overnight. Reserve the rest of the marinate to be reheated and served with chicken. Bake at 350° for 1 to 1 ½ hours, or until reaching an internal temperature of 160°. Serve with heated marinade. **NOTE:** *To butterfly chicken, use a shape knife or a pair of kitchen shears and cut down along the backbone of the chicken so that the bird can be spread out flat. You can ask your butcher to do this for you.

Roast Duck with Orange

Servings: 4

I have served this for Christmas, and the family enjoyed it very much. Duck is rich, however, so serve a light meal around it.

4-5 lbs.	Long Island duckling
1	Orange, quartered
1 medium	Onion, quartered
Fresh ground	Black pepper
	Salt
½ cup	Orange marmalade

Score the entire skin of the duck with a sharp knife to allow the fat to drain while cooking. Rub the cavity of the bird with salt and pepper. Put the orange and onion inside. With skewer, fasten neck skin over back. Close body opening and tie butcher cord around the legs to keep the body closed. Place bird on a rack in a baking pan and put in a pre-heated 325° oven for about 2 ½ hours. DO NOT add water. DO NOT cover. DO NOT baste. Bake until the thick part of the leg feels soft when pressed and legs can be easily moved up and down. About ½ hour before duck is done, increase oven temperature to 400°, brush skin with orange marmalade. When done, remove from oven. Remove orange and onion. To serve, use kitchen shears to cut the duck into serving pieces. **NOTE:** Keep an eye on the accumulation of the fat in pan. The duck should never sit in the fat. Remove excess fat if necessary. Be careful with fat so you do not catch the oven on fire. **NOTE:** A *Wild Rice* stuffing is nice with duck, but I make it outside the duck in a baking dish. **NOTE:** You can remove the fat from the pan and make gravy with the drippings and the browned pieces left in the roasting pan.

Roast Turkey

Servings: 10

Something we always have for Thanksgiving. Turkey is really an easy dish.

12-14 lbs.	Hen turkey
	Stuffing (optional)

I like to use this size turkey to have sweet, fine grain meat. I roast the bird on a rack in a baking pan. Wash the turkey and dry it. Rub salt and pepper inside, then stuff with filling, including the neck capacity. I use skewers to keep the neck and cavity closed. The legs can be trussed as well, using butcher's twine. Rub the outside of bird with oil and place on rack breast DOWN. This keeps the breast meat moist. Bake at 350° for 25 minutes per pound, stuffed, or 20 minutes per pound unstuffed. About 30 minutes before turkey is done, turn the bird breast side up to continue browning all over. You may need help to lift turkey and hold on to pan at the same time. Do not add water or baste. Remove turkey from oven when done and let sit for 15-20 minutes before serving. To make gravy, add ½-1 cup of water to pan and bring to a boil on stove scraping scraps from the bottom. Make a paste with 3 Tbsp. flour and ¼ cup of cold water, and add slowly to hot liquid, stirring until thickened, adding water to get the desired consistency. Add salt and pepper to taste; serve very hot. **NOTE:** I only use hen turkeys that weigh up to 14 lbs. If I need more meat than this, I cook two birds. The larger the bird, the more grainy the meat. The meat is often tough and strong in taste. That is what I learned from Ma and I am always pleased with the quality of the turkey when I follow this rule.

Tarragon Chicken

Servings: 4-6

A delicious way to prepare chicken for baking or grilling.

6 pieces	Chicken, boneless, skinless breasts
	Course salt
	Freshly ground black pepper
	Virgin olive oil
	Tarragon, dried or fresh
	Rice wine vinegar

Lay the chicken breast on a cutting board. Hold the meat flat with your hand and, using a sharp knife, slice the meat into two layers. Layer the chicken in a bowl with a light sprinkling of salt, pepper and tarragon. Drizzle a bit of olive oil over each layer. Cover the layered chicken with the vinegar. Marinate for 2 to 4 hours. Lay the chicken in a baking dish in one layer and bake at 350° for 20-25 minutes, turning once. Do not over-cook. **NOTE:** This marinade can be used for bone-in chicken, and then baked or barbecued.

FISH

Even though fish was something that we had very often as children, I have not included many recipes for fish. The ones I have are the recipes that Ma made often. I don't enjoy cooking much fish except poaching, but I often order it when I eat out.

Cod Fish Cakes

Ma
Servings: 6

Ma made these a lot. Sometimes she would get dried Hake fish from down home and make it the same way.

1 box	Codfish, dried
	Mashed potato
1 or 2	Eggs
A pinch	Black pepper
1-2 Tbsp.	Onions, grated

Dried Codfish can be purchased in a box. Sometimes you can find dried fish in the Italian markets. The recipe is on the container. You can follow it. Roughly, the fish needs to be soaked and drained, twice. Then it is mixed with the ingredients, made into patties and fry. Simple, salty, (that is why you soak it), and tasty.

Crab Cakes

Ma

Servings: 4

This is how we had them. Simple so that the favor of the crab come through.

1 lb.	Blue crab meat, picked
1	Egg, slightly beaten
1 heaping Tbsp.	Mayonnaise
Dash	Black pepper
Dash	Cayenne pepper
2 Tbs.	Butter

Mix everything together, except butter, lightly, Form into patties and sauté in melted butter. Lightly brown on each side. Serve with cocktail or tarter sauce.

Fried Fish

Ma
Servings: 4

On some Friday's Ma would make fried fish. Fish was usually the freshest on Friday because in those days Catholics were not allowed to eat meat on Friday. This meant the stores where stocked with fresh fish.

1/4-1/2 cup	Flour
1/2 tsp.	Salt
Dash	Pepper
Pinch	Cayenne pepper, optional
1 pound	Fish fillets
3-4 Tbsp.	Oil

Put the flour and seasoning in a plastic bag and shake. Add fillets of fish and shake. Heat oil in frying pan when hot place fish in hot oil, browning on both sides. Don't over cook the fish (3-4 minutes on each side according to thickness of fish.) **NOTE:** Any fillet of fish is good fried but another fish to try is smelts. They are fried whole. They take a few minutes longer to cook but are tasty and make a nice fish dinner. **NOTE:** On the menu Ma served, stewed tomatoes with onions, *mashed potatoes* and fried apples.

Fried Oyster

Ma
Servings: 6-8

Ma cooked oysters in a batter.

1 2/3 cups	Flour
2	Eggs
½ cup	Milk
½ cup	Liquid from oysters
1 ½ tsp.	Baking powder
1 tsp.	Salt
	Black pepper to taste
1 qt.	Oysters large
	Oil

Mix up batter using liquid from oyster as part of the liquid. Dip the oysters in the batter and fry in oil until they are brown on both sides. Drain on paper towels. I like oysters with ketchup but tartar or cocktail sauce are good as well. **NOTE:** Locally we go to ham and oyster dinner sponsored by a fire company. Their menu contains ham, fried oysters, potato salad, pepper hash (a sweet and sour cabbage relish), baked beans, bread, butter and ice cream for dessert. Some combination, but we enjoy it just the same. It is all you can eat and they keep filling the platters and bowls until the long table of people says stop!

Hard-Shell Crabs

These crustaceans are so good, but so mush work. Get ready for a mess but a delicious one.

Quantity desired (At least 4 per person)`	Blue hard crabs
	Old Bay seasoning

Plunge the live crabs into a large pot of seasoned boiling water, quickly putting the lid on. Boil for 8-10 minutes. Remove from the water and cool. To clean the crabs, break off the claws. Pull off the back and remove all spongy parts underneath. Turn the crab over and pull off the apron and split the body in two. Pick out the meat from the body and from the legs. Crack the shell of the legs with a nutcracker and remove the meat with a small pick or seafood fork. I like to dip the meat in vinegar and eat on saltines. Something cold to drink goes well. **NOTE:** There are many seafood seasonings, use your favorite. **NOTE:** If you are making this for a party where everyone is picking their own, cover the surface of the table with a thick layer of newspaper so the mess can be easily removed. If you are picking the meat to use in a recipe, you may want to buy the meat already cooked and picked in a can. Make sure you pick through the meat for any pieces of shell.

Paella

Servings: 6-8

This dish is a traditional Spanish dish. I served it with a Portuguese menu as well. However you use it, you and your family will enjoy it immensely.

3 lbs.	Chicken parts
	Olive oil
2 dz.	Mussels
2 dz.	Clams
8 oz.	Chorizo sausage*
4 cloves	Garlic
A few strands	Saffron
3 cups	Long grain rice
1-8oz. Bottle	Clam juice
	Salt
1 lb.	Shrimp, peeled
1 lb.	Imitation crab meat
7 oz. Jar	Pimentos, drained, cut into strips
	Green and/or black olives, pitted

Lightly brown the chicken in olive oil. Scrub the shells of the mussels and clams, then steam in a small amount of water, saving the liquid. Keep the shellfish warm. Heat 2-Tbsp. oil in a paellera* or large frying pan and fry 1 mashed clove of garlic until lightly browned. Discard garlic. Add rice to oil and stir until it turns yellow. Mash the rest of the garlic with the saffron, then add to rice. Add bottle of clam juice, and the liquid from clams and mussels, adding enough chicken broth or water to make up a total of 6-7 cups of liquid. Place chicken around the edge of the rice. Cover and cook for about 15 minutes or until rice is tender. If you want to serve paella on a large platter, transfer the chicken to the edge and keep warm. Steam shrimp with salted water for about 5 minutes. Add to rice. Steam crabmeat for 2-3 minutes to heat, and then add to rice. If using platter, gently stir seafood and the rice together and mound in the center of platter. If you are using sausage, cut in half lengthwise and sauté until lightly browned. Add to dish. Add clams and mussels in their shells to dish, pushing into rice. Decorate with pimento and olives. If using a paellera, arrange everything in pan. Cover, let sit for 10 minutes, keeping warm. Serve. **NOTE:** Chorizo sausage is a smoked Portuguese sausage available in specialty grocery stores. **NOTE:** Squid can be used in this recipe if you like. Sauté cut squid and add with the chicken. Use any of the liquid with the liquid for the rice. **NOTE:** *A paellera is a pan with two handles in which to make paella. **NOTE:** If you can find a country, chewy, crusty loaf of bread and serve it all with a green salad you will lick your chops for days! Here is a chance to use your seafood forks to dig out those clams and mussels! If you have no seafood forks you can use one half of the shell to dig out the meat in the other.

Philippines Baked Salmon

Servings: 15

Nicole's friend shared her native way of preparing salmon and it is luscious! A whole salmon servers a lot, so it is good for a crowd.

1 Whole, 5-7 lb.	Salmon, head removed if you wish
2	Mango, peeled and sliced
2	Tomatoes. Sliced
1 large	Onion, sliced
1 2 inch piece	Ginger root, peeled, sliced
1 package	Banana leaves*

Rinse fish and dry well, inside and out. Put the mango, tomato, onion and ginger root inside fish. Salt and pepper to taste. Wrap with banana leaves and wrap in heavy-duty aluminum foil and seal well. Bake in a 350. oven for about 1 hour or until tender. To serve, remove foil and place on large platter, folding back leaves. Remove top skin and using two large serving spoons, break meat into serving pieces. To serve other side of fish: Remove stuffing, bones and continue to spoon flesh. This will melt in your mouth and the flavors are exquisite! Serve it with a vegetable and a starch or a country crusty loaf of bread. Mayonnaise is a nice condiment. **NOTE:** *Banana leaves can be purchased frozen in an Asian grocery store**. NOTE:** Another way to cook the fish is to put the whole package on the BBQ grill. It should be turned and watched so it will not burn.

Poached Fish
I prefer salmon but you can use any firm flesh fish.

Fish, whole or fillet (5-6 oz. Per person)
Lemon
Water
Dill weed
Hollandaise sauce

The best fish to poach is a lean fish such as, Cod, Haddock, Halibut, Salmon, Sea Bass, Shad, Weakfish, and Whitefish. Whole fish, slices or fillets may be used. To cook a whole fish a poacher would be great but since most of us don't have one, a large pan to accommodate the fish is needed. To handle the fish, you need to wrap it in cheesecloth so you can remove it from the broth without it breaking apart. For slices or fillets this is not needed. Fill large pot or a large frying pan for slices, with water to cover fish. Add 1/2 Tbsp. of salt and 1/2 Tbsp. lemon juice or vinegar for each quarts of water. If using less water adjust proportion. I like to add some dill, fresh if you can, dry if you can't. You can use bay leaf and peppercorns as well. Bring seasoned water to the boil, slip fish into the water reduce heat to a simmer and keep it there, do not boil fish. Allow 6 to 10 minutes per pound for whole fish depending upon thickness. Allow 10 to 20 minutes for slices or fillets. Serve fish with any kind of sauce you prefer. *Hollandaise*, dill, and lemon but many are good. On salmon a simple dollop of mayonnaise is good. Homemade mayonnaise is great! **NOTE:** Any leftover of pouched fish is good to use in a sandwich or a salad or make a salad with it, the next day.

Salmon Japanese Style

Servings: 4

A treat to serve as a part of a Japanese style meal or a part of a simple menu.

2 lbs.	Salmon fillet
4	Scallions, chopped,
1/2 cup	Miso paste*
1 Tbsp.	Soy sauce
! tsp.	Oil, (sesame if possible)
1/2 cup	Sake
1 tsp.	Sugar

Mix ingredients to make a marinade. Pour over fillets in a flat dish. Marinate in the refrigerator for at least two hours or overnight. Remove fish from marinade and broil salmon until just firm, careful not to overcook. **NOTE:** *Can be found in an Asian grocery or health food store.

Soft-shelled Crabs

Ma

I have never cooked these but of course I saw Ma do so many times. This recipe is how it is done.

4 small per person.	Soft-shelled crabs
	Flour
	Black pepper
	Salt
About 4 Tbsp.	Butter

Ma always cleaned her own crabs, but if you can get the fish store to clean them for you so much the better. The face has to be removed and the lungs under the back need to be removed and rinsed under cool water. The crabs must be alive in order to be eatable. If you get them prepared make sure you use them right away. Dip the crabs into flour, patting the flour into the crab. Sauté them in the hot butter, browning on each side. The legs should be very crisp. Season them as they are cooking. The smaller the crab the better. Some restaurant will serve the large ones and they do not have the sweet flavor as the small one do. Soft crabs are only available certain months of the year. If you can find them fry them up and enjoy this delicate seafood.

EGGS AND CHEESE

Ma used eggs a lot in her cooking because we always had a fresh and plentiful supply. Here are a few ideas to use this versatile food, including, basic ways to cook them. See the Beverage section for Mr. Brandt's recipe for wonderful eggnog. Cheese is onr of my favorite foods. I have included my opinion about the cheese I like to use as well as how I use them. Many of these recipes call for both eggs and cheese. Enjoy.

EGGS

Poaching Eggs: In a frying pan, bring an inch of water to a boil. Break an egg into the boiling water carefully. Have a large spoon at hand, and immediately pick the egg up and turn it over. If you are cooking more than one egg, add one at a time, repeat the same process. Let simmer for about 3 minutes, then lift the egg out with a slotted spoon. Use a clean tea towel to pat under the spoon to catch any water. Place in bowl on an English muffin, or on toast.

Soft boiled or hard-boiled eggs: Place large eggs in a small saucepan, coving them with cool water. Place on fire and bring to a boil. Just when the eggs begin to boil begin timing. For soft boiled, three to three and one half minutes will give you cooked whites and soft yolks. Experience will tell you how long you like your eggs cooked. Remove pan from heat and drain. Run cold water over egga so you can handle them but not long enough to cool them. Use a spoon and strike the egg in the middle and scrape out the egg into a small bowl. Season the egg with salt, pepper and a pat of butter if you wish. You can serve them the old fashion way and use an eggcup. Place the cooked egg in the small egg of the cup with the small end of the egg up. Serve it this way on a small plate with a spoon. To eat it, tap the end of the egg with the spoon cutting off just the tip. Use salt and pepper in the egg and a pat of butter if you wish. Use the spoon to stir in the favoring and eat it out of the shell. You can use the large end of the cup to hold one or two eggs removed from the shell.

To hard boil, continue cooking for five to seven minutes. Turn fire off and let eggs sit for about ten minutes more. Drain and run cool water over the eggs. You can remove their shell at this point and use them as you wish or refrigerate for later use.

A quick trick for chopping hard-boiled eggs is to use an egg slicer. Put the egg through the tool the usual way, then, holding the egg together, place it in the slicer across the wires, and slice again. Instant chopped egg!

Another way to quickly cut up hard-boiled eggs is to use a potato masher. Just a few smashes of the tool and the eggs are chopped.

When beating egg whites and whipping cream, make sure that the bowl, beater, and rubber spatula are absolutely clean and free of any grease in order for these foods to beat well. If any yolk gets in whites they will not whip to a stiff peak. It is best to separate each egg in a small dish first, so that any bit of yolk that might get into the white can be used for something else and not added to a bowl of whites for whipping.

Meringue: When adding meringue to a pie, make sure to touch the edges of the pie with the meringue to keep it from shrinking.

Cheese

I am no more a connoisseur of cheese than I am of wine. I guess you could say that I know what I like, and I am willing to taste test and experiment. I will give you a short run-down on my favorite cheeses.

These are only a few cheeses that are available in the market. These are the ones I have used, liked and used again. I hope I help in your choices.

HARD

Cheddar: There are different levels of cheddar, from mild to extra sharp. I keep a consent supply of white extra sharp New York cheddar cheese. I use it for eating with fruit and crackers as well as cooking. When I refer to cheddar cheese in my recipes, this is what I mean. Mac and cheese is so tasty, using extra sharp. Cheddar is a must on any cheese tray.

Longhorn: This is mild cheddar and I like this cheese for melting and putting it on a cheese tray. This was a big favorite, I remember, with my Smith Island family.

Monterey Jack: We like this cheese in Mexican dishes, for cheese trays, melting on sandwiches or sliced in a sandwich. This cheese combines with other cheeses well.

Gouda: This has a smoky flavor that is a favorite to eat with fruit or with hardy mustard.

Munster: A softer cheese, mild in flavor but distinctive from other cheeses.

Swiss and Jarsburg: These cheeses are nutty. Jarsburg is the stronger in flavor of the two. These two cheeses range in flavor and texture from smooth and creamy to firm and bitty. They mix well with other cheeses, are good to cook with and make great sandwiches.

Edam: A mild cheese but with its own flavor. I think that eating with fruit shows off its flavor to best advantage,

Provolone: An imported wedge of this cheese is so flavorful, that it will take your breath away. I am crazy about it. You really have to like the flavor of strong cheese. As it ages, it gets harder and can only be used to grate. Some crusty bread, a bit of butter, fresh imported provolone and a glass of red wine, you can't get any better that that! The slicing kind found in the deli is much milder, but is wonderful in sandwiches and hoagies.

Parmesan: This is a wonderful grated cheese Grate it fresh for the best flavor.

Romano: Another fine cheese for grating and a different flavor than other hard cheese for grating. Good mixed with Parmesan.

Pecorino: This is my favorite grated cheese. But try all three of these cheeses and see which you like best.

SEMI-SOFT

Blues

Danish: I think that this is the mildest of the blues.

French Roquefort: This is a bit stronger but has a smoother flavor.

English Stilton: I find this cheese to be smooth and powerful in flavor and one of my favorites.

Italian Gorgonzola: This was a favorite of the children when they were young, and I still include it as an after dinner cheese. It has a zesty flavor.

Melt any of the blues on a hamburger and enjoy the snappy flavor it brings to this sandwich.

Fontana: A lovely dessert cheese. It is sweet and I have seen many dessert recipes calling for Fontana.

Brie: You will find a recipe in this book for baked Brie. I think it is excellent. I like this cheese any way it is served. You can eat the crust that is formed on the cheese but make sure you serve it at room temperature so the center is very soft. This cheese is traditionally served with white wine.

Limburger: Now you really need to like strong cheese to try this one. I like the Limburger spread purchased in glass jars. It gives you the flavor of the cheese but is not so over powering in fragrance. When using the pure cheese, make sure you seal it well because it will flavor everything in your fridge. I seal it in a plastic container. They say if you can get past the odor of Limburger, then you can enjoy the cheese. I like it.

SOFT

Cream cheese: There are many types and flavors for you to choose from. It is soft, smooth and sweet. There are recipes in every category from appetizers to dessert for cream cheese. This is a very versatile cheese.

Cottage cheese: Also a versatile cheese found in many flavors and textures. If you blend it until it is smooth and let it drain, it can be used in place of cream cheese with fewer calories. I like to use it with vegetables, but it is very good with fruit also.

Feta: This cheese is very versatile with an olive flavor. I like to use it for different flavors in salads. What would Greek salad be without Feta?

Mozzarella: If you can find an Italian deli that carries fresh Mozzarella you will find a real treat. Use this in your Italian recipes and see the difference. It is softer and sweeter. In the summer, we enjoy thick slices of this cheese and Jersey tomatoes layered with fresh basil. Drizzle it all with olive oil and season it with course salt and fresh ground black pepper. Yum!

Ricotta: This is the Italian cottage cheese. It is a ticker and richer flavor and oh so good in many dishes. I like to use it like cottage cheese and eat it with vegetables and fruit. Find my Rice Pie in this book and try this recipe for a rich dessert.

CHEESE TRAY

I like to serve my cheeses on a large wooden board. You can use a basket lined with real or paper grape leaves. I try to give a variety in flavor and texture, ranging from mild to strong. Plain but tasty crackers are best. Flavored crackers interfere with the flavors of the cheese. Wedges of crisp apple or pears dipped in water, flavored with lemon juice, helps keep the fruit from turning brown. A variety of grapes and nuts are nice. Wedges of melon are very good. Fresh figs would be exquisite if they are available. Use unsalted nuts for best flavor compliments. Wine is, of course, great with cheese, but punch and coffee is nice as a beverage as well. Put a cheese tray on a buffet, serve it as a light meal, or use it as a last course of a meal. Anyway you use cheese, people love it.

I try to buy the best quality cheese I can afford. Some imported cheese is preferable but many American cheeses are very good as well. Many of the grocery stores have a large selection of both imported and domestic cheeses. Ethic delicatessens usually have a nice selection too. If you can frequent a cheese shop, so much the better. They often will give you samples of cheeses you are considering to see if you like them. You will find the type and brands you like by experimenting.

It's important to serve hard and semi.—soft cheese at room temperature so you can taste its full flavor. Take it out of the refrigerator about one hour before serving.

Use nice tools, specific tools made for each type of cheese like a cheese shaver for hard cheese or a cheese spoon for blue cheeses. Cheese shops have a variety of tools to make it easier to work with and serve cheese.

Cheese food or imitation cheese is available, but I like to use real aged cheese even to slice for sandwiches and burgers.

One of my favorite memories of cheese happened on one of our trips to England. George and I went shopping in the famous Harrods Department Store. We shopped their wonderful food departments and purchased a wedge of Stilton, a few whole grain rolls, and some fresh lecchie nuts. We took our purchases and walked a short way to the legendary Hyde Park, where we had a picnic. We ate our lunch as we watched the riders on the bridal path.

Cottage Cheese

Ma
Servings: About 1 lb.

This is how Ma made her own cheese after the milk had gone sour. She never threw anything away!

1 qt.	Milk, soured
3 qt.	Water, warm

Heat the milk to lukewarm. and then pour into a cheesecloth bag placed in a colander. Pour 1quart of warm water over the milk and let drain. Repeat twice more. Tie the bag and let drip until the whey is gone and the curds are firm. Ma hung her cheesecloth bag on the clothesline to drip in the summertime. Refrigerate and enjoy freshly made cottage cheese.

Deviled Eggs

Servings: 12 pieces

I use these all year long. It fills the menu out very nicely.

6	Eggs, hard cooked
2 Tbsp.	Mayonnaise
1 rounded tsp.	Mustard
	Salt
	Pepper
	Paprika

Cut eggs lengthwise into halves. Combine egg yolks with mayonnaise, mustard, (I prefer Dijon), salt and pepper to taste. Sprinkle the egg white lightly with salt. Fill whites with yolk mixture. Sprinkle with paprika, refrigerate until needed. **NOTE:** Top with a small, cooked shrimp cut in half lengthwise or a dollop of red or black caviar. Decorate with a small sprig of parsley or dill. Add some chopped ham, crumbed bacon or snipped dried beef to the yolks. To create an extra kick to your deviled eggs add some curry power to the yokes. For 6 eggs I would start with ¼ teaspoon and add more to suit you taste buds.

Eggs Benedict

Servings: 1

This is the breakfast most requested by my family.

1	English muffins, split
2	Eggs
2 slices	Canadian bacon
	Cheddar cheese
	Hollandaise sauce

Toast muffin and set on baking sheet. Heat bacon in the microwave for 20 seconds or in a frying, pan, and put on muffin. Poach eggs place on top of bacon. Slice cheese and cover egg. Put baking sheet in a 350° oven to melt cheese. When cheese is melted, remove muffin to serving dish and top with warm *Hollandaise Sauce.* **NOTE:** Check at beginning of this topic to learn how to poach eggs easily. For a quick sandwich, substitute mayonnaise for hollandaise sauce. Spread mayonnaise on toasted muffin before assembling sandwich.

French Toast and Variations

Servings: 2

We enjoy French Toast very much. I am including the many different ways I have served this toast. This item is great for breakfast, brunch or lunch.

6 slices	Bread
2	Eggs
2 Tbsp.	Oil
2 Tbsp.	Butter

Mix eggs and milk together with a fork. Soak bread in egg mixture for a short time. Heat oil and butter in large frying pan to a medium heat. Sauté until bread is golden. Serve topped with more butter and syrup. **Variations:** I like to use a dense white bread for making this dish. Other breads are good as well. Try halvah, Brioche, French or Italian sliced at an angle, 1 ½ inch thick. A local restaurant serves a cinnamon swirl bread to make their French toast. It is excellent. Raisin bread is nice too. **For a different flavor** try adding a teaspoon of vanilla extract to the egg mixture or other extracts such as orange or almond. Using ½ teaspoon. A teaspoon of sugar adds a nice touch and so does a dash of cinnamon. **Toppings:** To top the toast try different flavored syrups or a dusting of 10x sugar. A warm orange juice syrup is tasty. 1 cup OJ, 3 tbsp. sugar. Simmer until the juice thickens slightly. We like to add a serving of bacon, sausage or a grilled slice of ham. **For a differ sandwich try this:** Make a sandwich of ham and cheese then soak it in the egg mixture and sauté in butter slowly so the meat heats and the cheese melts. Can be served with syrup as well.

Quiche

Servings: 6

This is my recipe for many varieties.

1 crust	Pie crust
2 cup	Cheddar cheese, shredded (about 4 ounces)
See note	Flavoring, meat or vegetable
2-3 Tbsp.	Onion, chopped fine
4	Eggs
2 cups	Evaporated milk
1/2 tsp.	Salt
2-3 drops	Hot sauce

Line a 10-inch quiche pan or pie pan with pastry. Sprinkle flavoring* over pastry then, cheese and onion. Beat eggs slightly and add milk, salt and pepper. Pour mixture over other ingredients. Bake at 425° for 15 minutes reduce oven to 300° and bake 30 minutes more, or until knife insert in center comes out clean. Let stand for 10 minutes before serving. Can be served at room temperature or even cold. Cut into wedges to serve. **NOTE:** *Flavoring *Amounts*: Quiche *Lorraine:* 12 slices of bacon, cooked and crumbled. Quiche *Florentine:* 1-10 oz. box of spinach, cooked, chopped and squeezed very well. Quiche *Seafood:* 8 ounces of imitation crab, crab, or shrimp, chopped. *Broccoli* Quiche: 1-10oz.-box broccoli cooked, drained.

ONE-DISH MEALS

Casseroles are a blessing. Ma used to fix them early in the day when she had other work to do or when she had to feed a lot of people. I continued the practice and love the convenience. Casseroles certainly fit into today's busy lifestyle.

ONE-DISH—

Beef Bourguignon

Servings: 12

A stew that can be served for company

5 lb.,	Beef, chuck cut in chunks and remove all fat
1/3 cup	Flour
1/4 cup	Butter
1/4 tsp.	Black pepper
1/2 lb.	Bacon, diced
4-5 cloves	Garlic, chopped
2	Carrots, chopped
2	Leeks, chopped. just the white part
2 cups	Onions, chopped
	Parsley
2	Bay leaves
1 tsp.	Thyme
2 ½ cups	Burgundy wine
2lbs.	Small white onions
2 lbs.	Mushroom
2 tsp.	Lemon juice

Roll beef in flour and brown on all side in hot butter in Dutch Oven. Sprinkle with salt & pepper. Heat oven to 350°. Add bacon, garlic, carrots, leeks chopped onions, 1 Tbsp. snipped parsley, bay leaves, thyme and 2 cups of wine. Bake covered 2 to 2 1/2 hours or until beef is tender. Remove meat from pan and put vegetables and liquid through a food mill. Return strained liquid and meat to pan. Can be refrigerated at this point and then reheated when you want to finish dish. Reheat by putting Dutch Oven on a low flame. Add 2 Tbsp of butter to a frying pan and brown whole onions well on all sides. Add 1/2 cup wine. Cook covered 15 to 20 minutes or until onions are tender. Add 1/4-cup water if needed. Add onion to meat with liquid. In a frying pan, add 2 Tbsp. butter and sauté half of the mushrooms caps until golden brown. Sprinkle with 1/2 of lemon juice and add to beef. Repeat with other half. Serve e in a 3-quart casserole dish and garnish with parsley. **NOTE:** Serve with a loaf of crusty bread to dip into this delicious sauce. **NOTE:** Serve with buttered wide noodles, as these make a lovely base to place the beef.

Chili

Servings: 10-12

A wintertime dish. Each time the chili is reheated the flavor improves.

2 Tbsp.	Oil
2 large	Onions, sliced
1	Red bell pepper, diced
2 lbs.	Ground beef
1 Tbsp.	Chili powder
1/2 tsp.	Cayenne pepper
1 1/2 tsp	Salt
2 large cans	Whole tomatoes, crush
2 cloves	Garlic, crushed
2 cans, without sugar	Kidney beans, undrained
1/2 tsp.	Cumin
1/2 tsp.	Basil
1/2 tsp	Coriander

In a large pot heat oil and sauté onion until soft. Add red pepper garlic and meat, brown. Add chili powder, cayenne pepper, salt, pepper and other spices. Stir. Add tomatoes and bring to a simmer. Simmer for 15 minutes and add beans, cover and simmer for 45 minutes. Serve in bowl topped with sour cream, and/or grated cheese. Add corn chips, cornbread or spoon bread to eat with the chili.

Corned Beef and Cabbage

Servings: 8

A March meal to celebrate our Irish roots.

1 4-5 lb.	Corned beef brisket or for a wonderful treat, use a corned eye roast
1	Onion, cut in half
4 whole	Cloves, stick into onion
1	Bay leaves
6	Peppercorns
1 rib	Celery
1	Carrot
1large head	Cabbage
8-10 whole	Potatoes, peeled

Boil with spices, onion, celery and carrot for 3 to 4 hours. Remove meat and keep warm. Discard vegetables and add potatoes to liquid and cook for 10 minutes. Cut cabbage into wedges, removing some of the hard core, and place on top of potatoes, continue cooking for 10 minute until vegetables are tender. Serve with sliced meat. **NOTE:** I use a *Mustard Sauce* to serve with corned beef. A nice loaf of *Irish Soda Bread* is good **NOTE:** For leftovers see *Corned beef hash.*

Corned Beef Hash

Servings: 6

What to do with the leftovers.

1/2 cup	Onion, minced
1 Tbsp.	Oil
1/8 tsp.	Black pepper
3 cups	Potato, cooked, diced
2 1/2 cups	Corned beef cooked, chopped
6	Eggs

In a skillet heat oil, brown onion, add pepper, potatoes and cored beef mix and sauté in skillet. Serve with a poached egg on each portion. NOTE: See *Tips of Food* for pouching eggs.

Creamed Dried Beef

Mrs. Scott
Servings: 8

Ma make this for us, however, Mrs. Scott made it a little different for my children. We all loved it. Here is her recipe

4 Tbsp.	Butter
2 4-oz. Packages	Dried beef, cut into strips
2 condensed cans	Mushroom soup
2 cans	Milk
1-4 oz. Can	Mushrooms, sliced

Heat butter in large frying pan, add dried beef and brown. Add soup, milk and mushrooms, and simmer covered for 10 minutes. **NOTE:** If you want to make, a Plain Dried Creamed Beef like Ma did, brown the beef and sprinkle 4 Tbsp. flour over meat and stir well. Slowly add 4 cups of scalded milk and stir until thick and creamily. Serve. Good served for breakfast over toast or biscuits, for lunch or dinner over mashed potatoes.

Enchilada Casserole

Servings: 6

When you want something different and spicy.

6	Corn tortillas, soft
2 1/2 cups	Cheddar cheese, grated
1-10 oz. Can	Enchilada sauce
2 cups	Chicken cooked and chopped OR
1 lb.	Ground, browned and drained
1/4 cup,	Green onion, chopped including some green tops
1/4 tsp.	Cumin
1 cup	Sour cream or plain yogurt

Combine filling of meat, sour cream, green onion and cumin. Dip the tortillas into enchilada sauce. In a 1 1/2 quart baking dish layer tortillas, filling and cheese. Top with a tortilla. Before adding the last tortillas add the remaining sauce to the dish. Bake 350° for 40 minutes.

Moussaka

Servings: 6

A Greek dish, rich and tasty. Am interesting way to use eggplant.

2 medium	Eggplant
	Salt
2 Tbsp.	Butter
1 lb.	Ground beef or lamb
2 small	Onions, chopped
1 Tbsp.	Tomato paste
1/4 cup	Red wine
2 Tbsp.	Parsley, chopped
3 Tbsp.	Water
Dash	Cinnamon
1 large	Egg, beaten
1/4 cup	Parmesan cheese
1/4 cup,	Breadcrumbs, flavored
White sauce	
3 Tbsp.	Butter
3 Tbsp.	Flour
1 1/2 cups	Hot milk
4	Egg yolks, lightly beaten
	Oil
	Parmesan cheese

Cut stem from eggplant and cut into thick slices, lengthwise. Sprinkle with salt, place in a colander and cover the eggplant with a plate. Weight it down with a heavy can for 30 minutes. Melt 4 Tbsp. butter in a frying pan and sauté meat and onion until meat is browned. Add tomato paste, parsley, wine, salt, pepper and water. Simmer until liquid is absorbed. Cool. Stir in cinnamon, eggs, cheese, and half the breadcrumbs. Make the white sauce by melting the butter and adding flour. Stir until well blended. Gradually stir in milk, stirring until sauce is thick and smooth. (I use a whisk.) Combine egg yolks with a little of the hot sauce, (tempering), then stir the egg mixture into sauce and cook over low heat for 2 minutes, stirring constantly. *Don't boil.* Rinse and drain eggplant. Brown both sides in hot oil. (Eggplant can absorb a lot of oil. Brown fast and add oil as needed.) Grease a casserole and sprinkle bottom with remaining breadcrumbs. Cover with layer of eggplant slices, then a layer of meat and continue until all eggplant and meat is used. Finish with a layer of eggplant. Cover with sauce, sprinkle with Parmesan cheese. Bake in a 350° oven for 1 hour.

Nachos

Servings: 4

This is one of those recipes that is flexible, according to your available ingredients and preferences. We like a plate high with all the goodies and go to it!

1 lb.	Ground beef
2 Tbsp.	Onion, finely chopped
1 package	Taco seasoning
1 can	Refried beans
	Corn chips
1 cup	Cheddar cheese or Monterey Jack, grated
2	Tomatoes, chopped
1/4-1/2 cup	Onion, chopped
1/3 cup	Black olives, sliced
1/2 recipe	Guacamole
1/2 to 1 cup	Salsa
1/2 to 1 cup	Sour cream
1/4 cup	Red or green pepper, diced fine (optional)
	Jalapeno peppers to taste

Sauté ground beef and 2 Tbsp. onions until brown, add taco seasoning cook for 3-5 minutes. Drain any fat off. Heat refried beans. Put a very generous amount of chips in a flat microwave dish. Spread grated cheese over chips and microwave long enough to heat chips and melt cheese. Spread meat over chips, and then add tomato, onions, olives and peppers if desired. Put portions of the guacamole and refried beans around the edge of the plate. Top with mild and/or hot salsa, then make a large dollop of sour cream on top. Serve. **NOTE:** Chips and cheese can be heated in the oven as well. These proportions are general, adjust to your taste. **NOTE:** To serve Nachos at their best, prepare everything ahead of time then assemble just before you are ready to serve.

Stuffed Cabbage

Servings: 8

Ma made this and I followed. It is an old fashion dish and it sticks to the ribs.

1 large head	Cabbage
1 lb.	Ground beef
1/2 cup	White rice, uncooked
1 small	Onion, grated
2	Eggs
1 tsp.	Salt
1/4 tsp.	Pepper
1 large	Onion, sliced
2—large cans	Tomatoes, whole
2-8 oz. Cans	Tomato sauce
1 tsp.	Salt
1/4 tsp.	Black pepper
2	Lemons, juiced

Remove 12-15 large leaves from cabbage. Trim off thick part of each leaf. Put leaves in a large pot of boiling water and let sit for a few minutes so the leaves become easy to fold. Remove leaves and drain. Combine meat, rice, grated onion, eggs, 1 tsp. salt, and 1/4 tsp. pepper. Place a heaping tablespoon of mixture in cup part of each leaf. Loosely fold over sides of each leaf, then roll leaf up, securing it with a wooden toothpick. Heat oven to 375°. In bottom of heavy Dutch oven place a layer of the remaining cabbage leaves. Arrange layers of stuffed cabbage with seam sides down and sliced onion in dish. Mix tomato sauce, tomatoes, lemon juice, salt and pepper and pour over cabbage. Bring to a boil on top of range. Bake, covered 1 hour. Uncover the dish and bake for 2 hours more.

Tamale Pie

Servings: 8

South of the border taste!

1/2 cup	Tofu, frozen, thaw and crumbled
2 cups	Kidney beans, cooked
1/2 cup	Onion, finely minced
1 Tbsp.	Oil
2 tsp.	Chili powder
1 tsp.	Soy sauce
2 Tbsp.	Tomato paste
1/2 cup	Corn
1/2 cup	Green pepper
1/2 cup	Parsley, fresh, chopped
3/4 cup	Celery, chopped
	Crust
2 1/2 cups	Water
1 tsp.	Salt
1 1/2 cups	Cornmeal
1 tsp.	Chili powder
1 cup	Monterey Jack cheese, grated

Mix and mash tofu and beans together. Brown in oil, onion and chili powder. Add soy sauce, tomato paste, corn, pepper, parsley and celery. Sauté for a few minutes, add to bean mixture. **Crust:** Mix and boil the ingredients together. When cool roll crust between wax paper and line rectangular dish. Fill with bean mixture. Top with another crust or with grated Monterey Jack cheese. Bake for 30 minutes at 350°.

ONE-DISH LAMB

Lamb Stew

Servings: 6

A red stew. If you aren't fond of lamb try this recipe. Dad, who did not like lamb, loved this recipe.

1 ½ lbs.	Lamb, cut into 1 1/2-inch pieces
2	Carrots, sliced
2 medium	Onions, slices
1 medium	Green pepper, sliced
2 chopped	Tomatoes or 1-lb. can, drained
1 tsp.	Seasoned salt or salt and pepper

Quickly brown meat in its own fat. Place in saucepan with vegetables and salt. Cook covered over low heat for one hour or until tender. If stew gets too dry, add tomato juice or bouillon. Serve over cooked rice or boiled noodles.

ONE-DISH PASTA

Baked Lasagna

Servings: 8

This is a wonderful meal.

1 lb.	Lasagna noodles
4 Tbsp.	Oil
1 qt.	Pasta sauce
Dash	Nutmeg
1/4 cup	Parmesan cheese
1 lb.	Ricotta cheese
8 oz.	Mozzarella cheese, shredded
1 lb.	Ground beef, optional
1 Qt.	Pasta sauce
2	Onions, sliced
8 oz.	Mushrooms, sliced

If you want to add the meat to this dish then sauté the meat in the oil into breaking it into small pieces. Add the pasta sauce to the meat and cook for 15 minutes or longer. Season with salt and pepper to taste. Cook noodles as directed on package. Mix the ricotta and mozzarella cheeses, nutmeg salt and pepper to taste together to make the filling. Sauté onions and mushrooms in a small amount of oil in separate batches. Set aside. In a 9x13-inch dish, layer sauce, noodles, filling, mushrooms, onions, then repeat this layering twice again. End with noodles, and sauce and sprinkle of grated cheese. Bake at 375° for 40-45 minutes until top is brown and sauce is bubbling.

Mac and Cheese

Servings: 4-6

The first thing I taught my kids to cook from scratch, when they were about seven.

1 lb.	Pasta elbow, shells or spirals
3 Tbsp.	Butter
3 Tbsp.	Flour
2 cups	Milk
4-5 oz.	Cheddar cheese (about 2 cups,) grated
1 Tbsp.	Mustard jared or 1 tsp. dry
1-14 oz. can	Evaporated milk
1 tsp.	Salt
	Black or white pepper to taste

Cook pasta as package directs. Drain. In same pot melt butter, when melted add flour and stir. Slowly add milk, stirring with a whisk. When thicken add cheese, stir until melted, add evaporated milk and mustard. When hot add pasta stirring until coated if more liquid is needed add some water or milk. Serve. **NOTE:** A fast way is to stir in Velveeta cheese instead of cheddar cheese. I like to use Dijon mustard. **NOTE:** We like to serve canned tomatoes with Mac and cheese. Stewed tomatoes are good to. Just open a can, heat and dinner in ready!

Pasta and Asparagus

Martha Davis

Servings: 4

Martha gave me this easy recipe and I have added to it.

1 lb.	Pasta, spaghetti
1 lb.	Asparagus, fresh or frozen
1Tbps.	Salt
6 qts.	Water
6 Tbps.	Olive oil
3 cloves	Garlic, chopped
¼ cup	Parmesan cheese, grated
To add chicken	
3 pieces	Chicken breast, boneless, skinless. Cut into 1-inch cubes
1 medium	Onions, chopped
1 tsp.	Salt

Boil water with salt. Add pasta and asparagus. Cook for 7 minutes or until pasta is al dente. Drain and place in serving dish or bowl. Heat oil while pasta is cooking and heat garlic in oil. Pour oil over cooked pasta, sprinkle with cheese and toss. Serve with more cheese if you wish. *To add chicken to this recipe:* when oil is heated add chicken, garlic and onion and sauté until the chicken is done, about 10 minutes. Process as above. **NOTE:** To add a little different flavor to this dish try adding the zest of one orange to the oil. To make the dish spicy add 1-2 tsp. of hot pepper oil or a pinch of hot pepper flakes to the oil.

Stuffed Shells

Serving: 6-8

George loves anything made with pasta. I like to make this recipe and putting it into smaller baking dishes and freezing all but the amount I want for that night. Defrost before baking. I sometimes have to increase the length of baked to compensate for any ice crystal that may form.

1 Box	Jumbo shells
1-2 Quarts	Pasta sauce, mushroom or marinara
2 lb.	Ricotta cheese
1-15 oz.	Part-skin milk mozzarella
¼ cup	Parmesan chasse
3	Eggs, beaten
2 Tbsp.	Parsley, chopped
1 tsp.	Basil
1 tsp.	Salt
Dash	Black pepper

Cook the pasta according to package directions. Drain well. I then lay the shells out onto clean tea towels to make sure all the water is out of the pasta. In a large bowl mix the 3 cheeses, eggs, spices and flavoring. Heat the pasta sauce, then make a nice layer of the sauce on the bottom of the pan or pans. Use cheese mixture to stuff each shell, placing them, in the sauce. Add more sauce over the shells. Bake, uncovered in preheated oven at 350° for 25-30 minutes or until the sauce is bubbling.

ONE-DISH POULTRY

Baked Chicken Curry

Servings: 6

The flavor of curry makes this dish stand out.

1-4 lb.	Roasting chicken, dressed for baking
2 tsp.	Curry powder
1 cup	Water
2 cup	Rice, uncooked
2 cups	Water
	Salt
4 Tbsp.	Butter

Place chicken in roasting pan with 1-cup water with curry powder mixed in. Bake in 350° oven adding more water if necessary, basting occasionally. Cook slowly for about 30 minutes. Drain liquid from chicken, save and replace with 2 more cups of water. Continue cooking chicken. Wash rice, and add the chicken dripping with enough water to total 4 cups to a medium saucepan. Cook for about 20 minutes. Keep warm on very low flame for another 20 minutes. (Carefully not to burn.) When chicken is browned, remove from roaster. Combine rice with butter and gravy from the cooked chicken. Spread rice on the bottom of roasting pan and replace chicken on top. Continue cooking for about 1/2 hour or until chicken is done and a crust a formed on bottom of rice. To serve, smother chicken with rice, crust side up on a large platter.

Chicken Curry

Servings: 6

Use lamb in place of chicken for a change. Lamb is the English influence on the Indian cuisine and Curry on the English.

1/4 cup	Flour
2 tsp.	Salt
To taste	Pepper
1	Chicken cut into serving pieces or 2 lb. Lamb cut into cubes
4 Tbsp.	Oil
2 medium	Onions, cut into quarters
6-8 medium	Potatoes, cut in half
4-6	Carrots, cut in half
	Water
1to 2Tbsp.	Curry paste*
6 cups	Rice, cooked

Put chicken or lamb flour, salt and pepper into plastic bag and shake. Shake excess flour off meat and brown in oil. Put into large pot with vegetables; curry paste and enough water to almost cover the ingredients. Stew slowly covered for about 1 hour or until very tender. Add water if necessary to have nice gravy. Serve with rice. **NOTE:** *Curry paste can be found in an Asia grocery store. **NOTE:** For a complete meal *serve Split Pea Dal, (soup) Tomato Chutney* and flat bread. Serve small bowls of some or all of grated coconut, salted nuts, raisins, diced dates, sesame seeds, and fresh very small hot peppers. Don't forget a bowl of plain yogurt or *Cucumber Raita.*

Chicken Pie

Ma

Servings: 8

I was very young when this was one of the first things I made, by myself, for company.

Double	Pie crust
4-5 cups	Cooked chicken, cut into large chunks
2-3	Carrots, cut in ¼ inch rounds
2 ribs	Celery, cut in 1/4-inch slices
1 cup	Onions, diced
2-3	Potatoes, peeled, cubed
4 cups	Chicken broth
1/4 cup	Parsley, fresh chopped
3 Tbsp.	Butter
3 Tbsp.	Flour

Heat broth, add vegetables and cook until soft about 10 minutes. Drain vegetables, saving broth, and place vegetables in 9 x 13 inch baking dish with chicken. Melt butter in saucepan, stir in flour and cook for 2 minutes; do not brown. Add hot broth slowly until smooth, using vegetable broth to get right consistency. Add parsley to gravy; season with salt and pepper to taste. Add gravy to meat and vegetables. Roll out piecrust into rectangle. Cover baking dish with crust, seal around edges by crimping. Make slits in top of crust. Bake in 350° oven for 45 minutes or until crust is brown and juices bubble. **NOTE:** If you want to cook raw chicken in broth first, use about 2 whole chicken breasts.

Chicken Quick Supper

Servings: 4

I used to make this very often when I was in a hurry and George and Nicole loved it. You can use chicken or pork chops.

2 Tbsp.	Oil
4 pieces	Chicken breast or 4 pork chops
1 can	Mushroom soup concentrate
1 can	Milk
1 4oz can	Mushrooms, drain and save liquid

Brown chicken or pork in oil in an electric frying pan if possible. Add soup, mushrooms and milk to meat, reduce heat to simmer and cover. Simmer for 30 minutes or until tender. Serve. **NOTE:** Save mushroom liquid to add to dish if the gravy gets to thick. You can substitute cream of chicken or cream of celery for the soup if you wish. *Menu:* Serve over mashed potatoes and a green vegetable. Quick!

Chicken Tetrazzini

Servings: 6

This casserole is nice for an easy meal. I use it for lunch, brunch or dinner.

3 cups	Chicken, cooked
1 lb.	Spaghetti, cooked
2 cans	Mushroom soup
1-8 oz. Can	Mushrooms, drained
4 Tbsp	Dry sherry
1 cup	Chicken broth
1/3 cup	Parmesan cheese

Mix all ingredients except Parmesan cheese. Pour into 9x 13-inch baking dish and top with cheese. Bake in 350° oven for about 30 minutes or until brown on top.

Jambalaya

Servings: 12

Another dish I learned in Louisiana. A country dish you can vary as to the ingredients available. But the trinity of celery, onion, and pepper is the standard vegetable in all jambalayas.

1/4 cup	Oil
1 whole	Chicken, cut up
4 cups	Onions, chopped
2 cups	Celery, chopped
2 cups	Green pepper, chopped
4-5, cloves	Garlic, chopped
4 cups	Rice
5 cups	Chicken broth
2 tsp., heaping	Salt
1 tsp.	Cayenne pepper
2 cups	Green onion, chopped
1 1/2 to 2 lbs.	Andouille sausage, or smoked hot sausage
1 lb.	Shrimp, peeled or other seafood like, crayfish, imitation crabmeat or combination
2 Tbsp	Kitchen Bouquet
1	Bay leaf
1 tsp.	Basil

Season and brown chicken in oil. Or boil a whole chicken, cool and pull meat off bones. Sauté sausage. Set meat aside. Sauté onions, celery, green pepper and garlic in the same pot until tender. Return chicken and sausage to pot. Add broth, salt, pepper and other desired seasonings, Kitchen Bouquet and bring to a boil. (For red jambalaya, add 1//4-cup paprika, or 1/2-cup tomato juice in place of Kitchen Bouquet) Add rice and return to boil. Cover and reduce heat to simmer. Cook for 10 minutes remove cover and stir rice. Cover and cook for 20 minutes more. Add green onions and seafood 15 minutes before end of cooking. **NOTE:** (For a red Jambalaya, you can add 2 cups of chopped tomatoes with green onions.)

ONE-DISH VEGETABLES

Eggplant Parmesan

Servings: 6

A long time favorite with the family. I like it cold on Italian bread the next day.

1 large	Eggplant
1 cup	Dry breadcrumbs or flour
2	Eggs, beaten with 1 tablespoon water
	Olive oil
1 qt.	Pasta sauce with basil
8 oz.	Mozzarella cheese, grated
1/4 cup	Parmesan cheese, grated

Wash eggplant and slice into 1/4-inch slices, crosswise. Season with salt and let drain 1/2 hour in strainer. Rinse eggplant with cool water and pat dry. Season with pepper. Dip in egg wash and then in breadcrumbs or flour. Heat 2-3 tablespoons of oil and fry eggplant until soft and brown on both sides. Add more oil as needed. Cover bottom of 2 quart baking dish with some pasta sauce. Layer eggplant, two cheese and pasta sauce, twice. Sprinkle with Parmesan cheese and bake in a 350° oven for 25-30 minutes or until the sauce bubbles and top is brown. **NOTE:** To make this dish more flavorful, add a large onion and/ or 8 oz. mushrooms, slice and sautéed and add to sauce.

German Onion Pie

Servings: 6

Use for a first course or for a lunch.

6 slices	Bacon
2 cups	Onions, chopped
2	Eggs, well beaten
1 cup	Sour cream
1 Tbsp.	Flour
1/2 tsp.	Salt
A few grinds	Black pepper
1 single	Pie crust

Sauté bacon until slightly crisp. Drain all but 1Tsp. of fat and sauté onions in it but do not brown. Cool. Beat eggs with sour cream; add flour and salt and pepper. Spread the onions and bacon over the piecrust and pour the sour-cream mixture over the onions. Bake at 400° for 15 minutes reduce oven to 350° and bake another 15 minutes or until browned. Best served hot.

Vegetable Chili

Servings: 6

I make this for my friend Jane, who is a vegetarian, and we all love it.

2 Tbsp.	Olive oil
1 large	Onion, chopped
1 medium	Green pepper, chopped
1 small	Zucchini, sliced
1 cup	Corn cut, fresh or frozen
1 can	Tomatoes, with liquid
1-6 oz. Can	Tomato paste
3 Tbsp.	Light soy sauce
1 Tbsp.	Chili powder
1 tsp.	Cumin
1/2 tsp.	Cilantro
1/2 tsp. or to taste	Basil or 3-4 leaves, chopped
2-16 oz cans or 1 cup raw	Kidney beans, cooked
	Extra sharp cheese grated for garnish
3 cups	Rice cooked, (optional)

Heat oil in large pot. Sauté onions on medium until translucent. Add green pepper and sauté until softened. Add all ingredients except cheese and simmer over low heat for 30 minutes. Serve with cheese sprinkled on top. Can be served over rice. I like brown rice the best.

SIDE DISH

Ma used them to stretch a meal and to add interest. They can make or break a nice menu. These dishes add the zest. I choose them to blend with the meal. If they clash, you can lose their effectiveness.

SIDE-DISH—FRUIT

Curried Baked Fruit

Servings: 12

A variation on Ma's sweet pickled peaches.

1/3 cup	Butter
3/4 cup	Dark brown sugar, packed
4 tsp.	Curry powder
1-lb. Can	Pears
1/4 cup	Maraschino cherries
1-1 lb. can	Peaches, or apricots halves
1 1lb. Can	Pineapple, slices or chunks

Heat oven to 325°. Melt butter and add sugar and curry. Drain fruit well, pat dry, and place in 1 1/2 quart baking dish, add butter and sugar mixture. Bake for 1 hour uncovered. Serve warm.

Fried Apple Rings with Brown Sugar

Servings: 6

This is a nice complement to ham, and sausage.

4	Apples, crisp, cored
	Dark brown sugar
	Butter
	Sour cream

Cut apples in 1/2-inch slices and press the brown sugar onto each side. Melt a couple of Tbsp. of butter and sauté each side of the apple until tender. Serve warm. Can top with a small dot of sour cream.

Fried Apples

Ma
Servings 6

Ma often added this to her meals to use apples that were no longer wanted for eating out of hand. It makes a lovely addition to pork or ham.

3	Apples, cored and sliced
2 Tbsp.	Sugar
1/2 tsp.	Cinnamon
3-4 Tbsp.	Butter

Sauté the apples in the melted butter. As they soften, sprinkle them with the cinnamon and sugar. Continue cooking until the sugar caramelizes but be careful not to burn the sugar. Serve warm. **NOTE:** For a country flavor, fry out 4 pieces of bacon and use the fat as a substitute for butter. Crumble bacon on top. Yum!

Green Apple Sauce

Servings: 3 cups

Tangy, and good with pork or chicken.

12	Crisp, tart green apples
	Sugar
	Cinnamon (optional)

Wash and quarter apples. Place in a saucepan with enough water to keep from sticking. Cook over low heat, covered for 30 minutes. Check to be sure that you don't scorch the apples. Put apple thought food mill or sieve. Add sugar to taste, reheat sauce to melt sugar. Cool, chill. Can add a dash of cinnamon for an extra flavor. **NOTE:** To make a chunky applesauce, peel and core apples, cook and mash with a potato masher. Continue with the recipe.

Red Apples

Ma
Servings: 6

Serve with meats.

1 cup	Water
1 cup	Sugar
3 tsp.	Lemon juice
4-6 crisp	Apples, quartered and pared
Few drops	Red food coloring

Boil water and sugar together for 5 minutes. Add red food coloring and apples. Cook until the apples are soft. Serve room temp. or cold.

Rhubarb and Fruit Sauce

Ma
Servings: 6

Here is an easy and good side dish or a dessert.

4-6 stalks	Rhubarb*, cut into 1 inch pieces
1 qt.	Strawberries, pared or use
4.	Apples, peeled and pared
1 cup or to taste	Sugar
1 tsp.	Lemon juice

Combine fruit and sugar and slowly cook in saucepan until soft. Rhubarb can still hold its shape but still be soft. Stir until well mixed. Taste for sweetness. Adjust if necessary. Cool and stir in lemon juice. Eat with meal or for dessert with cream. **NOTE:** *Never use any part of the leaves of rhubarb, as they are poison.

SIDE DISH SEAFOOD

Scalloped Oysters

Ma

Servings: 6

A wonderful side dish I still fix for Thanksgiving. I have had this dish on a Hunt breakfast buffet down South.

1/2 cup	Butter, cut into pieces
1/2 tsp.	Salt
1/4 tsp.	Black pepper
Dash	Cayenne pepper
1 qt., fresh	Oysters
1 box	Unsalted crackers, thick
	Milk

Preheat oven to 400°. Drain oyster and save liquid. Layer crackers, butter and oyster in a greased casserole dish. Top with butter on crackers for the last layer. Combine liquid with salt, pepper, and cayenne. Pour liquid over layers in dish using milk to just cover the layers. Put in oven and bake until brown about 30 minutes. **NOTE:** I use Nabisco Undeea cracker for this dish if you can find them. Unsalted saltines can be used if you need to.

SIDE DISH VEGETABLES

Cucumber Raita

Servings: 4

A wonderful cooling salad to serve with any spicy dish. A must to use with Indian foods.

2	Cucumber, peeled, sliced
2 cups	Yogurt, plain
1/2 tsp.	Dill weed
1/2 tsp.	Lemon juice

Slice cucumber and salt heavily. Put in strainer and let drain for an hour. Rinse and drain again for 15 minutes. Add to other ingredients and refrigerate for at least one hour. Stir well before serving.

Hot Slaw

Ma
Servings: 4

A dish Ma made often. Try it. It is different!

1	Egg
1 tsp.	Mustard
1/2 tsp.	Salt
	Pepper, to taste
1 tsp.	Sugar
1/2 tsp.	Corn starch
1/2 cup	Hot water
2-3 cups	Cabbage, shredded

Mix ingredients except cabbage together to make a paste. Bring to a boil stirring constantly. Pour over shredded cabbage. Serve.

Rice Cakes

Servings: 6

Ma made these from leftover rice as the starch dish for the meal.

2 cups	Rice, cooked
2	Eggs, beaten
1/2 cup	Flour
1/2 tsp.	Salt
1 tsp.	Baking Powder
1/2 cup	Milk
	Oil or butter
1/2 tsp. for each cake	Jelly or jam

Mix flour, salt, baking powder and add eggs. Stir in milk, then add rice. Drop large tablespoon of mixture into hot oil. Lightly brown on both sides. Remove to a warm platter, press a dent into the cakes with your thumb and put jelly in the indention. Serve warm with the meal. Especially good with ham or pork.

Spanish Rice

Servings: 6

A favorite side dish.

6 slices	Bacon, diced
1/4 cup	Onion, chopped
1/4 cup	Red pepper, chopped
3 cups	Rice, cooked
1-1 lb. Can	Tomatoes
To taste	Salt
1/8 tsp.	Pepper

Fry bacon in large skillet until crisp. Remove bacon and drain. Pour off drippings saving about 2 Tbsp. Use this to fry onions and pepper until tender. Stir in bacon and rest of ingredients and cook uncovered over low heat for 15 minutes. **NOTE:** Spanish Rice Meal to make this into a main dish add cut, and cooked chicken, sausage or seafood when adding bacon and other ingredients.

Stuffing

Isabella Meddings
Servings: 6

This old fashion English sage and onion dressing is from my Grandmom Meddings.

1 loaf	Unsliced stuffing bread, English toasting or Italian bread
2 cups	Chopped onions
2 cups	Chopped celery
6 Tbsp.	Butter
1 Tbsp.	Sage
1 14-15 oz. can	Chicken broth
To taste	Salt and pepper

Tear bread into small pieces and set aside. Heat frying pan and melt butter, add onions and celery and cook until soft but not brown. Season to taste with salt and pepper. Add vegetables to bread. Add sage and chicken broth and stir until well incorporated. Put in a baking dish and bake at 350° for 45-60 minutes. Can be used to stuff in a chicken or turkey and bake. **NOTE:** Here are some different flavors to add to this basic recipe: **Fruit and Sausage Stuffing:** Add 2 tart apples, peeled, cored and chopped, and/or ½-1 lb. of loose sausage, that has been fried out. **Stuffing Balls:** To serve stuffing as a side dish use flavored crouton stuffing mix in place of bread and continue with recipe. Add 2 eggs and mix thoroughly. Form stuffing into ball a little smaller than tennis balls and place on a cookie sheet flatting each ball with the palm of your hand. Bake at 350° for about 30 minutes. **Corn Stuffing:** Add 1 ½ cup corn. **Cornbread Stuffing:** Use a pan of cornbread, crumbed in place of bread. **Oyster Stuffing:** Add 1 pint of oyster to stuffing using oyster liquid as part of the liquid for stuffing. **Chestnut Stuffing:** Add ½ to 1 pound of cooked and chopped chestnuts. **Giblet Stuffing:** Place giblets in a small saucepan. Add a slice of onion, a piece of celery and a small piece of carrot ½ teaspoon salt. Cover with water and cook for about 30 minutes. Pick meat from neck bone and place in blender along with rest of giblets, vegetables and liquid. Blend, add to stuffing. **Raisin Stuffing:** Add 2/3-cup dark or golden raisins or a combination to the basic recipe. A nice addition is some peeled, pared and chopped apple along with the raisins.

Sweet Potatoes and Apple Casserole

Servings: 8

Try to use sweet potatoes. If not available, yams do work.

3 medium	Sweet potatoes
4 large	Apple, crisp, tart, peeled, corded and sliced
1/2 cup	Light brown sugar, packed
1/2 tsp.	Salt
4 Tbsp.	Butter
1/2 cup	Orange juice

Bake sweet potatoes until tender about 40-50 minutes at 400°. Peel the potatoes and slice diagonally into 1/2-inch pieces. Make 3 layers of potatoes, apples, sugar and salt in a 9x11-inch baking dish. Dot top with butter and pour orange juice over the mixture. Bake in a 350° oven for 30-40 minutes until the apples are soft. **NOTE: Sweet Potato, Ham, Apple Casserole:** To add meat to this recipe add a layer of sliced smoked ham with potatoes and apples.

Wild Rice Stuffing

Servings: 4

Good with duck or serve baked in a casserole with meat.

1/4 cup	Butter
2 medium	Onions, chopped fine
1/2 cup	Celery chopped fine
1/2 cup	Raisins
3 cups	Brown and wild rice, cooked
1 tsp.	Salt
2 cup	Chicken broth

Sauté onions and celery until tender, add other ingredients and place in a greased baking dish or stuff a bird. Bake in 350° for 45 minutes in casserole. **NOTE:** Wild and brown rice can be purchased in a package or you can purchase the two separately and cook together.

VEGETABLES

Ma just steamed most of our vegetables. I have found that green beans and potatoes must be cooked with salt in order for them to absorb the flavor, salting them after doesn't seem to work. Other vegetables should be lightly dusted with salt and pepper just before serving. Ma did not cook her vegetables with meat or fat either. Just a pat of butter before serving keeps the flavors sweet and fresh.

Baked Limas

Servings: 12

A Forth of July must, but good any time

1 lb.	Dried large lima beans
2 tsp.	Salt
2 Tbsp.	Butter
2	Onions, sliced
1/2 cup	Ketchup
1/2 cup	Molasses
2 Tbsp.	Vinegar
1/2 tsp.	Hot sauce
2 tsp., dry	Mustard
1/2 lb.	Bacon, cut into pieces

Rinse beans and place in pot. Cover with water and bring to a boil. Cook for about 1 1/2 to 2 hours or until done, but not mushy, adding more boiling water if needed. In butter, sauté onion until tender. In a bowl mix ketchup, molasses, vinegar, hot sauce, and mustard. When beans are done, drain and save liquid. Add a cup of the liquid to the ketchup mixture. In a 3-quart casserole or bean pot, arrange in layers, limas, onion, and bacon, topping casserole with bacon. Pour the ketchup mixture over the top of bean casserole. Bake uncovered in a 325° oven for at least 4 hours (up to 6 if baking a large batch). Serve hot and enjoy! **NOTE:** Can be cooked for a few hours, cooled, refrigerated until needed. Remove from refrigerator a few hours before starting to bake in order to reach room temperature. Bake for at least 1 hour to finish cooking and reheat.

Casserole of Yellow Squash

Servings: 8

This is the Southern way of using up that supply of summer yellow squash. If the squash has grown too large so it is no longer tender, this is just the recipe for you. You can now find this veggie all year long. No matter if you are using young or old squashes, the dish is still delicious.

2 lbs.	Yellow squash, cut into ½ inch slices. (Zucchini can be used)
1 large	Cooking onion, chopped
1 Tbsp.	Salt
1 1/3 cups	Fresh breadcrumbs*
1 1/3 cups	Sharp cheese, grated
3 large	Eggs, beaten
1 cup	Heavy cream or evaporated milk, undiluted
1 tsp.	Salt
1 tsp.	Black pepper
½ tsp.	Thyme
Pinch	Cayenne pepper

Place squash, onion and 1 Tbsp. salt in a saucepan, cover with water. Bring to a boil and reduce heat to a simmer. Cover and cook for about 25 minutes until very tender. Drain very well for about 15 minutes. Preheat oven to 350°. Place drained squash in a large bowl. To squash, add just 1 cup each of breadcrumbs and cheese. Add the rest of the ingredients and stir well. Place in a shallow casserole and top with the rest of the breadcrumbs and cheese. Cover and bake about 30 minutes. Uncover and bake until the top is brown, about 10 minutes. Everyone will love squash after they eat this dish! **NOTE:** To make fresh bread crumbs tear 2-3 bread slices, place in blender or food processor and pulse until bread is just loose crumbs

Collard, Kale, Turnip Greens

Servings: 6

Usually, all of these dark green vegetables we enjoyed, were cut from Aunt Ruth's garden each fall. Otherwise, we had to go to the city to find them since they were not common in NJ food markets. Now you can buy them fresh all year long.

3 to 4 lbs.	Greens
	Water
	Salt

Wash greens thoroughly using several changes of water. Pull the leaves down off the stems and place in a large pot with about 1 or 1 1/2 inches of salted, boiling water. Cook for about 15 to 20 minutes or until tender, collards often take longer. Drain, saving the pot liqueur for delicious hot soup, and place in a bowl. Cut through the greens and top with a pat of butter. **NOTE:** Down South it is traditional to add meat to greens. If you like the taste of meat in your greens, add a bit of chopped ham, cooked ham hock, or some cubed pork rind to the water (Our sin-in-law, Anthony Weal likes to add 2-3 smoked turkey wings also,) plus one or more of the following a pinch or more of crushed red pepper flakes, a few shakes of hot sauce, a small onion, chopped, your favorite herb i.e., basil, oregano, bay leaf, as well as minced garlic. The southerners like all of these then simmer for a couple of hours. I do like this way but, Ma didn't use meat in her vegetables and that is how I usually like them. Everyone to their own taste!

Creamed Vegetables or Vegetable Soufflé

Servings: 4

This is an easy formula to cream any vegetable.

2 cup	Cooked vegetable
	Salt
	Black pepper
	Cream sauce

Make 1 cup of a medium *Cream Sauce* and add the cooked vegetables. The different way to handle the vegetables is to suit your taste. You can puree them, cut in small pieces or, leave them whole such as baby carrots, or small white onions. To make creamed spinach use frozen chopped spinach cooked and well drained, then add the cream sauce. However you can puree the spinach and get a different texture. You can use your imagination and divvies your own style. A bit of spice can change the flavor as well. **NOTE:** Soufflés can be made from this basic idea as well. To each cup of sauce and 1 1/2 cups of pureed vegetable to which you add 1 chopped onion, as vegetable was cooking. You need to add a pinch of spice, such as nutmeg for spinach, and to broccoli and cauliflower a 1/4 cup of Parmesan cheese. Stir all of this together and add 4 egg yolks, 1 at a time, mixing well. Beat 6 egg whites until very stiff and fold them into the vegetable puree. Prepare a casserole with straight sides by buttering the bottom and side and coating the butter with dry breadcrumb, using about 2-3 Tbsp. discarding any loose crumbs. Pour mixture into the dish. Mix together 1 Tbsp. of breadcrumbs, and 1 Tbsp. Parmesan cheese, and sprinkle on top. Bake at 350° for 25 minute or until brown and firm. Serve immediately. Vegetable soufflés do not rise like cheese or sweet soufflés do. You may add a paper collar to the dish if you like, but it usually is not necessary. *Most important about soufflés is:* you mush wait for the soufflés, it cannot wait for you. You must serve and eat it right away. Make sure you are ready for the dish before you start to cook a soufflé.

Creole Okra

Servings: 6

Southern, zesty and delicious.

2 lbs.	Okra, sliced across
	Oil
2	Onions, chopped
1/2 tsp. or 4 fresh	Basil leaves
1-1 lb. Can	Tomato
To taste	Cayenne pepper
2 cloves	Garlic, minced
To taste	Salt
1 Tbsp.	Corn starch
2 Tbsp.	Water

Sauté the okra and the onions in a small amount of oil. Add the rest of the ingredients, except the cornstarch and water, and cook until tender about 10 to 15 minutes. Mix cornstarch with water and stir into the juice of the vegetables. Cook for 2 to 3 minutes until the juice thickens. Serve.

Fried Eggplant

Servings: 6

Ma made this a lot. Dad liked his eggplant sliced thin. I like it with the skin on. You can fix it as you like.

1 medium	Eggplant
	Flour
	Salt
	Pepper
	Oil

Cut the top and bottom of eggplant off. Peel or not. Slice across the vegetable as thin as you like. If you like the eggplant in chunks, slice the eggplant lengthwise in half then in thick slices then turn the slice on it side and make thick slices again to make thick sticks. Each stick can then be cut into a desired length. Place in layers in a colander, sprinkling each layer with salt. Let drain for an hour. Rinse the eggplant with cold water. Drain. Use about 3/4 cup of flour seasoned with salt and pepper. Dip the moist vegetable in the flour mixture and fry in hot oil. Eggplant can use a lot of oil so use it sparing, only as the pan requires. I like my eggplant with ketchup. You can make thicker slices to be used in *Eggplant Parmesan*. Keep warm as you fry the slices to serve it all together and hot.

Fried Tomatoes

Ma

Servings: 4

Something Ma made very often each summer. George would not let a summer go by without gobbling up a few platters of these delicious vegetables.

4 medium	Tomatoes, ripe
1/2 cup	Flour
1 tsp.	Salt
1/4 tsp.	Pepper
4 Tbsp.	Oil. (You can use butter instead)
1/2 cup approx.	Milk

Cut tomatoes in ¾-inch slices. Stir flour, salt and pepper together and dip each slice in flour. Heat oil in pan adding a few slices at a time until lightly browned on each side. After browning all slices scrape browned pieces from bottom of pan and stir milk in slowly until the flour bits thicken the gravy. Serve over tomatoes. **NOTE:** The gravy is George's favorite way to eat these vegetables but Ma never used gravy. She always sprinkled a light dusting of sugar over the tomatoes, and that is my favorite way. This recipe is just a base to work from; I always cook a lot more tomatoes for four people that this calls for but everyone to their own taste.

Fritters

Ma
Servings: 12-15 fritters

Ma's way of stretching vegetables.

1 cup	Flour
1 tsp.	Baking Powder
1/4 tsp.	Salt
1	Egg, beaten
1/2-3/4 cup	Milk
	Oil

Mix together to make batter. Add one of the following: 1 cup drained canned tomato using some of the liquid in place of some of the milk: 1-1 1/2 cups of cooked corn, canned or cut off cob: 1-11/2 cups grated zucchini. Heat a frying pan and add oil until hot. Drop about ¼ cup of batter into pan and brown on each side. Serve warm. **NOTE:** Adjust consistency of batter with milk or liquid from vegetables.

Harvard Beets

Servings: 4

Nicole's favorite dish, something she often requests.

4 cups	Beets, chunk or sliced, drained, save juice
1 Tbsp.	Corn starch
1 cup.	Sugar
1/4 tsp.	Salt
Dash	Black pepper
2/3 cup	Water, use water from beets
1/4 cup	Vinegar
2 Tbsp	Butter

In medium saucepan stir together cornstarch, sugar, salt and pepper. Gradually stir in water and vinegar. Cook, stirring constantly until mixture thickens and boils. Boil and stir 1 minute. Stir in beets heat through. Add butter. Serve warm. **NOTE:** I usually double or triple this recipe for 6 to 8 people or keep on doubling until you have enough for a crowd. This dish is usually very popular.

Mashed Potatoes

Ma
Servings: 6-8

Basic recipe that Ma passed on to me.

8 to 10	All purpose potato
1 tsp.	Salt
About 1/2 cup	Evaporated milk
1/2 stick	Butter

Peel potatoes and cut in chunks. Cover with water. Add salt and cook until tender. Drain liquid and save. Mash potatoes with a masher, for very smooth potatoes use a ricer. Add butter and milk, using an electric mixer, whip potatoes adding some of the saved liquid to make the preferred consistency. Add pepper to taste. **NOTE:** Always add salt to water when cooking potatoes. Adding salt after does not achieve the best flavor. **NOTE:** I also use red skinned potatoes and leave the skins on. The skins will go all thought the mashed potatoes and make a little bit of a texture (Again, use amount to your taste.) **NOTE: Garlic Mashed Potatoes:** Add 4-5 roasted garlic cloves to potatoes before mashing.

Parsnips

Ma
Servings: 6

Ma always fixed parsnips this way.

1 lb.	Parsnips
1 tsp.	Salt
	Water
3 Tbsp.	Butter
3 Tbsp.	Flour
1 cup	Milk
1/4 tsp.	Salt
Dash	Pepper
1/2 cup	Crushed corn flakes or breadcrumbs

Boil parsnips whole in boiling water with 1-tsp. salt until tender. Drain and plunge parsnips into cold water, let sit for 2 minutes. Remove vegetables from water and slip skin off the roots. Slice lengthwise in even thickness. Lay parsnips in a buttered baking dish making one layer. Melt butter and stir in flour, cooking for 1 minute, add milk slowly to make a thick white sauce. Spread over vegetables Ma always sprinkled it with corn flake crumbs. Bake at 350° for 40 to 45 minutes or until topping is brown and bubbling. **NOTE:** If the core of the parsnip is tough, discard. **NOTE:** This is another dish that Ma would make ahead and then bake before serving. Parsnips can be boiled, peeled and chopped crosswise and served with butter as a very tasty vegetable dish.

Peas with dumplings

Servings: 6

Something we had in the spring when the peas where freshly picked.

5-6 lbs.	Fresh peas
	Water
	Salt to taste
1	Dumpling recipe

Shell and wash peas. Prepare recipe for dumplings. Add salt to peas and cover with water 1 inch, bring to boil, Drop in small dumplings when water comes to the boil. Reduce heat to simmer. Cook 10 minutes uncovered. Cover pot and cook 10 more minutes. Uncover and serve in bowls with liquid. **NOTE:** Keep a check on water level. If too low after first 10 minute add boiling water before covering so peas and dumpling will not stick. **NOTE:** If you would like a little meat in this dish, add some cubed ham to peas before cooking.

Ratatouille

Servings: 8

This is a lovely combination of vegetables that will go with almost any meal.

1 medium	Eggplant
2 small	Zucchini
1 cup	Green pepper, finely chopped
1 medium	Onion, finely chopped
4 medium	Tomato, peeled* and quartered
¼ cup	Oil
3 cloves	Garlic, crushed
2 tsp.	Salt
¼ tsp.	Black pepper
1 tsp.	Basil

Cut eggplant and zucchini into 1/2-inch cubes. Sauté all ingredients in the oil until heated through. Cook over medium heat, covered. Stir occasionally for about 10-15 minutes until vegetables are crisp but tender. **NOTE:** *See *Tips About Food* for peeling tomatoes. **NOTE:** For any extra treat, sprinkle about 1/4 cup of grated cheese in vegetable before serving. **Ratatouille Casserole**: A second variety is to put ratatouille in a baking dish and top with 8 ounces of grated mozzarella cheese, baking in 350° over until cheese melts, about 10-12 minutes.

Red Cabbage

Servings: 8

This recipe is sweet, sour and goes very nicely with German dishes.

1 head	Red cabbage
1 cup	Cider vinegar
1 Tbsp.	Light brown sugar
2	Cloves
½	Bay leaves
¼ tsp.	Salt
2 tsp.	Onion, grated

Shred cabbage and steam until tender. Drain. Simmer other ingredients, except onion, for 5 minutes, strain and add onion. Pour over hot cabbage. Keep warm for 5-10 minute, stirring occasionally. Serve.

Rutabagas

Servings: 4

This very old vegetable is not used very much anymore. We still love this old time vegetable. I especially like it with lamb and duck, but it is good anytime.

1 medium	Rutabagas
	Water
1	Beef bullion cube

Peel rutabaga and cut into small chunks. Put rutabaga into pan with 1 inch of boiling water with bullion cube added. Cover and cook about 25 minutes or longer if the vegetable is cut in larger pieces or in slices. Serve drained or thicken the liquid with a water and flour combination. **NOTE:** Mashed rutabaga: After cooking vegetable, drain saving liquid. Mash with potato masher, add 3-4 tablespoons of butter and some canned milk using saved liquid to bring vegetable to desired consistency. For another ideas mix equal parts of white cooked potatoes or carrots to the rutabaga and proceed as above. I enjoy them anyway I cook them, I hope you will try them and enjoy them also.

Rutabaga Casserole

Servings: 6-8

We had rutabagas a lot as a child and I still like to use them in different ways. Try this casserole for a hearty winter dish.

2 med. (2 lb.)	Rutabagas
1	Beef bouillon cube
2	Eggs, beaten
¼ cup	Dry breadcrumbs
¼ cup	Half & half cream, heavy cream or undiluted evaporated milk
1/2 tsp.	Honey
¼ tsp.	Fresh ground nutmeg
1-2 Tbsp.	Butter

Peel rutabagas and cut into small pieces. Add bouillon cube and just enough water to cover vegetables. Cook for about 20 minutes or until very tender. Drain, reserving ¼ cup of cooking liquid. Mash rutabagas with reserved liquid. Stir in rest of ingredients, except butter. Pour into a greased 1-½ cup casserole, dot with butter. Bake at 350° for 50 minutes or until top is lightly brown.

Scalloped Potatoes

Ma

Servings: 8

An old stand by that can be assembled before hand and baked just before serving.

10 medium	Potato, peeled and sliced thin
2 Tbsp.	Onion, finely grated
6-8 Tbsp.	Butter
1/2 cup (about)	Flour
2 cups (about)	Milk
To taste	Salt
1/4 tsp.	Fresh-ground black pepper
1/2 cup	Breadcrumbs

Preheat oven to 350° and butter a 9x13 inch-baking dish. Make 3 layers of potatoes, sprinkled with flour, salt, pepper and pieces of butter. Top the last layer with bread crumbs then butter. Fill dish to almost full with milk and bake for 1 to 1 1/4 hrs. or until potatoes are tender. Let the dish sit for 10 minutes before serving. **NOTE:** You can make this recipe for a smaller or larger group just use the layering method and allow for size of baking dish for time baked. **NOTE:** For **Potatoes A la Gratin**: While layers ingredients add a layer of grated shape cheese. Top the breadcrumbs with grated cheese and bake as above. This is one of Ma's favorite dishes.

Scalloped Tomatoes

Ma
Servings: 4

Ma always called this recipe "stewed tomatoes" but this title descries them better.

1-1lb. Can	Tomato or 4 or 5 fresh with skins removed
1/2 tsp.	Cinnamon
	Salt to taste
	Pepper to taste
2 Tbs.	Molasses
1 slice	Bread, torn into pieces

Mix all ingredients; simmer for 10 minutes. Check if thickening is needed. If so, use flour and water mixed together in a container, cover and shake. Pour flour into simmering tomatoes and cook for a minute or two to cook flour. Can be served at this point or can be put into greased baking dish. Refrigerated and reheated in a 350° oven for 30 minutes to serve later. **NOTE:** Can be doubled for larger group**. NOTE**: When using fresh tomatoes simmer just tomatoes for ten minutes before adding other ingredients and continue with recipe.

Stuffed Tomatoes

Ma

One way Ma used the abundance of tomatoes from Aunt Ruth's garden each summer.

At least 1 per person	Tomato, whole, ripe but firm
	Cheddar cheese cut into chunks
	Salt
	Black pepper
	Breadcrumbs
	Butter cut into chunks

Wash tomatoes and cut out core. Salt and pepper each tomato and push small chunks of cheese down into tomatoes, placing tomato into a shallow baking dish. Top each tomato with breadcrumbs and top with a piece of butter. Bake tomatoes in a 350° oven for about 45 minutes or until tomatoes are tender and cheese is melted.

Succotash

Ma
Servings: 6-8

This is the way Ma fixed this dish.

1 10 oz. box frozen	Corn
1 10-oz. Box frozen	Lima beans
2 Tbsp.	Butter
½ cup	Water
1/2 tsp.	Salt
Pinch	Black pepper
1 cup	Milk

Put all ingredients except milk in a saucepan, cover, and bring to a simmer. Cook on low until vegetables are tender. Add milk and bring just to the boil, but do not boil. Serve succotash in individual bowl with liquid.

Twice Baked Potatoes

Ma

Servings: 8

Ma used this dish all the time for company dinners, because she could make it the day before and just heat it at dinnertime.

5 large	Baking potato, scrubbed
1/3 cup	Milk
4 Tbsp.	Butter
1 Tbsp.	Parsley
1/2 tsp. or to taste	Salt
	Fresh-ground black pepper, to taste
	Paprika for topping

Preheat over to 400° and bake the potatoes for 45 minutes, or until tender. Let cool for 15-20 minutes. Cut the potatoes in half lengthwise. I use a potholder in my hand to hold half and scoop out the flesh, being careful to leave the skin in tack. Put the flesh in a mixing bowl with other ingredient and mash with a potato masher or ricer. Whip the potato mixture with an electric mixer to make fluffy. Spoon the mixture into the potato shell and sprinkle with paprika. Bake at 400° for 20 minutes or until the tops become brown. **NOTE:** After stuffing the potato skins you can cover the potatoes and refrigerate them. Take them out to come to room temperature before baking. **Twice Baked Potatoes with Cheese:** You can add 1 cup of grated sharp cheddar cheese to this recipe for a nice touch.

PICKELS AND REISH

I have included a few, but not all, recipes that Ma used. Canning and preserving is quite a time-consuming job. In this day and age, most people don't have the time or the desire to devote to this activity. If, however, you would wish to experience this old-fashion way of processing food, I recommend the *Ball Blue Book of Canning and Preserving* published by the Ball Canning Co. They produce a complete line of jars, lids and other canning products you will need to purchase to enter into this adventure. Ma saved her jars and rings from year to year. Each time she used them, they were inspected for nicks on the rim of the jar, because this would not allow the jar to seal. Of course, they were scrubbed with hot soap and water and then sterilized to be used again with fresh lids. Some jarred sauces and fruits come in canning jars that can be used to process with your own fine products as well. Other recipes in this section do not require canning.

Cranberry Relish

Servings: 2 cups

Mother and I have been making this old stand by for years and years.

1 bag, fresh or frozen	Cranberries
2	Oranges, quartered
2 cups	Sugar

Using a meat grinder is the best tool to use for a consistent texture for this recipe. If you don't have a grinder you can use a blender or food processor, but be careful not to turn the fruit to a paste by over working it. Process in small batches is the safest way to do this. Add the sugar and stir until well incorporated. Chill for at lest 4 hours before serving.

Pickled Fruit

Ma

Servings: 10-12 quarts

This is how Ma made hers. You need canning jars, lids, and rings. You will find that a large mouth funnel and tongs are helpful as well.

14 lb.	Fruit*
1 qt.	White vinegar
1 tsp.	Cloves, whole
1 large	Cinnamon, stick, broken in pieces
6 lbs.	Sugar

Peel fruit.** Cut in half and remove core or pit, or pickle whole as Ma did. Add spices to the vinegar and sugar and bring to a boil. Add fruit, cooking until tender. Remove fruit with a slotted spoon and place in sterilized jars. Boil the syrup until it becomes thick, and then pour it over the fruit and seal. **NOTE:** *Use canning pears, peaches or plums. **See *Tips on Food* for peeling peaches. Pears need to be peeled with a vegetable peeler. Plums do not need to be peeled.

Pickled Peaches

Servings: 1 quart

This is a short cut to Ma's recipe.

1 large can	Peaches, halves or slices
2 cups	Sugar
1/2 cup	Apple cider vinegar
3-3inch	Cinnamon stick
3	Cloves, whole
3 whole	Allspice

Place peaches in a jar or bowl. Heat remaining ingredients to boiling. Pour over peaches and cool. Cover and refrigerate at least 8 hours or overnight. **NOTE:** I like to use a combination of canned peaches, pears and pineapple to make this recipe. I usually double the sugar, vinegar and spice mixture for this amount of fruit. This side dish goes with ham, or lamb very well. For an entirely different taste, check out Curried *Baked Fruit* recipe.

Pickled Watermelon Rind

Ma

Servings: 3-4 pints

Another of Ma's summertime treats. She used the rind after we ate the flesh. Using pint jars is nice because you can use them for gifts.

5 lb.	Watermelon
3 lbs	Sugar
3 pt.	White vinegar
1-2	Cinnamon stick
5	Cloves, whole
4	Lemons, juiced

Cut the green skin off the rind of the melon leaving a very small amount of pink flesh. Cut in small chunks. Soak in water for 3-4 hours. Drain. Put the sugar and vinegar into a pot and bring to a boil. Add spices wrapped in a cheesecloth bag and cook 5 minutes. Pour hot syrup over melon. Let sit overnight. Bring to a boil and slowly cook fruit until it is clear. Add lemon juice and cook for three more minutes. Pour into sterilized jars and seal.

Sweet Pickled Cantaloupe

Ma

Servings: 8-10

When cantaloupes were plentiful Ma used this method to use some of the fruit.

6 lb.	Cantaloupe, cut
4 qt.	Water
1 oz.	Alum*
1 qt.	Vinegar
3 lbs.	Sugar
8-inch piece	Cinnamon stick
10	Cloves, whole
10	Allspice, whole

'Peel just the tan part of rind, cut very soft part of flesh off and discard. Remove seeds then cut cantaloupe into equal size pieces. Bring water and alum to a boil and drop fruit in, cook for 15 minutes. Drain fruit. In an empty pot put vinegar, sugar and spices. Place fruit into pot with mixture and slowly cook until the fruit is clear. It may take two hours. Place in sterilized jars and seal. **NOTE:** * Can be found in grocery store were canning products are located.

Tomato Chutney

Servings: About 2 cups

I use this when I make an East Indian meal.

1 tsp.	Oil
1/2 tsp.	Cumin seeds
1 tsp.	Fresh ginger root, grated
2 cloves	Garlic, chopped
1 medium	Onion, chopped
4	Tomato, chopped coarsely
1 Tbsp.	Sesame seeds, roasted
To taste	Salt
1 tsp.	Sugar
2 small	Red chilies, dried

Heat oil in a saucepan and fry cumin seeds until they darken a little, *do not burn.* Add each item one at a time quickly as not to burn. Cook for 10 minutes over a medium heat. Let cool slightly. Place n blender or food processor and blend until smooth. Serve in a small bowl. **NOTE:** Because you have to work fast it is best to have everything prepared and at hand before beginning.

SAUCES

Of the basic sauces, the white sauce is the most versatile of all. You will find it as the basics of many recipes. Once you master it you will find many uses for it. I remember when my childhood friend Lee got married at the young age of 18. One day, we were on the phone and she was trying to hone her cooking skills, (at that age she didn't have many). She asked me what a white sauce was and I tried to tell her how to make it over the phone. I don't think my descriptive skills were very good, because she just could not understand how to made the sauce. I, of course, was an old hand at it and thought everyone was also. Silly me!

Barbecue Sauce

Servings: 1 ¾ cups

Good to use in the oven or on the BBQ.

6 Tbsp.	Onion, finely chopped,
3 Tbsp.	Butter
1 cup	Ketchup
1/4 cup	Vinegar
2 Tbsp.	Dark brown sugar
2 tsp.	Mustard
2 Tbsp.	Worcestershire sauce
Pinch	Salt

Sauté onion in butter in saucepan. Add all other ingredients and simmer 10 to 15 minutes. Brush over meat 15 minutes before meat is finished cooking.

Cocktail Sauce

Servings: 4-6

For all your seafood dipping.

1 cup	Ketchup
2 tsp.	Horse-radish
1/2 tsp.	Lemon juice
1/4 tsp.	Worcestershire sauce
2-3 drops	Hot sauce
Dash	Black pepper

Mix together and let sit for 15-20 minutes. You may increase or decrease these amounts to suit your taste.

English Horseradish Sauce

Servings: 1 cup

Use this with a nice roast of beef. Serve *Yorkshire pudding* for a real English treat.

1/2 cup	Heavy cream
3 Tbsp.	Horse-radish, well drained
1/2 tsp.	Salt

Beat whipping cream until stiff. Fold in horseradish and salt. Chill until served.

Ham Glaze

Servings: 2 cups

I often use this recipe

1/2 cup	Honey
1/4 cup	Orange juice
1/4 cup	Pineapple juice, from pineapple
1-lb. Can	Pineapple, sliced
1 tsp.	Corn starch

Mix honey, juices and cornstarch, cook until thickened. Add pineapple slices. Pour sauce over the meat 1/2-hour before end of baking. Place slices on ham 15 minutes before end.

Hard Sauce

Servings: ¾ cup

This is sort of like the whiskey sauce I use for bread pudding but you use brandy and it is not cooked.

1/3 cup	Butter
3/4 cup	10x sugar
2 Tbsp.	Brandy

Cream butter and sugar, add brandy gradually and continue beating until smooth. Chill. **NOTE:** Just the thing for *English Plum Pudding*

Hollandaise Sauce

Servings: About 1 ¼ cups

A basic sauce with many uses.

3	Egg yolks
1 Tbsp.	Lemon juice
1/2 tsp.	Salt
2-3 drops	Hot sauce
1/2 cup, melted	Butter

In blender, mix egg, lemon juice, salt and hot sauce. Slowly pour butter into ingredients while blender is at low speed. The sauce will thicken quickly. Can keep warm over hot water. Refrigerate any leftovers.

Lemon Barbecue Sauce

Servings:

About 40 year ago the blender became a poplar kitchen appliance. I found a sauce that I loved and have made for years. This is my version of the original.

1	Lemon, seeded and quartered
1/2 cup	Olive oil
1 tsp.	Salt
1 small	Onion
2-3	Cloves of garlic
¼ cup	Chili sauce or salsa

Put all ingredients into a blender or food processor and process until smooth. Brush on chicken or fish 2-5 minutes before done. **NOTE:** Can be used on red meat as well. Use in grilling or broiling. To make a spicier sauce, use medium or hot salsa.

Pesto Sauce

Servings: 2 ½-3 cups

A lovely topping for pasta and to use in soup. You need a lot of basil for this recipe. If you grow it or have a friend like I do who grows it, this is a good use of this herb.

3 cups	Fresh bail leaves, packed, no stems
4 cloves	Garlic
1/4 tsp.	Salt
3/4 cup	Parmesan cheese
1/4 cup	Pine nuts, can use walnuts
1/2 cup	Olive oil

Puree everything together in a blender or food processor until it becomes a smooth paste. I use several tablespoons to coat one pound of pasta, but you can use more. The favor is very, very strong, so go easy. If using in a soup stir in at the last minute to keep its flavor. **NOTE:** I store in the refrigerator in a screwed top jar to keep the flavor from other foods. This sauce can be frozen for later use. Freeze in small quality so you have just the right amount to use in your recipe.

Pineapple Sauce

Servings: 1-cup

Use this sauce to top a cheesecake.

1-8 oz. can	Pineapple, crushed
1 tsp.	Corn starch
1 Tbsp.	Lemon juice

Combine pineapple and cornstarch and simmer until clear and thickened. Add lemon juice. Cool. Top cake. **NOTE:** Can be used as a filling for a cake as well.

Sauce for Watermelon

Serving: 1 melon

This simple sauce adds so much to a watermelon. It brightens the natural sweetness of the fruit.

2 Tbsp.	Honey
1 tsp.	Ginger, fresh, grated
2 tsp.	Lime juice

Mix together, set aside for 15 minutes to allow flavor to develop. Pour over melon slices.

Tarter Sauce

Servings: 1 14 cup

This is so easy I don't know why anyone would bother to buy it.

1 cup	Mayonnaise
1/4 cup	Sweet pickle relish
Dash	Lemon juice
Dash	Black pepper

Mix together and serve. Could it be any easier?

Whiskey Sauce

Servings: 1 cup

Don't forget this topping for the bread pudding. Umm good!

1 stick	Butter
1/2 cup	10x sugar
2	Egg yolks
1/2 cup, about	Bourbon

Cream butter and sugar over medium heat until all butter is absorbed. Remove from heat and blend in egg yolks. Pour in bourbon gradually to taste stirring constantly. Sauce will thicken as it cools. Serve warm over warm bread pudding. **NOTE:** You can substitute fruit juice or other liqueur to complement your bread pudding.

White Sauce

Servings: 1 cup

A basic sauce to be used in so many ways.

1 to 3 Tbsp.	Butter
1 to 3 Tbsp.	Flour
1 cup, hot	Milk
1/2 tsp.	Salt

Amount of butter and flour should be equal. 1Tbsp. for thin, 2 for medium, and 3 for thick white sauce. Heat milk. Melt butter in saucepan. Add flour, stirring continually for 1 to 2 minutes but don't brown. Slowly add milk and stir until the sauce thickens. Add salt if needed. To use cold milk: After butter and flower are cooked. Add milk very slowly; at little bit at a time. Make sure all the milk is absorbed before adding more.

DESSERTS

Ma always topped dinner with a desert. It wasn't always elaborate or fancy; sometimes it was plain. I have included a variety. A plain dessert was an old one, Junket. This is an old-time milk dessert that can still be found today in the gelatin and pudding section of the food store. Junket comes in table form that is dropped in warm, sweetened milk. When the milk cools it becomes solid. You can top it with a dab of jelly or a bit of whipped cream. Ma sometimes served it to someone who was not feeling well because it is easy to swallow and to digest. Another simple dessert was some of Ma's canned fruit or some fresh. If you want something a little more substantial than experience one of these.

DESSERTS CAKE

Applesauce Cake Theresa

Servings:
Aunt Theresa

Thanks to Vasso I got this applesauce cake recipe that her mother made so many times. It is excellent. It seams that this cake was served without any frosting. However Aunt Maggie would whip up her recipe and she always topped her cake with a *7-minute icing*.

1 cup	Walnuts
1 Cup	Dates
1 Cup	Raisins
½ lb.	Butter
1 ½ cups	Sugar
2	Eggs
2 Cups	Applesauce
2 tsp.	Baking Soda
1 tsp.	Cloves
1 tsp.	Cinnamon
3 Cups	Flour

Dredge fruits and nuts in flour and set aside. Cream butter and sugar until light yellow. Add eggs and cream until well mixed. Add applesauce and spices mixing well. Stir in flour with fruit and nuts. Butter and flour an angle food cake pan. Bake in a pre-heated 350° oven for1 to 1-½ hours. Turn out onto a rack and let cool.

Black Walnut Cake

Ma

Servings: 10

We had a black walnut tree in the yard and in the late fall we would gather the nuts and crack them open. Ma would make a delicious cake with the meats.

2 cups	Flour
2 ¼ tsp.	Baking Powder
¼ tsp	Salt
2/3 cups	Shortening
11/2 cups	Sugar
1 tsp.	Vanilla
3	Eggs, separated
¾ cup	Milk
1 ½ cups	Black walnuts, ground

Grease 2 9-inch cake pans. Beat egg whites until stiff, set aside. Sift flour, baking powder and salt together, set aside. Cream shortening with sugar and vanilla until fluffy. Add egg yolks to mixture and mix thoroughly. Add dry ingredients and milk alternately, beating well after each addition. Stir in nuts, fold in egg whites. Pour into greased pans and bake at 350° for 30 minutes. Cool and ice with a 7-*Minutes Icing*

Carrot Cake

Ma
Servings: 10-12

I like this recipe because it is a chewy, fragrant cake

1 1/2 cups	Oil
4	Eggs
2 cups	Sugar
3 cups	Grated carrots
1 cup	Walnuts, chopped
2 cups	Flour
2 tsp.	Baking Powder
1 tsp	Cinnamon
1/2 tsp.	Salt

Beat oil and eggs. Gradually beat in sugar. Add and thoroughly mix in carrots and nuts. Sift flour, baking powder, cinnamon and salt. Add to first mixture, mixing it in by hand. Pour batter into two greased and floured 9-inch cake pans. Bake at 350° for 55 minutes. Frost with *Cream Cheese Frosting*

Cherry Cheesecake

Servings: 10-12

Nicole's favorite. I usually make this for her birthday.

1 box	Yellow cake mix
1 Tbsp.	Oil
1 1/2 cups	Milk
2-8oz.	Cream cheese, softened
3 Tbsp.	Lemon juice
3 tsp.	Vanilla
1/2 cup	Sugar
4	Eggs
1 jar	Cherry pie filling mix

Pre-heat oven to 300°. Reserve 1 cup of dry cake mix. In large mixing bowl combine remaining cake mix, 1 egg and oil. Mixture will be crumbly. Press crust mixture evenly into bottom and 3/4 the way up the sides of a greased 13x9x2-inch pan. In same bowl blend cream cheese and sugar. Add 3 eggs and reserved cake mix, beat 1 minute at medium speed. At low speed slowly add flavoring; mix until smooth. Pour into crust. Bake at 300° for 45-55 minutes or until center is firm. When cool, top with pie filling. Chill well before serving. Store in refrigerate. **NOTE:** Pineapple Cheese Cake: Make *Pineapple Sauce* and top cake with this instead of Cherry pie filling.

Chocolate Mayonnaise Cake

Servings: 10-12

I think you will enjoy this, it is something different! A moist and rich cake which will keep people guessing as to how you made it.

2 cups	Flour
1 ¼ cup	Unsweetened cocoa
1/4 tsp.	Baking powder
1 ¼ tsp.	Baking soda
3	Eggs
1 2/3 cups	Sugar
1 ¼ tsp.	Vanilla
1 cup	Mayonnaise (do not use salad dressing)
1 1/3 cups	Cool water

Sift first 4 ingredients together and set aside. At high-speed mix the eggs, sugar and vanilla for 3 minutes. At low speed, add mayonnaise, and then add sifted ingredients alternating with the water until batter is smooth. Pour into greased and floured 9-inch cake pans. Bake in a 350° oven for 30 to35 minutes. Remove and cool on wire racks. Ice with *Chocolate Butter Icing* or *7-Minute Icing.*

Daffodil cake

Servings: 10-12

I entered this recipe in a baking contest given by Gimbels department store when I was a teenager. I won 1st prize in the junior division. All the entries were frozen and sent to the military fighting in Korea.

1 cup	Cake flour
1/4 cup plus 2 Tbsp.	Sugar
12	Egg whites
1 ½ tsp.	Cream of tartar
1/4 tsp.	Salt
3/4 cup	Sugar
6	Egg yolks
1 ½ tsp.	Vanilla
1/2 tsp.	Almond extract

Stir flour and 3/4 cup, plus 2 Tbsp. sugar and set aside. In large bowl, beat egg whites, cream of tartar and salt until foamy. Add 3/4-cup sugar, slowly beating at high speed until the eggs hold a stiff peak. Fold flavoring into egg whites. In small bowl, beat egg yolks until very thick and lemon colored, up to 5 minutes. Set aside. Sprinkle flour mixture, 1/4 at a time over egg whites, folding in just until flour mixture disappears. Pour half the batter into another bow. Gently fold egg yolks to this mixture. Spoon yellow and white batters alternately into an ungreased tube pan. Cut through batters to swirl. Bake at 375° for about 40 minutes or until top springs back when touched. Invert pan on funnel and let hang until the cake is completely cool. Use knife to go around all sides of pan. Remove to serving plate. Frost with *Lemon Butter Frosting.* To decorate, place a small container of daffodils in the center of the cake.

Dark Chocolate Cake

Servings: 1 9-inch cake

This is one of Mother's favorite. I have made it for her birthday cake.

2/3 cup	Butter
1/2 cup	Sugar
2 1/2 cups	Cake flour
2/3 cup	Unsweetened cocoa
1/4 tsp.	Baking powder
1 tsp.	Baking soda
1 1/4 cup	Water
2 tsp.	Vanilla

Heat oven to 350°. Grease and flour 2 9-inch round pans. Cream butter, sugar and eggs, together for 5 minutes, until fluffy. Sift dry ingredients together. Add, alternately, with water and vanilla. Pour into pans. Bake 35-40 minutes. Cool. Then frost with *Chocolate Butter Icing.*

English See Cake

Servings: 15 slices

Grandmom Meddings made her recipe from scratch. This is my shortcut.

1 box	Pound cake mix
2 Tbsp.	Caraway seeds
	ICING
1 lb.	10X sugar
1 Tbsp.	Fresh lemon juice
1 tsp.	Grated lemon rind

Prepare cake as per directions. Add the caraway seeds to the cake batter and bake, using a loaf pan, as directed. When cake is baked and cooled, mix the sugar, juice and rind together in a small mixing bowl, adding more juice if necessary to make icing thin enough to pour, (but not too thin.) Pour over cake. TO SERVE: Slice in thin slices or cut into fingers of cake. Serve with tea for a delicious combination.

Fruit Cake

Servings: About 2 ½ pounds

This is my short cut recipe. George loves to eat this cake in thick chunks. Ma always served her fruitcake in thin slices.

1	Egg
1 cup	Water
1 cup	Raisins
1 cup	Walnut or pecans, chopped
2 cups, (1 lb.)	Candied fruitcake mix
1 box	Bread mix, date or nut (if making a double batch use 1 box of each)
1 jigger	Rum
1 jigger	Apple Jack

Grease and flour two 8x5 inch loaf pans. If doubling recipe use a tube pan, or four loaf pans. In large bowl combine egg and water. Add remaining ingredients except rum and applejack. Stir until mixed well. Pour into pan. Bake 350° for 60-70 minutes or until toothpick inserted in center comes out clean. Cool 15 minutes, loosen edges, and remove from pan. Cool completely. Use rum and applejack to pour over cake. Wrap in a good layer of aluminum foil and store in a dark cool place. Best if stored for several weeks, adding rum and apple jack each week before serving. Cut into thin slices to serve. **NOTE:** Can decorate cake with candied cherries, pineapple and nuts before backing.

Gingerbread

Ma
Servings: 9

Ma often served gingerbread with *Apple Fluff* in the fall.

1 cup	Molasses, unsulfered
1 cup	Milk, soured*
2 1/4 cups	Flour
2 tsp.	Baking soda
1/3 cup	Sugar
1 tsp.	Ginger, ground
1/2 tsp.	Salt
1	Egg, well beaten
1/2 cup	Butter, melted

Mix molasses and milk. Sift dry ingredients together and add to liquids. Add egg and butter and beat until smooth. Pour into greased 9x9 inch baking dish and bake at 350° for 30 minutes. Good served warm. **NOTE:** *To sour milk see *Tips on Food.*

Jelly Roll

Ma
Servings: 8

Another dessert Ma made often. It is simple, easy and a nice treat.

5	Eggs, separated
1 cup	Sugar
1	Lemon, juice and rind, grated
1 cup	Cake flour
Pinch	Salt
1 cup	Strawberry, raspberry, apricot, or currant jelly or jam as desired
	10x sugar

Beat egg whites to a soft peak, add 1/2-cup sugar and continue to beat until stiff. Beat egg yolks until thick and lemon colored. Add the rest of the sugar and beat until stiff add grated lemon rind and juice. Fold yolks into egg whites. Combine dry ingredients and fold carefully into egg mixture. Line a jellyroll pan, 11x 16 inch, with waxed or parchment paper. Pour batter into pan and spread evenly. Bake at 350° for 15 minutes. Do not over bake. Sift 10x sugar heavily on a clean tea towel. Turn cake onto tea towel and remove pan and paper carefully. Trim edges so that the cake will roll easily. While still hot begin to roll cake using the towel to roll the cake away from you. Wrap the roll in the towel and let cool. When cool, unroll cake and spread the entire cake with the jelly. To make this easier, whip the jelly with a whisk. Roll again. Let rest before cutting. Can be refrigerated.

Orange Cake

Aunt Theresa given to me by her daughter, Vasso,
Servings: 16

When I asked Vasso for some of her mother's recipes, she gave me this one. Not only did she give me the receipt, she brought me the cake. I must say it is deliouse. Try it and you will agree!

1 recipe	Yellow cake mix
3	Oranges, quartered and seed removed
¾ Cup	Sugar
½ Stick	Butter
3 Tbsp.	Cake Batter

Bake cake as per directions. While cake is baking blend oranges in blender put all ingredients in a saucepan. Cook over low heat stirring constantly for 15-20 minuets until thickens. Ice cake when the cake is still warm, in between layers and on top. This keeps the moisture in the cake. Refrigerate any leftovers.

Orange Juice Cake

Uncle Harold
Servings: 1 9-inch

This recipe went around the family for years. Uncle Harold was the one who gave it to Ma.

2 1/4 cups	Flour
1 1/2 cups	Sugar
4 tsp.	Baking powder
1 tsp.	Salt
1 cup, concentrated	Orange juice
1 tsp.	Vanilla
1/2 cup	Shortening
3	Eggs

Mix all ingredients, except eggs, in a bowl. Beat two minutes. Add eggs, beat two minutes more. Pour into a greased tube pan and bake at 375° for 45 minutes. **NOTE:** On Smith's Island this cake is baked in 7 very thin layers and a orange juice glaze of juice and 10X sugar is pour over each layer and let stand until the glaze is set. Yum!!

Pineapple Upside-Down Cake

Ma

Servings: 8

Something Ma would whip up for a quick dessert.

1/2 cup	Butter
1 cup	Dark brown sugar, packed
1 can	Pineapple, sliced, drained, save juice
12	Pecans, whole pieces
12-15	Maraschino cherries
1 cup	Cake flour
1 tsp.	Baking Powder
Pinch	Salt
3	Eggs, separated
1 cup	Sugar
6 Tbsp.	Pineapple juice

Melt butter in a 10 inch baking dish. Sprinkle brown sugar over butter and arrange pineapple slices, pecans and maraschino cherries over sugar. Set aside and make batter. Beat egg whites stiff and set aside. Sift flour, salt, baking powder together. Beat egg yolks until light. Add sugar and beat. Add pineapple juice. Add dry ingredients slowly. Fold in egg whites and pour over pineapple. Bake at 375° for 30 to 35 minutes. Turn upside down on serving plate. Serve warm with whipped cream. **NOTE:** *See Food Tips* for whipping cream.

Pinwheel Cake

Servings: 10-12

I made this cake at a very young age. Everyone loved it and still does.

2 squares, (2-oz)	Unsweetened chocolate, melted
1 3/4 cups	Cake flour
2 tsp.	Baking powder
1/4 tsp.	Baking soda
1 1/2 cup	Sugar
1 tsp.	Salt
1/2 cup	Shortening, softened
11/4 cup	Evaporated milk
1 tsp.	Vanilla
2	Eggs
2 squares (2 oz.)	Unsweetened chocolate, melted

Sift dry ingredients together. Add shortening, 1 cup of milk and vanilla. Mix to dampen dry ingredients. Beat 2 minutes at high speed. Add eggs, 1/4 cup of milk and 2 oz. chocolate. Beat 1 minute. Pour into lined 9" layer pans. Melt 2 more squares of chocolate. Pour in a circle on top of the batter in each pan, about 1" from rims. With a rubber spatula, swirl the chocolate in continuous circles, once around the pan. Bake in oven at 350° for about 30 minutes. Cool. Split each layer into two layers. Spread *Fluffy Chocolate Filling* between the three layers only. Chill before serving.

Potato Cake

Ma

Servings: 24

I make this cake each Christmas. This cake is very large. Serve in thin slices, as it is so rich.

1 cup	Butter
2 cups	Sugar
1 cup	Potato, finely mashed, warm
4	Eggs, separated, well beaten
1/2 cup	Cream
4 oz.	Unsweetened chocolate, melted
1 tsp.	Vanilla
1 tsp.	Cinnamon
1 cup	Nuts, chopped
1 1/2 cups	Flour
2 tsp.	Baking Powder

Cream butter and sugar. Add potato, then egg yolks, then cream, melted chocolate and spices. Mix and sift the flour and baking powder. Dredge the nuts with the flour. Mix into batter. Fold in egg whites. Pour batter into greased and floured tube pan. Bake at 350-375° for 50-60 minutes. Cool and ice with *Chocolate Fudge Frosting.* **NOTE:** See *Food Tips* about nuts

Sauerkraut Cake

Servings: 10-12

Try it, it is great! Your quests will never guess what the secret ingredient could be!

1/2 cup	Butter
1 1/2 cups	Sugar
3	Eggs
1 tsp.	Vanilla
2 cups	Flour
1 tsp.	Baking soda
1 tsp.	Baking Powder
1/4 tsp.	Salt
1/2 cup	Unsweetened cocoa
8 oz. can	Sauerkraut rinsed, drained, and finely snipped

In large mixing bowl, cream butter and sugar until light. Beat in eggs, one at a time. Add vanilla. Sift together, flour, baking powder, baking soda, salt, and cocoa, add to creamed mixture alternately with water, beating after each addition. Stir in sauerkraut. Turn into greased and floured 13x9 in. pan. Bake at 350° for 30-35 minuets. Cool in pan. Frost with *Sour Cream Chocolate Frosting*. Cut into squares to serve.

Sherryl's Cherry Cheesecakes

Servings: 12

Sherryl always brings a large tray of these to a party. They are simple but oh so good.

12	Vanilla wafer cookies
2-8 oz. packages	Cream cheese, softened
3/4 cup	Sugar
2	Eggs
½ tsp.	Vanilla
1 jar	Cherry pie filling mix

Place a cookie in the bottom of lined muffin pan cups. Beat cream cheese, softened, sugar and eggs with an electric mixer until fluffy. Fold in vanilla. Spoon filling into each muffin pan cup, filling about 2/3 full. Bake at 350° for 30 minutes. Turn off oven, open door slightly. Let cool in oven for 30 minutes. Remove and cool completely. Top with cherry pie filling. Refrigerate at least 1 hour. **NOTE:** To vary, use different flavoring, like lemon, orange, rum etc. as well as topping, as blueberry, peach or use fresh fruit as a topping.

Steamed Fruit Cake

Ma

Servings: 25-30

This is the cake that takes a whole day to bake. It is dark and very good.

2 cups	Shortening
2 2/3 cup	Light brown sugar, packed
9	Eggs, beaten
1/2 cup	Molasses
1 cup	Strong coffee
1/2 cup	Fruit juice
1 tsp.	Vanilla
1/2 tsp.	Baking soda
5 1/2 cups	Flour
3 tsp.	Baking powder
2 Tbsp.	Cinnamon
1 Tbsp.,	Cloves
1 Tbsp.	Nutmeg
1 tsp.	Salt
2 lbs.	Raisins, chopped
3/4 lb.	Citron, candied, cut fine
1/4 lb.	Lemon peel, candied, cut fine
1/4 lb.	Orange peel, candies, cut fine
2 cups	Nuts, chopped

Cream shortening and sugar together. Add eggs, stirring until well mixed. Add molasses, coffee, juice, and vanilla. Dissolve the baking soda in a tablespoon of hot water, then add to the mixture and stir. Sift flour, reserving 1 cup to dredge fruit. Sift remaining flour with baking powder, spices and salt. Add the flour to the mixture and beat. Dredge* all the fruit and nuts in a large container. Add the batter to the fruit and stir very well until thoroughly mixed. Grease and lined with wax paper the container. You can decorate the top with whole almond and candied cherries or candied pineapple. Place in a steamer and steam for 3 hours. The large cake takes 5 hours. Remove to a 300° oven and bake 1 hour. Large cake can take up to 1 1/2 hours or until center comes out dry. Cool completely, even over night. Use a jigger each of dark rum and Applejack to pour over top. Wrap well will aluminum foil and put in a dark place to ripen, about 3 to 4 weeks. Using a jigger each rum and applejack to bath cake each week. Cut in thin slices. **NOTE:** Can use tube pan for one large cake or 2 large loaf pans or several small loaf pans. **NOTE:** *Dredge means to completely cover the fruit and nuts with flour so that they will not sink to the bottom of the cake.

Tomato Spice Cake

Jean Allen

Servings: 8-10

This is George Junior's favorite cake. I usually make it for his birthday.

1 box	Spice cake mix
1 can consented	Tomato soup, undiluted
1/2 cup	Water
2	Eggs
1 cup	Nuts, chopped, (optional)

Mix all ingredients together until batter is smooth. If desired fold in nuts. Bake as directed on cake mix box for 2 layers. Ice with *Cream Cheese Frosting.*

DESSERTS CANDY

Candy Mix

Women of the Fortnightly
Servings: About 20 cups

Great to package up for holiday or hostess gift.

4 cups	Corn Chex
4 cups	Rice Chex
4 cups	Cherrios
4 cups	Small round pretzels
12-oz. Jar	Dry roasted peanuts
1-16 oz bag	M&M candies
2-16 oz. Bags	White chocolate chips

Melt white chocolate chips. Pour over the other ingredients. Mix well. Spread out on cookie sheets to dry. Break up into small chunks and store in plastic bags.

Chocolate "Hay Stacks"

Servings: 25-30

This recipe comes from Joan Neilson a Woman's Club friend. It's easy and fun.

1 large can	Chinese noodles
8-oz.	Semi-chocolate chips
8 oz.	Butterscotch chips

Heat chips together until melted. Watch and stir constantly. "Crunch" noodles into mall pieces. Stir into melted chips. Stir to coat. Peanuts, raisins, or coconut can also be added now if wanted. Place on cookie sheets lined with foil in small walnut size mounds, Refrigerate until hard.

Then place in a container for you own use or package it nicely for a lovely gift.

Irish Potatoes

Servings: About 30

I double and triple this recipe for family and friends. They disappear very quickly.

6 oz.	Coconut
1 lb.	10x sugar
1 tsp.	Vanilla
About 3 Tbsp.	Milk
	Cinnamon

Mix together everything except cinnamon, adding more milk in very small amounts if necessary to make the sugar and coconut hold together in small balls. Roll in cinnamon, twice. Store in airtight container. Will get firmer as the candy ages.

Stuffed Dates and Prunes

Servings: 15-20

When I was a child this is something we served at the holidays for a nice sweet. It is still a yearly treat.

1 lb. Whole	Dates and/ or
1 lb. of seedless	Prunes
1 jar	Peanut butter, chunky
1/2 pieces	Walnuts, or pecans
	Coconut, Grated
	Candied cherries
	10X sugar

If the dates have seeds, cut open and remove. Stuff the dates or prunes with any of the ingredients above or a combination. I like to start with peanut butter then add your choice of fillings. When stuffed, roll fruit in 10 X sugar and place on a plate in a decorative manner. Refrigerate.

Sugared Pecans

Mrs. Emerine Long
Servings: 16

Mrs. Long was a long time friend of Mother. She lived to be 97. She served these nuts to me on my last visit and shared the recipe with me.

2 cups	Pecans halves
1	Egg white
1 tsp.	Water
1/2 cup	Sugar
1/4 tsp.	Salt
1/2 tsp.	Cinnamon

Beat egg white and water together until foamy. Mix sugar and cinnamon together. Mix everything together and spread on a cookie sheet. Bake at 225° for 1 hour. Remove from sheet or loosen immediately. Cool and store in airtight container.

Taffy or Pulled Sugar

Aunt Linda

This is something that Aunt Linda introduced us to. Taffy. We would have so much fun with this project and then we got to eat it.

4 cups	Sugar
1 cup	Water
1/4 tsp.	Cream of tartar
1 Tbsp.	Light corn syrup

Put the sugar and water in a saucepan and set in a warm place to dissolve. When thoroughly dissolved place on heat and add the corn syrup and cream of tartar. Cook as quickly as possible to 312° on candy thermometer. Or to the hard cracked stage. Dip the pan into cold water to stop the boiling. Then pour the syrup onto a slightly oiled slab or counter. As the syrup cools lift the edges toward the center with a knife. When the taffy cools enough to handle, roll it into a ball and begin pulling it from each side, pulling the taffy into the center. Work fast and keep the taffy warm. This is when two people can pull the candy. Pull and fold into the center, pull again, keep pulling. The candy will get whiter as you pull it. When the candy gets very white this is the time to make shapes with the taffy. Can cut pieces off and make sausage shaped pieces. Enjoy the fun but keep the candy warm or it will harden in one big piece. Work fast!

DESSERTS COOKIES

Aggression Cookies

Servings: 15 dozen

The children loved to make these at Christmas each year. I still make them yearly. The name comes from all the squeezing and pounding of the dough. You can get your Aggressions out!

3 cups	Light b Light brown sugar, packed
3 cups	Butter
6 cups	Oatmeal
1 Tbsp.	Baking soda
3 cups	Flour

Put all ingredients into a large bowl and mash, knead, squeeze, and beat until mixed well. Make into small balls the size of a walnut. Put on an ungreased cookie sheet, about 2 inches apart. Butter the bottom of a glass and dip into granulated sugar and mash each ball. Coating the bottom of the glass with sugar for each cookie. Bake at 350° for 12 minutes. Lift from cookie sheet when done and cool on rack. Store in a closed container. Can be frozen. Boy, that felt good! **NOTE:** The recipe makes about 15 dozen so you can cut in half if you don't want that many cookies.

Almond Oatmeal Wafers

Marjorie Evans
Servings: 4 doz.

This is Mothers recipe. She made them often for her grandchildren.

1/3 cup	Flour
1/4 tsp.	Salt
1/4 tsp.	Baking powder
1/4 cup	Butte, softened
1/2 cup	Sugar
2 Tbsp.	Corn syrup, dark
1 tsp.	Vanilla
2 Tbsp.	Milk
1/2 cup	Oatmeal, quick cook
1/2 cup	Almonds, blanched, finely chopped
3 squares (3 oz.)	Semi-sweet chocolate

Mix flour, salt and baking powder. In bowl beat butter, sugar, corn syrup and vanilla with wooden spoon or electric mixer until well blended. Stir in flour mixture alternately with milk until well blended. Stir in oats and almonds. Drop by level teaspoon 2 inches apart onto foil lined cookie sheet. Bake in pre-heated 350° oven 12-14 minutes until edges brown. Cool completely on sheet on rack. Remove from foil with thin blade spatula. Melt chocolate over hot water. Drizzle from spoon over cookies. Chill until chocolate is set. Store in tightly covered container in a cool place with wax paper between layers.

Brownies

Servings: 16

Orange rind gives the special zinger to this recipe. The juice keeps them moist.

1 cup	Flour
1/2 tsp.	Baking powder
1/2 tsp.	Salt
2/3 cup	Butter, softened
1 cup	10x sugar
2	Eggs
3 oz.	Unsweetened chocolate, melted
1 1/2 tsp.	Vanilla
1 cup	Nuts, optional
1/3 cup	Orange rind, grated

Sift together flour, baking powder and salt. Mix butter and sugar together. Beat eggs, one at a time into sugar mixture until light and fluffy. Stir in melted chocolate, vanilla and orange rind and nuts if used. Gradually add flour mixture while stirring. Turn into greased 9-inch square baking dish. Bake at 350° for 25 to 30 minute. Cut into squares; remove from pan to cool.

Chocolate Chip Heart Cookie

Servings: 1-10 inch cookie

For many years I have made George and both the children a large heart shaped cookie. For Valentine's day The recipe is very easily.

1 Recipe from the back of chocolate chip bag

Place entire recipe in a 10-inch heart shaped cake pan. Bake for about 30 minutes or until the cookie pulls away from the pan. Remove from pan and cool on rack. Can be decorated with frosting. Wrap with plastic wrap and present to your love!

Classic Butter Cookies

Servings: 2-4 dozen

This butter cookie recipe for cutout cookies, is the best I have found in all the years of my cookie baking

1 cup	Butter
1 cup	Sugar
1	Egg
1 tsp.	Vanilla
3 cups, about	Flour
2 tsp.	Baking powder
	Water, if necessary

Preheat oven to 400°. In a large bowl, cream butter and sugar. Add egg and vanilla, beat. Sift flour and baking powder, add to butter mixture, 1 cup at a time. Mix after each addition. This is a very stiff dough. If necessary to get all of the flour in the batter, use water, a teaspoon at a time. Don't chill dough. Make 2 balls of the dough. Flour surface and roll each ball out to a 1/8-inch thickness. Use desired cutter shape to cut out cookie. Keep cutter shape floured. Use ungreased cookie sheet to place cookies on. Bake according to size of cookie, starting at 5 minutes, and baking as long as 7-8 minutes pr until lightly browned. **NOTE:** Sometimes I like to ice and decorate these cookies.

Lemon Squares

Martha Davis
Servings: 16 squares

A very good recipe for this old time favorite.

1 cup	Flour
1/2 cup	Butter, softened
1/4 cup	10x sugar
	Filling
1 cup	Sugar
1/2 tsp.	Baking powder
1/4 tsp.	Salt
3 Tbsp.	Lemon juice

Preheat oven to 350°. Mix together first three ingredients and press into the bottom and up the side (1/2-inch) of an 8x8 inch baking pan. Bake for 10 minutes. Combine the rest of the ingredients in a bowl and mix for 3 minutes but do not make foamy. With crust in oven pour filling over baked crust. Bake for additional 20 min. sprinkle 10X sugar generously over filling while still hot. Cool. Cut into squares.

Magical Cookies

Servings: 24 bars

A quick cookie and oh so good.

1 stick	Butter
1 1/2 cups	Graham cracker crumbs
1 can.	Condensed milk (Do not use evaporated milk)
1-6 oz bag,	Semi-sweet chocolate chips
1 cup	Coconut
1 cup	Pecans
1/2 cup	Cranberries, dried (optional)
1/2 cup	Cherries, dried, (optional)
1/2 cup	Candied cherries, chopped (optional)

Preheat oven to 350°. Put butter in a 13x9-inch baking dish and melt in oven. Sprinkle graham cracker crumbs over butter and press on the bottom of dish. Sprinkle the chocolate chips over crumbs, then sprinkle coconut then nuts. Add any one of the optional items. Press down lightly. Top layers with condensed milk, bake for 30 minutes or until lightly browned. Cool thoroughly before cutting into bars.

Peanut Butter Cookies

Servings: 2 dozen

If you like peanut butter cookies, make many batches of these easy cookies. I won a Blue Ribbon for this recipe at District 3 of Federated Woman Club of NJ, achievement day.

1 cup	Peanut butter, chunky (I use Skippy)
1 cup	Sugar
1	Egg, beaten
	Candied cherries cut in half

Mix peanut butter and sugar. Stir in egg, Drop on ungreased cookie sheets, top with 1/2 candied cherry. Bake 350° for 12-15 minutes. **NOTE:** I make this recipe and multiply it by 4 to suite the appetites of the family. **NOTE:** You can use chocolate chips to use in place of the cherries. I often make some of each.

Russian Butter Cookies

Servings: 2 dozen

I have made this cookie at Christmastime since I was a teenager. I usually have to at least double the recipe to keep everyone with enough cookies.

½ cup	Butter
2 Tbsp.	Honey
1 cup	Flour
¼ tsp.	Salt
1 tsp.	Vanilla
1 cup	Pecans or Walnut, finely chopped
	10X Sugar

Beat butter until creamy. Stir in the rest of the ingredients except 10X sugar. Chill 1 h our. Roll into balls the size of a walnut. Place 2 inches apart on a greased cookie sheet in a 300° oven for 35 minutes or until lightly brown. Remove from cookie sheet and roll in 10 X sugar, place on rack to cool. Roll again in 10X sugar after cookies are cooled. Store in airtight container. Cookie improves in flavor with time.

Scottish Shortbread

Servings: 12-15 cookies

This is another recipe I took from a cookbook while I was in England. This is why the measurements are as written.

4 oz.	Flour
2 oz.	Rice flour*
Pinch	Salt
2 oz.	Sugar
4 oz.	Butter
	10x sugar for dredge

Heat oven to 325°. Lightly grease a baking sheet and dust with rice flour. Do the same with a 7-inch mold. Sift the two flours and the salt into a large bowl. Stir in the sugar with a dinner knife. Cut the butter into the flour until the mixture resembles very large breadcrumbs and clings together. Knead the mixture into a smooth crack-free ball. If the dough becomes sticky cover with foil and refrigerate for 10 minutes. Press the shortbread into the mould with flour on your hands. Holding the mold close too the prepared baking pan too the base and the shortbread will come out. Mark shortbread into portions on top using a sharp knife. Do not cut all the way though. Bake in center of the oven for 45 minutes until very pale golden in color and firm to the touch. Do not remove shortbread from baking sheet. Cool on a wire rack for 10 minutes. Transfer shortbread to a wire rack to finish cooling. Dredge with sugar and cut on lines into pieces. **NOTE:** * Rice flour can be found in health food stores

DESSERTS CUSTARD

Banana Pudding

Ma
Servings: 6-8

Uncle Ellsworth's favorite.

2 cups	Bananas, ripe, mashed
1 cup	Milk
2/3 cup	Sugar
4	Eggs, separated
1/2 cup	Butter, melted
1/4 tsp.	Cinnamon
1/4 tsp.	Nutmeg
1 tsp.	Vanilla
Pinch	Cream of tartar

Beat egg white with 1/4 cup of the sugar and a pinch of cream of tartar into firm peaks, set aside. Mix rest of ingredients well, pour into a greased 1-½ quart baking dish. Bake at 350° for 1 hour. Top with egg whites, making sure that meringue touches all sides of dish. Bake for a few minutes more until meringue is slightly brown. Cool. Serve room temperature or cold.

Caramel Custard

Servings: 6

A wonderful sauce for baked apples

2	Eggs, slightly beaten
1/8 tsp.	Salt
1/4 cup	Dark brown sugar, packed
2 cups	Milk, scalded
1/2 tsp.	Vanilla

Combine eggs, salt and sugar. Add milk slowly and cook over low heat until mixture coats a spoon. Add vanilla. Divide equally into 6 dishes and chill. Top with warm baked apple, serve.

Egg Custard

Ma
Servings: 4

Ma's easy custard and George's favorite.

1 pint	Milk
3	Eggs
1/3 cup	Sugar
1 tsp.	Lemon juice
1 Tbsp.	Vanilla

Beat eggs separately. Mix other ingredients together. Stir in beaten egg yolks, then fold in whites. Bake in a greased baking dish set in a larger dish filled 1/2 way up the custard dish with hot water. Bake at 400° for 30 minutes. Test with a knife inserted near the center. It should come out clean, Serve warn or cold.

Flan

Servings: 6

Dorothy Brandt's favorite and her brother's as well.

3 cups	Milk
1	Lemon rind
1	Cinnamon stick
3/4 cup	Sugar
1/3 cup	Water
4	Eggs, whole
4	Egg yolks
3/4 cup	Sugar

Scald the milk with the lemon rind and cinnamon stick and let stand in a warm place for 15 minutes to infuse. Use water and sugar to make the syrup by heating until the sugar melts then boil the mixture, without stirring, until it is a dark golden caramel. Immediately remove and pour caramel into a 5-cup soufflé or baking dish, quickly tilting the dish around until the bottom and sides are coated. Thoroughly beat the whole eggs, egg yolks and sugar together, stir in the hot milk. Strain this mixture into the prepared baking dish and place in a pan filled 1/2 way up the dish with hot water. Bake in a pre heated 350° over for 40 to 50 minutes or until knife inserted near center comes out clean. Remove from oven and from water bath. Let cool. Before serving loosen sides with a knife and invert onto a server plate with a rim to hold the caramel sauce.

Snow Cream

Ma

Servings: 6-8

A childhood favorite I made for my children as well. First you make the custard, then send the children out for the snow. Add to the custard and serve.

1 qt.	Milk, scalded
4 Tbsp.	Corn starch
1	Egg
1/2 cup	Sugar
1 tsp.	Vanilla
Large bowl of clean, dry	Snow

Mix small amount of milk with cornstarch and beaten egg. Add mixture to hot milk and sugar. Cool and add vanilla. Add snow until mixture thickens. Eat immediately.

DESSERTS FROSTING

Chocolate Butter Icing

Servings: 1-9 inch cake

This is very rich icing. If you love chocolate, this is for you.

1/3 cup	Butter, softened
3 cups	10x sugar, sifted
1 1/2 tsp.	Vanilla
3 squares (3 oz.)	Unsweetened chocolate, melted
3 Tbsp	Cream

Blend butter and sugar. Add cream and vanilla. Stir until smooth. Blend in melted chocolate. For extra richness, add 1 egg

Cream Cheese Frosting

Jean Allen
Servings: 9-inch cake

Great for tomato spice cake, spice cake, carrot cake.

2-3 oz.	Cream cheese, softened
1 lb.	10x sugar, sifted
1/2 tsp.	Vanilla

Blend cream cheese until smooth. Gradually blend in 10x sugar and vanilla. If needed to thin for spreading consistency, use small amount of milk.

Fluffy Chocolate Filling

Servings: 1 9-inch cake

This filling goes with the pinwheel cake.

1 square (1 oz.)	Unsweetened chocolate, melted and 1 cooled
1/2 cup	Shortening
1/2 cup	Sugar
1/3 cup	Evaporated milk
1 Tbsp.	Water
1/4 tsp.	Salt
1 tsp.	Vanilla

Using a small bowl, combine all ingredients. Beat on high for 10 minutes or until fluffy.

Fudge Icing

Servings: 1-8-inch cake

Try this recipe for a lush topping for your favorite cake.

2 cups	Sugar
2 Tbsp.	Corn syrup, light
3 ounces	Unsweetened chocolate
1/2 cup	Milk
1 tsp.	Vanilla
2 Tbsp.	Butter

Cook sugar, corn syrup, chocolate and milk, stirring constantly to 232° on a candy thermometer. Remove from heat, add vanilla and butter. Cool to lukewarm without stirring. Beat until creamy and thick enough to spread. Will cover top and sides of two 8-inch layers. **NOTE:** If you don't have a candy thermometer, the test to determine the temperature is to drop a small amount of the syrup into cold water and it should form a very soft ball.

Lemon Butter Frosting

Servings: 1 9-inch cake

This is so simple and easy.

1/3 cup	Butter
3 cups	10x sugar
2 Tbsp.	Lemon juice

Blend butter and sugar. Stir in lemon juice beating until smooth.

Penuche Icing

Ma
Servings: 1 9-inch cake

My all time favorite icing.

½ cup	Butter
1 cup	Dark brown sugar, packed
2 cups	10x sugar, sifted
¼ cup	Milk

Melt butter in saucepan. Add brown sugar. Bring to boil over low flame for 2 minutes, stirring constantly. Add milk stirring constantly. Remove and cool to lukewarm. Gradually add 10x sugar until thick enough to spread. If too stiff, add a little HOT water. Good on spice or date/nut cake

Seven Minute Frosting

Servings: 9-inch cake or 34 cupcakes

This fluffily frosting requires some work but very well worth it.

1 1/2 cups	Sugar
Dash	Salt
2 tsp.	Light corn syrup
6 Tbsp.	Water
2	Egg whites
1 tsp.	Vanilla

Combine all ingredients except vanilla in the top of a double boiler. Beat at high speed for 1 minute then place over boiling water and beat for 7 minutes. The frosting should stand in high stiff peaks. Remove from heat, pour into a large bowl and add vanilla. Beat for another minute until thick enough to spread. Wonderful for spice, applesauce, or chocolate cakes.

Sour Cream-Chocolate Frosting

Servings: 1 9-inch cake

Delicious frosting for Sauerkraut cake or for any cake.

6 oz. Package	Semi-sweet chocolate
4 Tbsp.	Butter
1 cup	Sour cream
1 tsp.	Vanilla
1/4 tsp.	Salt
2 1/2 to 2 3/4 cups	10x sugar

Heat chocolate chips and butter together. Remove from heat, blend in sour cream, vanilla and salt. Gradually add 10x sugar to make spreading consistency. Beat well. Ice cake.

DESSERTS FRUIT

Ambrosia

Ma
Servings: 6

One of Ma's quick desserts

6 Orange, peeled, sliced
10x sugar
Coconut freshly grated or packed flaked

In a bowl layer orange slices, 10 X sugar and coconut. Refrigerate until well chilled. Serve.

Apple Fluff

Servings: 6

This is what Ma would serve with warm *gingerbread*

1 2/3 cups	Applesauce, cold, unsweetened
Dash	Nutmeg
Pinch	Salt
1 tsp.	Vanilla
2	Egg whites
1/4 cup	Sugar

Beat egg whites until fluffy, then add sugar, beat until stiff. Mix all other ingredients together and fold egg whites into the mixture. Chill and serve in bowls. You can top with whipped cream if desired. **NOTE:** Make sure you use very fresh eggs.

Baked Apples

Servings: 6

Serve warm in a custard sauce, top with the juice of the apples.

6	Winesap or other crisp, tart apples
2 Tbsp.	Raisins
2 Tbsp.	Pecans
2 Tbsp.,	Apricots, dried, diced
2 Tbsp.	Lemon rind, candied
1/4 tsp.	Nutmeg
1/4 tsp.	Cloves
2/3 cups	Dark brown sugar, packed

Core and peel an inch from the top of apple. Chop fruits and nuts. Mix fruits, nuts, spices and sugar together and stuff in apple. Make sure that the apple is full to the bottom. Place in baking dish and just cover the bottom of dish with water. Bake at 350° for 1 hour. **NOTE:** If juice is to thin, remove from baking dish, place in small saucepan and boil to reduce to 1/2. Serve apples warm in cold *custard sauce* with juice from apples.

Banana Pancakes

Ma
Servings: 14-16 cakes

Ma's special treat.

2 cups	Baking mix
2	Eggs
¾ to 1 cup	Milk
2-3	Very ripe bananas
1 recipe	Vanilla Pudding

OR

1 lg. Boxed, cooked	Vanilla pudding,
½-1 cup	Milk

Mix baking mix, eggs and milk or your favorite recipe for pancakes and add the bananas that have been mashed well. Place about 1/2 cup of batter on hot griddle or frying pan. Turn when bubble form on top. Brown other side and remove to platter. Keep warm. Cook as recipe calls for. Mix pudding, adding 1/2 to 1 cup more milk than recipe calls for. Cook. Keep warm. Spoon the warm pudding over the pancakes to serve. Enjoy!

Broiled Grapefruit

Servings: 2

Another quick dessert Ma used. Also very nice served for breakfast.

1	Grapefruit, cut in half
2 tsp.	Sugar
2	Maraschino cherries

Sprinkle sugar on grapefruit and put a cherry in the center of each. Put under broiler for a few minutes, just until sugar turns a light brown. Serve. **NOTE:** Ma would cut around the sections of the fruit. I serve the fruit with a serrated spoon.

Brown Betty

Servings: 6

When the apples were available and there was stale bread it was just the time for Ma to make this dessert.

4, lb.	Apples, sliced thin
2 cups	Bread cubed,
3/4 cup	Dark brown sugar
1 Tbsp.	Butter
	Cinnamon

Brush a baking dish with melted butter. Place a layer of apples on the bottom, then a layer of bred cubes; sprinkle with half the sugar. Make another layer of apples, bread and then a layer of apples. Cover with the other half of the sugar, sprinkle with cinnamon and top with any butter left. Add 1/4 cup of hot water and cover with aluminum foil. Bake in a 350° oven for 30 minutes. Remove cover and brown. Serve with a *Hard Sauce.*

Fruit Cobbler

Ma

Servings: 8-10

Ma always made peach, but I like to use other fruits as well. So here is the basic recipe and your choose of fruits.

6-8	Peaches peeled, sliced
3/4-1 cup	Sugar
1/2 tsp.	Cinnamon
Double batch	Baking powder biscuit dough*

Mix the sugar, cinnamon and peaches together. Put in a 9x13 baking dish. Top with the baking powder batter. Bake in a 350° oven for about 1 hour or until brown and the center of batter is baked through. Serve warm with whipped cream or vanilla ice cream or just plain. **NOTE:** *Use a biscuit mix for dough or make from scratch. **NOTE:** To use blueberries or other fruit or combination of fruits, use enough to have a deep layer of fruit on bottom of dish. and continue the recipe.

Homemade Ice Cream

Serving: 2 Quarts

This is a basic recipe for ice cream made in a hand turned churn. There are cookbooks devoted just to ice cream for those who want to become an ice cream aficionado. There are counter top electric makers available. You can cut this recipe in half to make it in a small electric maker. This is how we make ice cream in the summer, as a group effort. We have had a lot of fun though the years churning this frozen delight by hand.

4 cups	Pureed fresh fruit*
½ tsp.	Salt
1 cup	Sugar
4 large	Eggs
3 cups	Half and half
1 cup	Heavy cream
2 tsp.	Vanilla extract

Puree the fruit with the salt in a food processor or blender. Measure and set aside. (I like to leave some of the fruit chunky, so don't over process.) Beat the sugar and eggs together in a bowl until they are thick and pale yellow. Set aside. Heat the half and half to a simmer and add to the egg mixture. Place everything back into the pan and over a low heat, stir constantly with a whisk until the custard thickens. Do not let the mixture boil or the eggs will curdle. Pour the hot custard into a strainer over a bowl. Cool slightly. Stir in the fruit puree, cream and vanilla. Cover and refrigerate overnight. Put the paddle into the cylinder, pour the cold custard into the churn's chamber, cover with lid, and set into the bucket. Layer crushed ice and rock salt around the cylinder. Attach the handle and begin to turn. We started with the youngest child and worked up to the adults as we continued turning until the custard thickens. The handle should be very difficult to turn. This is where the strongest of the group is put to work. When it is very difficult to turn handle the ice cream is done. Remove the cylinder from the ice and wipe off the outside of the container so that the salt doesn't contaminate the ice cream. You can serve the ice cream now, or if you can persuade everyone to wait, you can pack the container in ice and wrap in padding, then wait for it to freeze harder. Good luck! **NOTE:** * Use about 2 quarts of strawberries or blueberries, or 6 cups of peeled, sliced peaches to get 4 cups of puree.

Chocolate Ice Cream:

1 ½ cup	Sugar
5	Eggs
1 ½ cup	Cocoa powder
2 ¼ cups	Whole milk
2 cups	Heavy cream
1 ½ Tbsp.	Vanilla

In a blender or food processor, blend the eggs, sugar and cocoa together. Set aside. Bring the milk to a boil in a large saucepan. Slowly pour most of the hot milk into the egg as the blender or food processor is running. Return everything to the pan and heat over a low heat. DO NOT BOIL or the eggs will curdle. Stir constantly until the mixture is thickened. Pour mixture though a strainer into a bowl. Let sit until cool, then stir in the cream and vanilla. Cover and refrigerate overnight. Process as in vanilla ice cream instructions. **NOTE:** For **Rocky Road Ice Cream,** about half way through the freezing process, add ¾ cup mini—marshmallows and ¾ cup chopped, roasted nuts (almonds, walnuts, pecan, or unsalted peanuts.) Continue churning until very thick. A very favorite of the ice cream makers.

Peach Crisp

Servings: 8-10

This easy dish is wonderful for many fruits. I like it with ice cream but everyone to his or her own taste. Use this recipe all year long as the fruits** come into season.

10	Peaches, ripe
1 cup	Sugar
¾ tsp.	Cinnamon
3 Tbsp.	Lemon Juice
1 cup	Flour
¼ tsp.	Nutmeg or cinnamon
6 Tbsp.	Butter, cold and cut into cubes
	Whipped cream or vanilla ice cream

Peel* and slice peaches. In a 9X13 inch baking dish place fruit and sprinkle with the ½ cup of the sugar mixed with the cinnamon. Drizzle the lemon juice over fruit. In a food processor, place flour, ½ cup sugar, nutmeg or cinnamon and pulse until blended. Add chunks of butter and pulse until the mixture has turned into crumbs. Sprinkle topping over fruit and bake at 375° for 1 hour until bubbling in the middle and brown on top. Serve warm or room temperature. Top with whipped cream or ice cream. **NOTE:** *To peel peaches easily, check "*Tips on Food*" section. ** To use other fruits you need about 5 cups of: apples, peeled, cored and sliced. Other fruits to use are, blackberries or blueberries; plums; rhubarb; combos of peaches and blueberries: rhubarb and strawberries; rhubarb and apples.

Poached Pears in wine

Servings: 6

A wonderful dessert or can be served with a cheese course.

6	Bosc pears, firm, ripe
1-2/3 cup	Sugar
3/4 cup	Red wine
3/4 cup	Water
Zest of 1	Lemon
Small piece	Cinnamon, stick
11tsp.	Cornstarch
1 Tbsp.	Water

Dissolve sugar in wine and water in a pan, adding cinnamon stick and lemon rind. Bring to boil and cook for 1 minute. Keep the stems on pears and peel. Using a melon baller remove the "eye" from the bottom of fruit. Place pears in syrup so the pear is completely covered. If not possible, cook pears on one side then turn and cook on the other until tender. Cook about 25inutes each side. Drain pears and arrange on a serving plate. Reduce liquid to about 1 1/2 cups, removing cinnamon stick. Stir the cornstarch into water and use to thicken syrup. Cook until slightly thickened and pour over each pear. Chill thoroughly. Can be served with whipped cream and a sprinkle of toasted almonds.

Prune Whip

Ma
Servings: 4

An economical dessert Ma often made.

1 cup	Cooked and pureed prunes
1/8 tsp.	Salt
1/2 cup	Sugar
2	Egg whites, beaten
1 Tbsp.	Lemon juice

Heat prunes, salt and sugar together until sugar dissolves, stirring well. Slowly pour hot puree over the beaten egg whites folding well until all the ingredients are incorporated. Stir in lemon juice. Pour into dishes and serve warm. **NOTE:** Make sure the eggs are very fresh. **NOTE:** Can top with a bit of whipped cream.

Raspberry Parfait

Servings: 4

A very elegant desert and quite delicious.

1 pt. fresh	Red raspberries OR
2 cups of frozen	Red raspberries without sugar
2	Egg whites
1/2 cup	Sugar
1 1/2 cups	Heavy cream

Put raspberries in blender and blend, then put puree through a fine strainer to remove seeds. Put puree in a flat dish, covered and freeze overnight. About an hour before serving, beat the egg whites until they hold a soft shape. Gradually beat in the sugar until the mixture holds a stiff peak. Whip the cream in a separate bowl until it is very stiff. Remove frozen raspberries from freezer and transfer it to a bowl and beat with a spoon to a consistency that the cream and eggs can be whisked together. Pile the parfait into tall glasses and keep it cold until ready to serve. **NOTE:** For an extra treat, layer the parfait with a chocolate sauce and top with a bit of whipped cream. Extra special dessert when you want something to impress

THINGS TO KNOW ABOUT PIES

I like pie the best. I find them easy to make, and they are so welcomed as a dessert.

I have not noted all of this information in each and every recipe for a pie. I am putting general information for pies here at the beginning of the section so everyone is familiar with the art of pie making.

Single crust to be filled. To fill a pie pan with a bottom crust you need to lay the crust into a pie pan and lightly press the dough into the form. If a small amount of crust hangs over the edge of the pan you can fold it under and crimp the edge by using a fork to press down around the edge or by pinching the edge with your fingers to form a crimped edge. Fill crust and bake.

Single piecrust pre-baked. (Blind) After putting the crust in the pan, you need to prick (dock) the bottom of the crust with a fork. Make marks over the bottom of the crust so the crust will not bubble up as it bakes. Some people use a layer of dried beans on a sheet of parchment paper on the bottom of the crust to do the same thing. The beans can be used over and over. Store them in a glass jar, sealed.

Double crust. Follow the instruction for a single crust until the sealing of the edge. Fill. Place top crust over pie. Then continue with the directions. You can tuck the top and bottom crusts under and then finish. Another way, if you have an excess of crust, is to cut crust even with edge of pie pan then continue. Some like to moisten, with water, the bottom lip of crust before adding top. Make a few slashes in the top of the pie to allow the stem to escape. Before placing the crust on top you can use a small cutter to make a design in the center of the pie to accomplish the same thing. You can also use an old-fashioned pie "bird". This is usually a ceramic bird that is placed in the center of the pie to allow the stem to escape. The bird is removed after the pie cools.

Decorating the top of the pie. You can use extra crust to cut out small shapes such as leaves, fruit, animals or whatever idea you may have. Use an egg wash. (1 egg beaten with 1 tablespoon of water), to brush the back of the decoration to "glue" it to the crust. Brushing on an egg wash or heavy cream on the edge of a crust or the whole crust to give it a golden brown color and a shine. Sprinkling the top with some sugar gives it a crunch.

Criss-cross top. Roll crust out and use a very sharp knife, a pizza wheel or a crimped pastry wheel to cut the dough into 1-½ inch strips. Lay the strips over the filled pie with 1-½ inch spaces. Then at an angle or direct across the strips begin to lay the rest of the strips. Lift the first row up so you can weave the strips over and under, alternating each row so it forms a criss-cross pattern. When all the strips are in place, seal the ends of each strip. Brush the top with a wash or with cram and sprinkle with sugar if you wish. Bake.

Crumb Top Pie: Mix together 1/4 cup cold butter, 1/2 cup flour with 1/2 cup brown sugar, packed, until it is a rough crumb. Top pie with mixture and bake as directed.

Filling. In fruit pies, I find mixing the fruit, sugar, flour and spices together in a bowl and pouring the filling into the pie the easiest way to fill this pie. The ingredients are evenly distrusted. For very liquid filling, like pumpkin, I think that putting the crust in the oven first and then filling it there is the easiest because it avoids spillage.

Baking. The reason for two temperatures in most recipes is to brown the bottom of the crust with the higher heat, so it will not become soggy and then lower the temperature to cook the whole pie for a long time.

Topping the pies. Pie is often served with whipped cream or a scoop of ice cream of your favorite flavor, something that will complement the flavor of the pie. This is why vanilla is often used. Some other flavors compliment the pie very well also. Sharp cheese with apple, cranberry sauce or relish with pumpkin or sweet potato, a dusting of 10x sugar on fruit pies and drizzle of chocolate syrup on cheery pie are very nice. Of course, a freshly baked pie is good just as it is!

DESSERTS PIE

Apple Pie

Ma
Servings: 6-8

A old, simple recipe but still the best in my opinion,

6	Apples, crisp, tart, peeled, corded and sliced
1 cup	Sugar
1 tsp.	Cinnamon
1/4 tsp.	Salt
2 Tbsp.	Flour
2 Tbsp.	Butter
Double	Pie crust

Sift dry ingredients together and mix with apples. Line a 9-inch pie pan with pastry. Fill with apple mixture, dot with butter and cover with top crust. Bake at 450° for 15 minutes. Reduce oven to 350° and bake for 45 minutes more.

Blueberry Pie **Servings:** 8

From scratch.

4 cups	Blueberries, fresh or frozen
1 cup	Sugar
1 tsp.	Cinnamon
1/8 tsp.	Salt
1 1/2 Tbsp.	Lemon juice
Double	Pie crust
1 Tbsp.	Butter

Mix berries with sugar, cinnamon, and flour, salt and lemon juice. Line a 9-inch pie pan with crust and pour filling in, dot with butter then top with other crust. Bake 450° for 10 minutes. Reduce oven to 350° and cook for 30 minutes more. Cool.

Carrot Pie

Ma

Servings: 6-8

Ma's recipe when there was a bountiful supply of carrots

1/2 cup	Sugar
1/8 tsp.	Salt
1 tsp.	Cinnamon
1/2 tsp.	Nutmeg
2	Eggs, slightly beaten
1 2/3 cups	Milk
1 1/2 cup	Cooked, well mashed carrots
Single	Pie crust

Sift dry ingredients together and stir into eggs. Add milk and carrots. Line 9-inch pie pan and pour in filling. Bake at 450° for 10 minutes. Reduce oven to 350° and bake 35 minutes more. Cool. **NOTE:** A knife inserted in pie should come out clean to make sure pie is completely done.

Cherry Pie

Ma
Servings: 6-8

This recipe is for fresh cherries, see note for canned cherries. Ma would use the cherries from our tree and use the cherry pitter to process them. If you don't have a pitter, squeeze the fruit to remove the pits.

1 qt.	Cherries, washed and pitted
1 1/4 cups	Sugar
Pinch	Salt
21/2 Tbsp.	Flour
Double	Pie crust

Mix cherries together with sugar, salt and flour. Line 9-inch pie pan with crust and pour in filling. Top with other crust. Bake at 450° for 10 minutes. Reduce oven to 350° and bake 25 minutes longer. Cool. **NOTE:** For canned cherries use 1 can of pie cherries and reduce sugar to 1/2 cup and flour to 1 tsp. Bake as above.

Gooseberry Pie

Servings: 6-8

Mother's favorite. Since I was young we had a few gooseberry bushes that the fruit was used for pies. I liked to pick the ripe ones from the bushes. If you can fine fresh picked berries be sure to use this recipe for a great treat.

3 cups	Gooseberries
1 ½ cups	Sugar
1/2 cup	Water
2 Tbsp.	Flour
1/4 tsp.	Salt
1 tsp.	Cinnamon
1/8 tsp.	Nutmeg
1 Tbsp.	Butter
1 double crust	Pie crust

Combine gooseberries, 1-cup sugar and water and cook until berries are tender. Sift remaining sugar, flour, salt and spices together and stir into cooked mixture and cool. In a 9-inch pie pan with crust, pour in filling and dot with butter. Cover with top crust and bake in 450° oven for 10 minutes then reduce temperature to 350° and bake 25 minutes more.

Grape Pie

Servings: 6-8

In the fall if you can find Concord grapes this is the pie to make. Aunt Ruth grew concord and white Niagara grapes. Ma made grape juice, jam and jelly. Of course when the grapes were ripe we always had a dish of grapes on the table to snack on.

4 cups	Concord grapes
1 cup	Sugar
3 Tbsp.	Flour
1 tsp.	Lemon juice
1 Tbs.	Butter
1 double crust	Pie crust

Wash grapes and remove from stem, then measure. Remove skins from grape by squeezing the fruit. Save skins. Bring pulp to a boil, cool and rub the pulp through a sieve to remove seeds. Mix pulp with skins. Blend in sugar, flour and lemon juice, mix well. Put crust into a 9-inch pie pan and pour grape mixture into crust. Dot with butter and top with other crust. Bake at 425° 35-40 minutes. Cool.

Lemon Meringue Pie

Servings: 6-8

My son, George, very favorite pie. An old stand by that Ma often whipped up for an evening's meal.

1 cup	Sugar
3 Tbsp.	Corn starch
1 1/2 cup	Water
3	Egg yolks, beaten
	Rind of 1 lemon
4 Tbsp.	Lemon juice
1 Tbs.	Butter
6	Egg whites
1/2 cup	Sugar
1single	Pie crust

Blind* bake the piecrust. Mix sugar and corn starch together in a saucepan. Stir in water until smooth. Stir in egg yolks. Bring this mixture to a boil, stirring constantly, boil 1 minute. Remove mixture from the heat and add lemon rind, juice and butter. Cool. Pour mixture into a 9-inch piecrust. Beat egg whites until foamy then add sugar a little bit at a time until stiff peaks form. Put meringue on pie filling making sure meringue touches all edges so while baking the meringue will not pull away from crust. Bake at 350° for 15 minutes or until top is browned. Cool away from a draft then refrigerate. **NOTE;** Blind Bake See "Things to know about pies". Bake crust at 350° for about 10 minutes or until lightly brown,

Lemon Pie

Servings: 6

If you like lemon you will love this pie. I have given this recipe to very few people. I share it now with you.

1 double	Pie crust
1 1/2 Tbsp.	Sugar
1 tsp.	Nutmeg
3 Tbsp.	Flour
1 1/2 cups	Sugar
1/2 cup.	Cold water
1/4 tsp.	Salt
1/3 cup	Butter, softened
3	Eggs, beaten
3	Lemons, peeled and sliced paper thin
2 tsp.	Lemon peel, grated

Line a 9-inch deep pie pan. Roll crust out into a 9-inch circle and cut into 6 wedges. Place each wedge on a baking sheet and sprinkle with 1 1/2 tsp. of sugar and nutmeg mixed together. Bake at 350° for 10 minutes. Cool on wire rack. Mix filling ingredients together in a bowl and pour into piecrust. Bake at 400° for 25 minutes. Carefully lift the wedges onto the pie and bake for an additional 10 minutes. Cool. **NOTE:** *Make sure to remove all white peel from lemon before slicing.

Mincemeat for Pie Filling

Servings: 3 9-inch deep-dish pies

This is the recipe from scratch, and the one I use. It is meatless. If you have the time, it is worth the effort.

1	Orange (quartered, seeds removed)
1	Lemon (quartered, seeds removed)
1 1/2 cups	Golden raisins
1 1/2 cups	Currants
8	Apples, tart (quartered, core removed)
3/4 cup	Candied fruit, mixed
2 cups	Apple cider
3 1/2 cups	Dark brown sugar, packed
1 tsp.	Salt
1 1/2 tsp.	Coriander
1 1/2 tsp.	Cinnamon
1 1/2 tsp.	Allspice
1 1/2 tsp.	Mace
1 1/2 tsp.	Nutmeg
1 1/2 tsp.	Cloves
1/2 cup	Whiskey
1/3 cup	Rum
3/4 lb.	Walnuts, shelled

Put all fruit and nuts through the coarse blade of a food or meat grinder. Put in a large pot and add cider. Bring to a boil and simmer, uncovered, until the mixture is fairly dry, about 15 minutes. Add sugar, salt and spices and simmer until thick, about 15 minutes. Stir in whiskey and rum. Mincemeat can be used to make pies or can be canned, by the hot water bath process. **NOTE:** I make all my holiday pies at the same time. I bake them, cool, then wrap them well and freeze. Thaw before serving. This mincemeat makes nice tarts and cookie bars as well.

Mincemeat Pie

Ma

Servings: 10

This is the shortcut recipe (when not making it from scratch.)

2 boxes	None Such condensed mincemeat
3 cups	Apple cider
1 cup	Raisins1/2 dark and 1/2 light,
1 large	Apple, Winesap or granny Smith, (peeled, cored and chopped fine)
1 double	Pie crust

Crumble mincemeat in large pot. Add cider, raisins and the apple and bring to a boil, then simmer for 5 minutes. Remove from heat and cool. Line a 9-10 inch deep-dish pie pan with piecrust. Pour cooled filling into crust and top with second crust. Seal and crimp the edges. Put a few slashes in top. Bake at 450° for 35-45 minutes or until golden brown. Cool.

Peach Pie

Ma
Servings: 6

Ma made this each summer when the fruit was plentiful.

6-8	Peaches, peeled, sliced
1/2 cup	Sugar
1 tsp.	Lemon juice
2 Tbsp.	Flour
2 tsp.	Cinnamon
3 Tbsp.	Butter
1 double	Pie crust

Put peaches in a large bowl and add sugar, cinnamon, lemon juice and flour, mix well. Pour into crust and top with butter cut into chunks. Top with second crust, crimping around edges and cut slits in top. Bake at 450° for 15 minutes. Reduce heat to 350° and bake for 30 minutes or until top is brown and juices are bubbling. Cool. **NOTE:** See food tips for peeling peaches.

Pecan Pie

Servings: 6-8

I first had this in Maine in the late 60s. Now, I love to bake it in the fall, but it is wonderful anytime.

1 single	Pie crust
1 cup	Corn syrup, ½ light & ½ dark
1 cup	Dark brown sugar, packed
1/4 tsp.	Salt
1/3 cup	Butter, melted
1 tsp.	Vanilla
3	Eggs, slightly beaten
1 heaping cup	Pecans

Mix corn syrup, sugar, salt, butter and vanilla. Beat in eggs. Pour into unbaked crust, sprinkle with pecans. Bake at 300° for 45 minutes.

Pie Crust

I like this recipe because it is hard to make it wrong. It has been around for a long time, but still works. A short cut is to use the refrigerated kind and save time and energy. They are very good, but if you want to try a piecrust from scratch, here it is!

	ONE CRUST
1 cup	Flour, unsifted
1/2 tsp.	Salt
1/3 cup	Oil
2 Tbsp.	Cold water
	TWO CRUST
1 ¾ cup	Flour, unsifted
1 tsp.	Salt
1/2 cup	Oil
3 Tbsp.	Cold water

Mix flour and salt. Blend in oil thoroughly with a fork. Sprinkle all of the water over mixture and mix well. Press firmly into a ball. If too dry add very small amounts of oil. For two crusts, cut dough in half. Place ball between two pieces of wax paper and roll out into a circle to fit pie pan. To bake crust, bake at 450° for 12-15 minutes. For filled crust consult recipe.

Pumpkin Pie

Servings: 6

I have used this recipe for years and it is always a hit.

1—single	Pie crust
2	Eggs, slightly beaten
1 1/2 cups	Pumpkin, canned or fresh cooked
3/4 cup	Sugar
1/2 tsp.	Salt
1/4 tsp.	Ginger, ground
1/8 tsp.	Cloves
1 tsp.	Cinnamon
1/4 tsp.	Nutmeg
1 2/3 cups	Evaporated milk

Mix filling ingredients together in the order given. Pour into 9-10 inch piecrust and bake at 425° in a pre-heated oven for 15 minutes. Reduce heat to 350° and bake for 45 minutes more. Pie is done when a knife inserted in center comes out clean. **NOTE:** I find, putting the empty piecrust on the oven rack and filling it there, to be the easiest. The filling does not spill when using this method.

Raisin Pie

Servings: 6-8

This is differently George Senior's favorite pie.

1 cup	Raisins
2 cups	Water
1 1/2 cups	Sugar
4 Tbsp.	Flour
1	Egg, well beaten
1 Tbsp.	Lemon juice
2 Tbsp.	Lemon rind
1/4 tsp.	Salt
1 double	Pie crust

Soak raisin in cold water for 3 hours. Drain. Mix flour and sugar together and combine with 2 cups of water raisins, salt, lemon juice, rind and eggs. Mix thoroughly and cook over low heat for 15 minutes. Line pie pan with crust and pour in filling. Cover with a criss-crossed pastry topping and bake in a 450° oven for 10 minutes. Reduce heat to 350° and bake 30 minute. Cool on rack.

Strawberry and Rhubarb Pie

Servings: 6-8

One of our Spring favorites. Now with frozen fruits you can make it all year long.

1/4 cup	Flour
1 1/4 cups	Sugar
1 cup	Strawberries
2 cups	Rhubarb, diced
2 Tbsp.	Butter
1 double	Pie crust

Sift flour and sugar together. Use about 3/4 of the mixture to combine with the fruit. Place a piecrust in a 9-inch pie pan and sprinkle the rest of the sugar mixture on the bottom of the pan. Put fruit in pan and dot with butter. Cover with other crust and bake in a 350° oven for 35-40 minutes. Serve warm. Good with a dollop of whipped cream. **NOTE:** Never use any part of the leaf of rhubarb, as they are poisonous.

Sweet Potato Pie

Servings: 6-8

My famous pie I make in the fall. Try this one.

1 Tbsp.	Butter
1/2 cup	Sugar
3 Tbsp.	Lemon juice
1 Tbsp.	Lemon rind
3	Eggs, separated
1/4 tsp.	Cinnamon
2 cups	Sweet potatoes, cooked, peeled and mashed
1 cup	Evaporated milk
1 single	Pie crust

Beat egg whites until stiff, set aside. Cream butter until soft, add sugar and continue to cream. Until sugar is well blended. Add lemon juice, rind, beaten egg yolks, cinnamon, potatoes and milk. Mix thoroughly. Fold in beaten egg whites. Pour into a 9-inch pie pan lined with crust. Bake at 425° for 10 minutes. Reduce oven to 350° and bake for 40 minutes more or until knife inserted in the center comes out clean. Cool. **NOTE:** When doubled this recipe make 3 9-inch pies. **NOTE:** Try and use white sweet potatoes but if you cannot obtain them using orange yams will do.

The flavor will be different but still very good.

DESSERTS PUDDING

English Plum Pudding

Servings: 12

This is something my Grandmother Meddings made each year. Serve it with a traditional English hard sauce.

1/2 cup,	Fine breadcrumbs
3/4 cup,	Hot milk
3/4 cup	Cake flour
1 tsp.	Salt
3/4 tsp.	Baking soda
1 tsp.	Cinnamon
1/4 tsp.	Nutmeg
1/2 tsp.	Mace
8 oz.	Raisins
8 oz.	Currants
4 oz.	Citron, candied
2 oz.	Lemon Peel, candied,
2 oz.	Orange peel, candied
2 oz.	Almonds, blanched
8 oz.	Dark brown sugar
5	Eggs, separated
8 oz.	Suet, chopped
1/4 cup	Apple cider
1/2 cup	Red currant jelly

Soften crumbs in milk for 10 minutes. Sift dry ingredients together. Chop fruit and almonds and stir into dry ingredients. Combine suet and breadcrumbs, and stir into flour-fruit mixture. Beat egg yolks, adding sugar as you continue to beat, then fruit juice and jelly mixing well. Fold in stiffly beaten egg whites. Pour into greased mold, cover tightly with lid and steam for 3 1/2 hours. Remove pudding from mold and serve warm with hard sauce. **NOTE:** If mold does not have lid seal with a piece of cheesecloth, then a heavy cover of aluminum foil tightly tied with cotton string. **NOTE:** Can pour warm rum over pudding and ignite before serving.

Farina Pudding

Servings: 8

Another East Indian dish. I really liked the first time I had it and have made it for many years.

2 Tbsp.	Ghee or clarified butter
1 cup	Farina (Cream of Wheat)
6 cups	Milk
1 1/2 cups	Sugar
2 Tbsp.	Raisins
2 Tbsp.	Almonds, slivered and toasted
1 tsp.	Cardamom powder

Heat the butter and fry the semolina briefly but do not let it brown. Add milk and simmer 10 minutes over heat and keep stirring so it will not stick or burn Add sugar, raisins and almonds and boil 5 minutes more. Pour into bowl and sprinkle cardamom powder on top. Serve warm or cool. **NOTE:** I like it warm with a dollop of whipped cream.

New Orleans Bread Pudding

Servings: 8-10

I learned this recipe when I took a cooking class the first time I went to New Orleans. I learned two secrets, use stale French or Italian bread, and serve it warm. This has become a family favorite.

1 loaf	French bread, stale, crumbled
4 cups	Milk
2 cups	Sugar
1 stick	Butter, melted
3 or more	Eggs
2 Tbsp.	Vanilla
1 cup	Raisins, dark, light or mixed
1 cup	Coconut
1 cup	Pecans, chopped
3	Apples, crisp, tart, peeled and chopped
1 tsp.	Cinnamon
1 tsp.	Nutmeg

This is a country recipe so you can vary the ingredients according to what you have on hand. Combine all ingredients. Mixture should be very moist but not soupy. Pour into a buttered 9x 13 inch baking pan. Bake at 350°. For approximately 75 minutes or until top is brown. Serve warm with *Whiskey Sauce* or whipped cream.

Rice Pudding

Ma
Servings: 6

Ma usually made this from leftover rice. She would cook it up on the stove while she prepared dinner and serve it warm.

2 cups	Rice, cooked
1 qt.	Milk
1 cup	Sugar
1/2 cup	Raisins
3	Eggs, beaten
1/2 tsp.	Cinnamon
1 tsp.	Vanilla

Slowly cook milk, rice, sugar, and raisins in a large pot on low heat for about 30 minutes. Add a bit more milk if the pudding gets too thick. Just before pudding is done add small amounts of hot pudding into eggs, stirring until eggs reach the same temperature as rice. Just before pudding is done, add egg mixture to rice and stir well. DO NOT BOIL after eggs are added. Turn heat off, remove from heat and add vanilla. Top with cinnamon and serve either warm or cold.

Rice Pudding II

Aunt Theresa

Servings: 4-6

This is Aunt Theresa's version of an old-time favorite.

1 Stick	Butter
1 Cup	Rice
½ Gal	Milk
4	Eggs
2 tsp.	Vanilla
¾-1 cup	Sugar (to taste)

Rinse rice. Place rice in pan with 2 cups of water for 10 minutes. Drain, return to pan add butter, milk and cook. Beat eggs and add a small amount of hot rice until eggs reach the same temperature as rice mixture. Add vanilla and sugar. Cook on low flame for one hour. Stirring constantly. Serve warm or refrigerate before serving. Top with whipped dream if desired.

Steamed Duff

Ma

Servings: 6

An old-fashioned hardy dish that we had a few times a year.

4 cups	Blackberries*
2 cups	Sugar
1 Tbsp.	Butter
2 cups	Flour
4 tsp.	Baking powder
1 tsp.	Salt
3/4 cup	Milk
1 tsp.	Lemon juice

Sift flour, baking powder and salt together. Work in the butter, add the milk and mix thoroughly. Combine sugar, berries and lemon juice and mix with the flour mixture. Pour into a buttered mold, pan or bowl that can be covered tightly. Steam in a water bath for 45 minutes. Serve warm with whipped cream or a *Vanilla Sauce*. **NOTE:** *or blueberry, raspberries, cherries, peach.

Tapioca Pudding

Servings: 4

Tapioca is a very old pudding. I like the large pearls but any size will do.

1 box	Tapioca, I like the large pearl
1 cup	Whipped cream
1/2 tsp. for each serving	Jelly or jam

I follow the fluffy recipe on the box of tapioca. Beat the egg whites and fold them in last, is the version I prefer. A nice helping of whipped cream or a bit of jelly is a nice topping. **NOTE:** I don't like the consistency of Instant tapioca save this for pies.

Vanilla Cornstarch Pudding

Ma

Servings: 4

Ma made this from scratch, and then someone came along and put it in a box. I like it Ma's way and it really is easy and cheaper.

1/3 cup	Sugar
1/4 cup	Corn starch
Pinch	Salt
2 3/4 to 3 cups	Milk
2 Tbsp.	Butter
1 tsp.	Vanilla

Combine sugar, cornstarch and salt in a saucepan. Stir in the milk gradually until smooth. Bring the mixture to the boil over a medium heat, stirring constantly. Cook for 1 minute. Remove from heat. Stir in butter and vanilla. Pour into individual dishes and refrigerate. Simple? I think so! **NOTE:** To keep the top of the pudding from forming a skin, place a piece of plastic wrap directly on the pudding to cool. Serve with a dollop of whipped cream. To make **Chocolate Pudding** add 3 Tbsp. Unsweetened cocoa to the dry ingredients. **NOTE:** *Vanilla Sauce*: To turn this pudding into a sauce simply add ½ to 1-cup additional milk to recipe. Serve warm or cold.

BEVERAGES

Mother tells of her experience as a child of gathering dandelion flowers for her father so he could make dandelion wine. He made wine out of parsnips and elderberries as well. How he made them, she is not sure, but he did store them in barrels in the cellar. I came across a recipe for dandelion wine in an old country cookbook. It was quite a process that started with a gallon of flowers, then sugar and yeast cakes were added. It had to be processed several times and the mixture had to age for quite a while. I think I prefer to make my selection from the wine cellars of the liquor store!

Champagne Punch

Servings: 24

A sparking punch for a special party

1 pt.,	Fresh strawberries, sliced
1/4 cup	Bourbon
2 bottles	Champagne
1 litter	7 up
1	Ice ring

Pour bourbon over strawberries and let soak for 2 hours. Place ice ring in the bottom of punch bowl and then add strawberries. Add champagne and 7 up. Serve. **NOTE:** Ice ring can be made of 7 up and sliced strawberries.

Cranberry Shrub

Servings: 8

A nice first course for a fall or winter meal.

1 qt.	Cranberry juice
1	Cinnamon stick
3	Cloves, whole
1/8 tsp.	Allspice
	Raspberry sherbet

Put about 1 cup of the juice in a saucepan and add spices. Simmer for 5 minutes. Cool. Add to rest of juice and chill. **To serve:** Just before servings top each glass of chilled juice with a small amount of sherbet. **NOTE:** I use the large end of a melon baller to dip up the sherbet.

Eggnog Arno

Mr. Brandt

Servings: 18

As promised to many, this is Grandfather, Arno Brandt's recipe as told to me by his wife.

12	Eggs, separated
2 cups	Sugar
1 pt.	Heavy cream
1/2 gal.	Milk
1 Tbsp.	Vanilla
1 Tbsp.	Rum extract
	Nutmeg, grated

Separate eggs. Beat whites until foamy, then add 1 cup of sugar, beating until stiff. Put into large bowl. Using same bowl, beat egg yolks with 1 cup of sugar until fluffy and light yellow. Add to whites. Wash bowl and beaters thoroughly and dry. Beat heavy cream until thick. Add to eggs. Add milk to mixture and flavorings. Refrigerate for at least 3 hour. Just before severing grate fresh nutmeg on top. Serve in punch cups. **NOTE:** If you wish to use alcohol instead of extract use 2 oz. each of dark rum and whiskey. **NOTE** Each Easter I double this recipe and it is devoured. If any is left over refrigerate.

Frosty Punch

Servings: 12-15

Simple and easy. This recipe makes a fluffy, sweet drink. We had this when I was a kid and it still is a punch that people enjoy.

1 quart	Fruit sherbet (orange or raspberry)
2 liter bottle	Ginger ale

Place sherbet in punch bowl, pour ginger ale over sherbet. The color of the sherbet will become the color of the punch.

Fruit "Cocktails"

Servings: 1

George and I don't use alcohol much anymore, but we do like a cocktail time some evenings. I make a small tray of appetizers and these "Cocktails".

2 parts juice	Apple, orange, cranberry, apricot, or grape etc.
1 part	Seltzer water, plain or flavored

Pour juice and seltzer water over crushed ice and decorate with fruit, serve. **NOTE:** This reduces the caloric intake of the juice and increases you daily intake of water!

Fruit Punch

Servings: 24-30

This is a rich punch many people think it is spiked but there is no alcohol in this recipe.

1 qt.	Cranberry juice
3 cups	Pineapple juice
1 6 oz. frozen can	Orange juice, don't add water
1/2 cup	Lemon juice
1 liter	Ginger ale

Combine all the fruit juices and pour over an ice block. Add ginger ale just before use. **NOTE:** I like to use juice to make a block of ice so that when it is melting it doesn't dilute the punch. If the punch sits awhile, refresh it by adding more ginger ale.

Hot Cocoa

Ma
Servings: 6

Ma used this recipe and so did I each winter, when the children were young.

1/4 cup	Cocoa powder
1/2 cup	Sugar
1/4 cup	Hot water
Dash	Salt
4 cups	Milk, heated
1 tsp.	Vanilla
	Marshmallows

Mix cocoa, sugar, water and salt in a saucepan. Stir constantly over medium heat until mixture boils. Cook and stir for 2-3 minutes. Slowly stir in milk and heat for 2 minutes **DO NOT BOIL!** Remove from heat and stir in vanilla. Serve in mugs toped with marshmallows. **NOTE:** Can serve a cinnamon or peppermint stick if you want to add another flavor. **NOTE"** For a very rich cup of coco use evaporated milk in place of the milk.

Hot, Mulled Cider

Servings: 12-15

A fall and winter drink that will warm you up.

1/2 gallon	Apple cider
1 whole	Cinnamon, stick
4 whole	Cloves
2 whole	Allspice
1/4 tsp.	Ginger, ground
1 tsp.	Orange rind, freshly grated (Optional)

Put all ingredients in a pot and heat, but not boil. I put this in a warm crock-pot and keep it on low to stay warm while serving. Serve in punch cups or mugs. **NOTE:** If you wish, after about 30-40 minutes you can remove the whole spices from cider.

Ice Tea Punch

Mildred Brandt
Servings: 10-12

Nice for a crowd, but you can make it by the glass as well.

8	Tea bags
1	Orange, sliced
1/2 cup	Sugar or to taste
1 liter bottle	Ginger ale

Put the tea bags, sugar and the sliced orange in a large container, cover with 2 quarts of boiling water, stir and let steep for 20 minutes. Remove tea bags, squeezing all liquid from them. Pour liquid over an ice block and add ginger ale. **NOTE:** To make just a glass or two, make strong, sweetened tea, put a slice of orange or a bit of orange juice in tea pour over ice and add ginger ale. **NOTE:** I have used Red Rose tea for years and years. I think it makes wonderful flavored tea, hot or cold.

Iced Tea

Servings: 2 qt.

My friend Jane loves my ice tea. I have included it for her. I think the secret is in the brand of tea.

5	Red Rose tea bags
2 cups	Water

One Way: Steep the tea in boiling water for 5 minutes or longer. Pour the concentrate into a 2-quart pitcher. Squeeze all the water out of tea bags. Fill the pitcher with water. Serve in a tall glass with lots of ice, sweetener, and a wedge of lemon and/ or lime. Second way and the easiest: Place tea bags in a 2-quart pitcher, and fill with tap water. Sit on the counter or put into the refrigerator for an hour or longer, remove tea bags, squeezing out all the water. Serve as above**. NOTE**: I like to use an artificial sweetener in my ice tea. If you prefer using sugar I suggest adding the sugar with the tea concentrate. Make sure that the sugar is dissolved before adding cold water. I like the flavors of fresh lemon and lime, so I pass a bowl of wedges of the fruits so everyone can choose for himself or herself. For an extra flavor add fresh mint leaves that have been crushed as you put the leaves into glass or pitcher by rubbing the leaves or giving a twist to release the oils.

Sangria

Servings: 6-8

Dot liked this traditional Spanish wine drink. Lovely in the summertime for a picnic, a meal or an evening entertainment.

1 bottle (1 liter)	Dry red wine
2	Oranges
1	Lime
1	Lemon
½ cup	Bing cherries, pitted

Several hours before serving, pour the wine over the fruit that has been sliced with the skins on and let it steep. Traditionally it is served in a pitcher. Pour over ice.

LOST RECIPES

Ma made a cooked, dark chocolate icing that the family talked about for years. The icing was cooked, and then spread on the cake and, when it cooled, it became hard and shiny. When you cut into the cake the icing would crack, sort of like the chocolate on an ice cream bar. Unfortunately, Ma forgot how she made it. She wrote to food companies, trying to locate the recipe, but no one was ever able to find it. I still look in any new cookbook for this recipe but have not found it yet. If anyone has a suggestion let me know.

I made an Apricot Bavarian dessert for years. Aunt Ruth made a fruit Bavarian as well. I lost these recipes and I have never been able to find them again. If you find a recipe that you enjoy, make sure you make a permanent record of it because you may never be able to create it again.

TIPS AND INFORMATION ABOUT FOOD, IT'S PREPARATION AND OTHER IDEAS

COOKING

When I make chicken soup, I like to use homemade or canned chicken broth in which to cook the chicken. It makes the flavor strong and delicious.

Chicken liver: Adding liver to gravy or stuffing seems to give it a bitter taste. When using a whole chicken, I usually sauté the chicken liver from a packet of giblets. I like to add a bit of onion to cook slowly with the liver. Serving the liver on crackers or toast is a nice treat for the cook. **NOTE: A** drop or two of white wine and a bit of pepper adds a nice flavor.

Pasta Sauce: I made my own sauce for years but with the quality of the sauces on the market today I prefer to open a jar and not spend the time and effort cooking up my own. After much experimentation I have selected on Classico Pasta Sauce. I like the tomato/ basil or the sauce with mushrooms the best. This sauce uses no sugar, I hate sweet pasta sauce, and there is some texture to this brand. I sometimes add 1 1lb. can of diced tomatoes and a drained 8 oz. can of mushroom bits and pieces to a jar of Classico for a little different flavor or consistency. This is what I prefer. You need to fine your own flavor that satisfies you. **NOTE:** I have heard people say to put sugar in the sauce because it cuts the acidity. But I think the reason the sauce gets acidity is because people cook the sauce to long. Tomatoes have their own sugar and adding more just gives you a sweet sauce. If you make your sauce from scratch you only need to cook it long enough to blend the flavors. If you add mea tit only needs to cook until the meat is done.

Vegetables: Dropping a bullion cub in root vegetables gives them a nice flavor. You don't have to season them, but do a taste check before adding any salt.

Tomatoes or Peaches: **To** peel these fruits easily drop them in boiling water and let them sit for about 30 seconds. Remove and drop into cold water for one minute, remove. Skins will slip off very easily.

To peel garlic easily, place a clove on a hard surface and use a large knife. Lay the knife flat over the garlic and, with a sharp blow with the heel of your hand, strike the blade. The paper skin will come off. Then you can chop, mash or crush the garlic clove.

Butter: I keep a stick of butter in a covered butter dish on the counter so that I have soft butter for spreading on toast and other foods. In the heat of the summer, it is not advisable to do this, unless your kitchen is air-conditioned all the time.

Ghee: To make this form of clarified butter, melt a quantity of unsalted butter slowly. When melted, slowly pour the clear butter into a crock, seeing that none of the solid gets into the clear part. (You can use a piece of cheesecloth to catch any bit of solid.) Discard the solid matter. The ghee does not need to be refrigerated. Just sit it on the counter to be used as oil.

Quick tip: Aunt Linda use to save the wrappers from the butter or margarine sticks, and stack them in the refrigerator. Some thought her thriftiness had gone too far, but she used them to grease a pan or baking dish.

Whipped cream: When beating whipping cream and egg whites, make sure that the bowl, beater, and rubber spatula are absolutely clean and free of any grease in order for these foods to beat well. For whipped cream, chilling the bowl and beater lets the cream whip up faster. When whipping cream, don't forget not to leave it unattended, because it can quickly turn to butter if whipped too long.

Scalding milk: Heat milk until just before boiling. Bubbles will form around edges. DO NOT BOIL. Remove from heat and use as recipe directs.

To sour milk: Put ½ to 1 teaspoon of vinegar in the measuring cup, and add milk called for in the recipe.

Crumbs: I find that making your own bread, both dry and fresh, cracker, graham cracker and corn flake crumbs to be very easy to make by using your blender or food process. It is thrifty too.

Meringue: When adding meringue to a pie, make sure to touch the edges of the pie with the meringue to keep it from shrinking.

Cinnamon sugar: I keep a small jar of cinnamon sugar in my spice cupboard to use in recipes or to sprinkle on toast, French toast, waffles and many other treats. An old jelly jar works fine. Fill the jar with sugar and add 2 tablespoons or more of ground cinnamon. Put the lid on tight and shake until the cinnamon is dispersed throughout the sugar. To make this yourself is very thrifty.

Melting baking chocolate in the microwave is very easy and a lot less mess than using a double boiler.

Nuts: To understand a recipe when calling for nuts, use this guide: 1-cup nuts "chopped" means measure the nuts first, then chop them. 1 cup chopped nuts means the opposite.

When cooking with wine, choose the best wine you can afford. Sometimes the same wine can be served with the meal. Cooking wine is not anything you want to use in your cooking. Sometimes the liquor store can recommend a good wine to go with your food.

SEASONING AND HERBS

Kosher or sea salt. You need to adjust a bit in handling it, but I pick up a pinch of the salt with my fingers and gently sprinkle it over the food. Use the measurement it calls for in a recipe. Kosher salt has a slightly different flavor than table salt. I like to taste the salt when eating something directly salted.

Salt in the summer: Salt can cake in a saltshaker in the humid weather. Ma's solution was to put uncooked rice in each saltshaker, about ¼ way, and add the salt. This trick kept the salt from clumping up and it was free pouring all summer. It makes a nice sound too!

Black pepper: I like freshly ground black pepper. I use a mill that coarsely grinds the corns. You can find mills that grind fine as well, if that's your choice. There are different colors of peppercorns, black is the most potent.

Spices are defined as seeds, berries, bark or buds, whole or ground. I like to use spices and I have quite a collection. I learned to distinguish among each of the flavors over many years of cooking and eating. Experiment with recipes and see what spices meets your taste. Using spice does not mean that the food will be hot, but it will be interesting. Use spices in layers. Put some in the breading or while browning meat, and then use more when liquid is added to the dish. This way you don't over spice a dish. Of course, you need to taste all along the way. Some spices do not release their flavor right away. Sometimes the flavor grows stronger as it cooks or even the next day after it has set and the flavor penetrates the foods. Cooking with spice is a trial and error process. You just have to accumulate the experience. Start with the recommend amounts in a recipe and adjust the amount to your liking. Good luck!

Are your spices and herbs too old? Don't keep them for long periods of time; they lose their flavor. I like to find a store, sometimes a health food store that sells their spices and herbs loose. You buy by the ounce and the prices are usually better than bottled spices. Using whole spice and grinding them when ready to use gives even a fresher flavor.

Where to store spices and dried herbs. Not next to or over the stove. They should be stored in a cool, dry and dark place.

These are some of the spice I use and were.

Allspice is a complex flavor (thus it's name) and it can stand on it's own or be used in combination with other spices.

Cardmond has a subtle sweet and lemon flavor. Ethic cooking often calls for this spice as well as some baked goods.

Caraway Seeds. Try these in a pound cake to create the taste of an *English Seed Cake.*

Cayenne Pepper. Hot, hot, hot! A spice you will want to use with caution. The flavor builds as the food cooks. Go lightly until you are sure how much you want to use.

Celery Seed is good with potatoes and in any mayonnaise based salad like egg or seafood.

Chili Powder, a combination of flavors and of course a must for chili, but used in other dish as well. Small amounts of cayenne pepper cam bring out the kick of the powder.

Cinnamon is another very versatile spice. I use it so much both in ground and stick form.

Coriander the seed of the plant it can be best tasted when crusher or heated until the seeds pop open.

Cumin. Mexican and other ethic foods use this distinct flavor. Again a lemon flavor is among its fragrances.

Fennel Seed has a licorice flavor. Grinding or crushing the seed releases the flavor.

Ginger. This is a wonderful addition to food and the dried as opposed to the fresh taste different. Look for the many ways I use ginger.

Mace: Did you know that mace was the outer shell of the nutmeg? If you want a milder flavor, use mace.

Nutmeg. You will find this spice in a variety of recipes form soup, main dishes, drinks to desserts. I like to use the whole nut and grate it fresh when needed.

Turmeric, a necessary spice in Indian cooking to create a beautiful color in the food especially rice. Turmeric also adds a distinct flavor in combination with other spice.

Herbs: Herbs are defined as the leaves of a plant. When you only have dried herbs, use about 1/2 the amount called for if the recipe calls for fresh herbs.

Fresh herbs can make quite a difference in the taste of your dish. Many fresh herbs are available year round, and I encourage you to try and use them more often. Some people enjoy growing their own and keep a pot or two of their favor herb growing on their windowsill all year long.

Some uses of fresh herbs that I like are as follows:

Basil. Can be used with fresh or cooked tomatoes. This herb is the base of the wonderful pesto sauce.

Bay leaves. If you can find fresh bay leaves, they are better than the dry, but the dry ones are fine to give a dish its particular flavor. Can be used in tomato sauces, soups, stews and in numerous other dishes

Chives. A subtle onion flavor I like to use as a topping for a dish and to also add color and design.

Cilantro is a flavor you like or don't like. The fragrance is very pungent. This plants seed is Coriander, another potent flavor. I like both to use in my East Indian and Mexican dishes as well as other recipes. What would salsa be without Cilantro?

Dill Weed is used in seafood. I use it with chicken and with cucumbers as well. I like eating the fresh dill along with the prepared dish. Sprinkle the leaves in a salad or use for decoration.

Lemon grass is used frequently in Thai foods. The flavor is sweet, but has the taste of lemon. The grass is fragrant and distinctive. It is good to use when cooking fish or chicken.

Mint is refreshing in tea, hot or cold. Put a few leaves in the water when cooking peas. The mint brings out the sweetness of the peas. I like mint in salad dressing, finely chopped to release their oil. And what would tabbouleh be without lots of mint leaves?

Parsley can be used in vegetables, soups, stew, and dumplings. To use as a decoration, either chopped or whole, is a standard in cooking. I also like to eat a sprig of parsley at the end of the meal. Some say that parsley aids in digestion and freshens your breath, but I just like the flavor. Place a sprig or two in a seafood salad sandwich!

Rosemary, along with garlic, is a must for lamb. It adds a sweet fragrance to potatoes and chicken too. Rubbing the leaves allows the oils to be released.

Sage is used in stuffing and is good with chicken and eggs.

Tarragon in poultry, baked and poached, is excellent.

Thyme is used in soups and meats.

TOOLS:

Fresh citrus juice: I use an old-fashioned glass citrus juice extractor. The juice falls into a troth around the reamer. Then you use the handle to pour the juice from the spout. They are easy to use, and to clean, and they are attractive to display. You can find them in antique, consignment, and thrift stores. Sometimes you can find them at flea markets or tag sales. I have both clear and green.

Kitchen tools: I have a collection of old kitchen tools that can still be used. A cherry pitter, a hand, metal eggbeater with a painted wooden handle, a metal drum cheese grater with a handle, and old-fashioned eggcups. Some things are not useable, like my great-grandmothers wooden potato masher. I also have a black cast iron flat iron. I have a glass scrubbing board my mother gave me. It is in a willow laundry basket with wooden clothespins and a cotton cloths line. They are fun to see and to remind you how woman worked in their kitchens and households many years ago.

I use a thermometer when roasting meat to make sure it cooks as I expect. Using this tool is the only way to be assured of this. Remove the meat from the oven when it reaches 5 degrees less that desired because the meat will continue to cook after it has been removed from the heat. Let the meat sit for 15-20 minutes, partially covered, in a warm place so that the juice can set. If it is sliced right away, the juice may pour out of the meat.

The cake tester, a small, thin, metal rood, is a handy kitchen tool for testing cakes, puddings, spoon bread etc. to see if they are done. Try it to test root vegetables.

Wire whisk is an essential tool for whipping up scrambled eggs, sauces even for foaming a pot of hot chocolate, as well as beating egg whites, cream, and other things. I own a variety of sizes, from a very small to a large balloon sized one. If you use instant flavored coffee, use a small whisk, which will disperse the coffee crystals very well in your cup.

Pots and pans: I have used the same cooking pots for over 40 years. I received most of them as wedding gifts. They are stainless steel with aluminum bottoms. Stainless steel does not conduit heat evenly, which is why the aluminum, which does a better job, is on the bottom. I don't see any reason why I would not use them for many more years. I have burned things in these pots and I just soak them for a while and scrub them clean. I don't like the coated pans at all. I do use a cast iron frying pan, which I have aged and keep on the stove at all times. After use, I simply rinse it out, rub it with a paper towel and heat it to dry the pan, so that it doesn't rust. You never use soap in a cast iron pan once it has been aged. It is the only way I can cook fried eggs without using a ton of fat to keep them from sticking. I use it to fry almost everything. I do, however, like my electric stainless steel frying pan for cooking large quantities of food so you can keep an even temperature, then keep the food warm. I use my electric frying pan on a buffet to keep food warm also.

Kitchen tools: I got tired of buying cheap cooking tools, so a few years ago I bought one-piece stainless steel tools. I wish I had started out with them. I guess what I am saying is buy quality and they last a long time.

CLEANING

Odors on hands: To quickly and easily remove fish, onion, garlic and other strong food odors, even bleach, just wash your hands with soap and water and rinse. While your hands are still wet, rub them over the chrome faucet of your kitchen sink. It works!

Odors in the air: Ma always would burn a little cinnamon on her stove when she was cooking strong foods like cabbage, fish and onions. You can sprinkle some cinnamon in a pan and heat it on the stove. Add other spices if you wish. (Allspice, or ginger, etc.) It works very quickly. I have a small electric potpourri container. You place water in it and spice or citrus rinds and heat.

It gives a nice fragrance to the air. I don't care much for sprays or perfumed candles. The smell is too powerful and strong for my nose.

Bolweevil: Those little bugs that get in your grains and cupboards are destructive After having to discard packaged products and scrubbing my cupboard several times, I got tired of dealing with these pesky insects. I began storing grains, flours, and pasta in my freezer. I have not been "bugged" since!

Keep an open box of baking soda in the refrigerator and freezer to absorb any odors. Don't forget to change the boxes every 3 months or so. Use the old baking soda to put down the garbage disposal to help freshen it too.
Baking Powder is a good scrubbing agent for Formica counters to get the food stains out with out scratching the tops. So is a drop or two of dishwasher detergent.

STORAGE:

I keep my coffee in the freezer after the container is opened to keep it fresh, especially when it is a coffee I don't use as often, such as espresso.

***Quick tip:* I** keep cooking chocolate, chocolate chips, nuts, and shredded coconut in the freezer to keep them fresh, especially because I don't use them as often as other foods. I can also buy these items on sale and keep them on hand to have for the holidays or other special occasions.

Bell peppers: I like to use red bell peppers in some recipes. If you have priced them lately you know they can be very expensive, especially in the winter. In the fall, I buy a small basket of red bell pepper at the farm market and wash and dry them. I then cut them into chunks, removing the stem and core. I place the peppers in a plastic bag and freeze them. Whether I want just apiece or a whole pepper, I have a supply in the freezer all season long.

ENTERTAINMENT

CHAPTER ONE

HOW DO YOU DO IT?

How do you do it? This is a question I often get when I entertain a group. Everything seems to go smoothly, and the food gets done on time so that everything is appropriately hot or cold. So how do I do it? Planning. It is as simple as that. Weeks or even months ahead of a party, I formulate a plan that I write down. Which meal you will be serving will dictate you chooses as well.

The theme of the party is first. Is it a holiday, birthday, anniversary, or just a party? What time of the year will it take place? This determines where the party might be, inside or outside, which in turns helps to decide the menu.

The guest list is next. Putting people together is difficult sometimes, so you need to think out how people will mix. If it is a large gathering, you can be more daring, but a small party, gets a little trickier. Sometimes, a theme will bind a group together, everyone has a good time, and they don't have to worry about not fitting into the group. Invitations are extended at least three weeks ahead of the party, whether you make phone calls or mail invitations. With the ability of the computer and beautiful stationery, making a custom invitation to your party is much easier today. You can also tie your invitation into your theme or decorations. A simple rubber stamp is available in many designs to custom make the invitation to match your party theme.

Now, for the menu, which is the next decision. I get out my cookbooks and my book of pervious menus and start to research the food I think I want to serve. Often the theme dictates the menu. I depend on books to give me ideas as to flavoring, combinations of flavors, proportions, and techniques. I often devise my own recipe by reading those of others. The fruits, vegetables, and other seasonal things that are available help you to decide on a menu as well. You might think of a simple menu, such as salad, chicken, potatoes, broccoli, and pie for dessert. Simple, but cookbooks could spark your imagination and the menu might sound a little more special. For instance: Caesar salad, chicken Kiev, twice-baked potatoes, broccoli with lemon butter and fruit tarts with whipped cream for dessert. Sounds good to me!

WHAT'S NEXT?

After you plan your menu, you can make a shopping list from the menu. Your recipes and that list will help you figure out the rest of the plan.

Other lists that may be needed are, ones for the bakery for rolls or dessert, for the liquor store for wines or other spirits for cooking or serving, and for the party store for party products. *I like to use favors,* a little something for everyone to take home. I have used flowers, candy, cookies, refrigerator magnets, napkin rings, candles, etc. If I have a theme, this helps carry out that theme by tying the party together. You need a list of materials or objects to purchase for those favors. *Look around for things* that fit into your party. If you plan way ahead, you will have the time to gather what you need. Pick up odds and ends when you shop in your various stores with an eye on future plans. I like to plan ahead for large parties. I take my shopping list as I shop each week to keep an eye open for sale items and stockpile them for the upcoming event. That way, the cost of the groceries is spread out over a period of time so the cost does not accumulate all in one shopping. I find a place to put my gathered supplies so I can have everything together when I need it.

Next is how you are going to set the table. Is it a sit down party? If so, can everyone sit at one table? I have set a number of tables through the house or in the yard to allow a large group to sit at a table. If you are going to have a full meal, sitting at a table is the most comfortable option. It makes it easier for each guest to handle the food comfortably. If you can sit everyone at different tables, a buffet is still the easiest way to serve the food. Trying to serve the food at each table is too difficult. When I set more that one table, I think of a way to tie them together. Flowers are one way. Each table has to have its own combination of linens, dishes, glasses, silver or flatware, and a centerpiece. Different cloth, napkin and dish combinations may be necessary, as most people do not have matching sets of china and linens to feed thirty or forty people unless you rent these items or use disposable products.

Be creative. I try to make each table as attractive as the main table. I try to use cotton or linen tablecloths and napkins. Linen is so comfortable to eat on, to put your arm or hands on a fabric tablecloth or wipe your mouth and fingers on a linen napkin. I love old linen and find many kinds at yard sales, consignment shops and thrift stores. I also find brand-new tablecloths and napkins all the time in these same places. The old linens have developed elegance; they become very soft with use and iron beautifully.

Not everyone wants to wash and iron table linens. I happen to enjoy it. People like throwing away things; it saves a lot of work. Even if you use disposable items, there is a large choice of paper and plastic table settings available. The choice is lovely. You can set a great table with paper, if that is your style. Using colorful plastic dishes from the dollar store can set a nice table as well especially for the patio. I like to use terry cloth washcloths for napkins when eating outside. They are just the things for messy BBQs and they wash right up. New washcloths can be purchased inexpensively at discount linen and curtain stores, dollar stores or flea markets. It's the presentation that counts. I like to set a nice table everyday. Who is better to treat well than your family and yourself?

Setting a beautiful table, to me, is half the battle to accompany a wonderfully planned and prepared meal. I use mismatched items very often, even if I have enough of one pattern to set the table. I think it makes an interesting effect and is a topic for conversation. Again, I have all kinds of interesting serving pieces, bowls, platters, tureens, and plates to set an attractive table. Using napkins that are similar such as, the same color and size is fun as well. One Easter, I had twelve people for dinner. I used four different dish patterns; four different color napkins and tied it together with a single colored tumbler. Fun, humm?

To decorate the table is something to think about. You can do the traditional thing and put a beautiful floral centerpiece in the middle of the table. If you do this, remember that you need to be able to see over or under the arrangement. Candlesticks with white, off white, or colored candles are a classic way to set the table. Holiday and theme parties give you the perfect reason to be creative. There are books to help you create centerpieces and to teach you how to assemble other items to go on the table. I have used decorations like old bric-a-brac on the table, old things, like salters, and individual bouquets in the miniature vases I have. Different sizes, levels and colors of candles, shells, small collections of items like birds, animals, teddy bears and fish can all add to an attractive table. When I want to put decorative item at different spots on the table, I like to place my serving dishes on the table to make sure there is enough space for everything.

Napkin folding makes an interesting feature to the table. Dover Press publishes two books on the subject of napkin folding. If you want to be formal, the use of *place cards* can be used. Again, printed place cards are available; these can be hand lettered or you can print them on the computer. Sometimes, I make a printed menu to be circulated around while people are eating the hors d'oeuvres.

OK, the party is beginning to take shape. Now what dishes do you have to make your food presentation? From your menu, you can make a list of your serving pieces, don't forget the serving utensils. This tells you if you are missing something and if you need to purchase it or borrow it. Serving pieces can be rented as well. I like to be creative and use odd things to serve my food in. Think of a container as multi-purpose and use it in new and different ways. I have a collection of old chicken dishes. They make a wonderful presentation with one at each place setting to serve soup. Do you have enough tables and chairs? Again, as with serving pieces these can be borrowed or rented as well.

Now comes the countdown. When to send the initiation! At least 3 weeks before most parties when possible. For a wedding, 3 months in advance. When do you need to start any favor, decoration or construction of a centerpiece? When do you get your linens and dishes in order to be used? When do you need to clean everything so the house or the yard looks its best? Mark your daily calendar for these things. You need to determine how all of these things will fit into all the other things you need to do daily. Some things need to be done way in advance to accommodate your lifestyle.

To facilitate a smooth, last few days and hours before your event, you have to *plan the order of the food preparation.* I always try to plan some of the dishes so that they can be made or assembled a day or so ahead. Sometimes I purchase things that are too time consuming to make myself, like stuffed grape leaves, phyllo dough, croissants, and ethnic breads or desserts; I also use frozen vegetables rather than fresh ones. You need to work all of this around your normal schedule. For the day of the party I make a list of the times that the different foods need to start cooking, so it all gets done together. I find charts in any general cookbooks for the timing of meat and vegetables. The meat should set for fifteen minutes or so to let the juices settle in. I might remove the meat half hour ahead of serving and keep it warm on top of the stove; then, I have a half hour to cook something else like baking the rolls while I am making the gravy. Rolls and gravy are the last foods to be heated. It takes timing and juggling to have the top and oven space for everything to cook and keep warm. I also make use of crock-pots and heating trays to keep foods hot until it's time to serve them. I have changed my menu when I realized that I had no space to cook more food or that my oven would hold. I have used a neighbor's or my mother's oven or refrigerator in a pinch; I have solved the problem one way or the other. I have tried to keep an extra refrigerator in the garage or basement, even if it is a small one, to keep the overflow of food and prepared dishes for a party, or at harvest time when buying a larger quantity of fresh produce than normal. Sometimes, I can make something the day before and cook it and just heat it up for dinner; the microwave oven also works well. All of this needs to be thought out ahead of time so that you don't become frantic at dinnertime. Keep your menu posted to help you keep a check on your items as you cook. Especially when you serve dinner make a finale check of you menu to make sure you have not forgotten anything, like a cold dish in the fridge.

I usually set my table the day before the party because I like everything together in case I find something missing or I don't like the looks of something. Get this job out of the way because the next day is devoted to preparation, cooking and seeing that everything is just right and that you can enjoy your guests and party.

You need a good supply of tea towels, plastic bags, wraps, aluminum foil and plastic containers for storage. A supply of hand towels washed and in place in the bathroom is important to your guests. You might want a candle lit and some special soap in the dish and a small fresh bouquet of flower in the bath as well. Now you have a plan to give a party. I then have a schedule to help me to complete the project.

ORGANIZING MYSELF

When I cook, I like to conserve my energy, especially when I'm entertaining. I like to organize my plans; I also like to do the same for myself. I will gather all the ingredients in one place so I know where to locate things as they are needed. It also gives me a check to see that I have not forgotten anything. I also sit down, whenever I can, when preparing or assembling food. I arrange a layer of tea towels and paper towels on the table and put my cutting board on top. I gather my bowls, waste container, tools and food around my workspace and sit down to work. To clean up, I simply gather any peels or cuttings up in the paper towels to dispose of it. I will often wash a bowl, knife or other utensils to re-use as I continue; this reduces the accumulation of dirty dishes.

I like to have a clean trash bag and a clean dishwasher to fill up with items I soil as I work. I'm not always so efficient, but when I am, it does reduce the clutter and gives me more room to work. Don't forget to allow time in your party day schedule for yourself to dress and relax a bit before it is time to go back to the kitchen or to greet your guests.

It took me years to get proficient at this but it has always helped me to have time to enjoy my own parties. I often only spend half an hour in the kitchen while my guests are in the house. If I have a lot of people, I offer a snack like cheese and crackers, a salty snack, maybe small canapés and something to drink. This allows you to get everyone into the house and have time for greetings, hanging up coats, and introductions. I invite people about half an hour before I plan to serve the meal, unless I have a cocktail time, in which case I need at least 45 minutes to an hour.

GAMES

I like to have interesting conversation, but it is fun sometimes to offer a little entertainment. Games can be fun. I have researched games in the library. In the children's section, you can find books with games that will entertain adults. Don't be too ambitious, but a game or two will keep people interested for a while. There are board games to play but these require a clean table and quite a bit of time, but maybe that is what your group will enjoy. Then you can get ambitious and introduce physical games. Inside where people are restricted to movement, limits your choices. Outside, you can have a wider variety of games, anything from water games to team games. It is what your company is happy with and willing to do.

If you have a member of your party who plays a musical instrument, sings or does a bit of magic, you might ask him or her to favor everyone with a short rendition. I would ask them when you invite them, so you can determine how long you want them to perform. They can prepare and bring anything they might need. Everyone begging for someone to perform off the top of his or her head is intimidating and uncomfortable for everyone. If you find out the evening of the party about a guest's ability, ask them quietly to perform. If they say no, don't plead; ask if they would perform next time. And please, if you ask someone to perform, please be curious enough to be quiet when they do. Please see that your guests respect the performer as well. This is another reason to ask ahead, so you can settle on the length of time that your guest will have to do their thing. Someone going on and on will lose the attention of the guests no matter how good he or she may be. People with entertaining talents are almost always willing to entertain an audience. But some people do not know when to stop. This is why a time limit is suggested. Leave the audience wanting more should be a performer's goal.

AFTER THE PARTY

Cleaning up is a chore; I don't care for it very much. I do not want to take the time to clean up while I have guests. Sometimes, family and friends offer to help and I get them to carry things to the kitchen, I usually put any leftovers away and then return to the party. I clean up later and the next day. To spend all of your time in the kitchen preparing and cleaning up while your guests are roaming around without you is something I don't want to do. The dishes can wait.

This is my plan for a party, whether I am having a friend for lunch, or a table full of guests for a multi-course Japanese dinner; I use the same formula. That is how I do it.

CHAPTER TWO

TABLE SETTING

Some people are intimidated by setting a formal table or even by dining at one. A formal setting really is done in a prescribed way to make it comfortable and easier to know what to use and how to use it. If you learn in what order you use the implements at the most formal of tables and do it with ease and comfort, you can sit down to any table and feel at home. It really is simple. The secret is this: the knives and spoons are placed on the right and the forks on the left of the dinner plate. With the exception of the seafood fork, for some reason, at a very formal table, is placed on the right. Starting away from the plate, the tools are laid in the order that the food will be served. Example: If the first course is soup then the soupspoon is the first spoon on the right farthest from the plate. If the second course is a salad, then the salad fork is the first fork on the left farthest from the plate. Study the diagram for other placements. The dessertspoon or fork can be served with the dessert or it can be placed at the top of the plate. Note that the fork goes in the direction as if it were next to the plate and you just moved it up, the same for the spoon. Napkins are usually placed under the forks and, when using a flat fold, the open edge of the fold goes next to the plate so you can easily pull the napkin apart and across your lap simply without shaking the napkin out. For less formal settings the napkin can be folded in other ways and placed under the forks, on the dinner plate or in the wineglass.

Use a glass for each beverage that you will be serving. Now they are placed in the order they will be offered from the plate out. The glasses are placed on the upper right above the knife and usually form a triangle if you are using several glasses. The glasses do not have to match, but you should try to use the right size glass for the appropriate beverage. When serving juice, if it is not set with the other glasses, and served a first course, it can be served on a small plate and placed on the dinner plate. The cup and saucer are placed to the lower right. The salad can be placed to the lower left or on the dinner plate in front of you as a course. The bread and butter plate is placed to the upper left. If you use individual butter knives it is placed across the top of the bread and butter plate. Don't forget to use a small plate under the soup bowl when it is served. Always pass a bowl of soup or a cup on a plate or saucer. It is easier to handle and avoid spills from dripping on you, your guest, or your table. Chargers can be used under the dinner plate. This gives a nice look to the table setting.

Don't forget to add a butter dish, salt and pepper, creamer and sugar, a dish of lemon slices when appropriate, using the appropriate silver, such as butter knife, sugar spoon, lemon fork, etc., as well as serving spoons and forks. Try to provide a serving utensil with all dishes, if possible, so your guests are not forced to use their personal utensils or their fingers. Two sets of salt and pepper, sugar and creamer and a butter dish are convenient on a long table.

SERVING

Wait for everyone to finish a course, then remove everyone's dishes including the under plate and all used silver before serving the next course. At the end of dinner, remove all plates and serving pieces, like salt and pepper and all food. Of course, leave cups, glasses, any silver meant for dessert or coffee, and napkins (unless badly soiled in which case a small napkin for dessert should be placed at each setting.). Coffee can be served with the meal if your guests prefer, but it is often served at the end of the meal with dessert. Dessert plates or bowls can be placed on the table if the dessert is to be passed. If it is to be served on the plate or bowl, serve each guest with his or her own plate placed in front of him or her. Don't forget a small plate under the bowl.

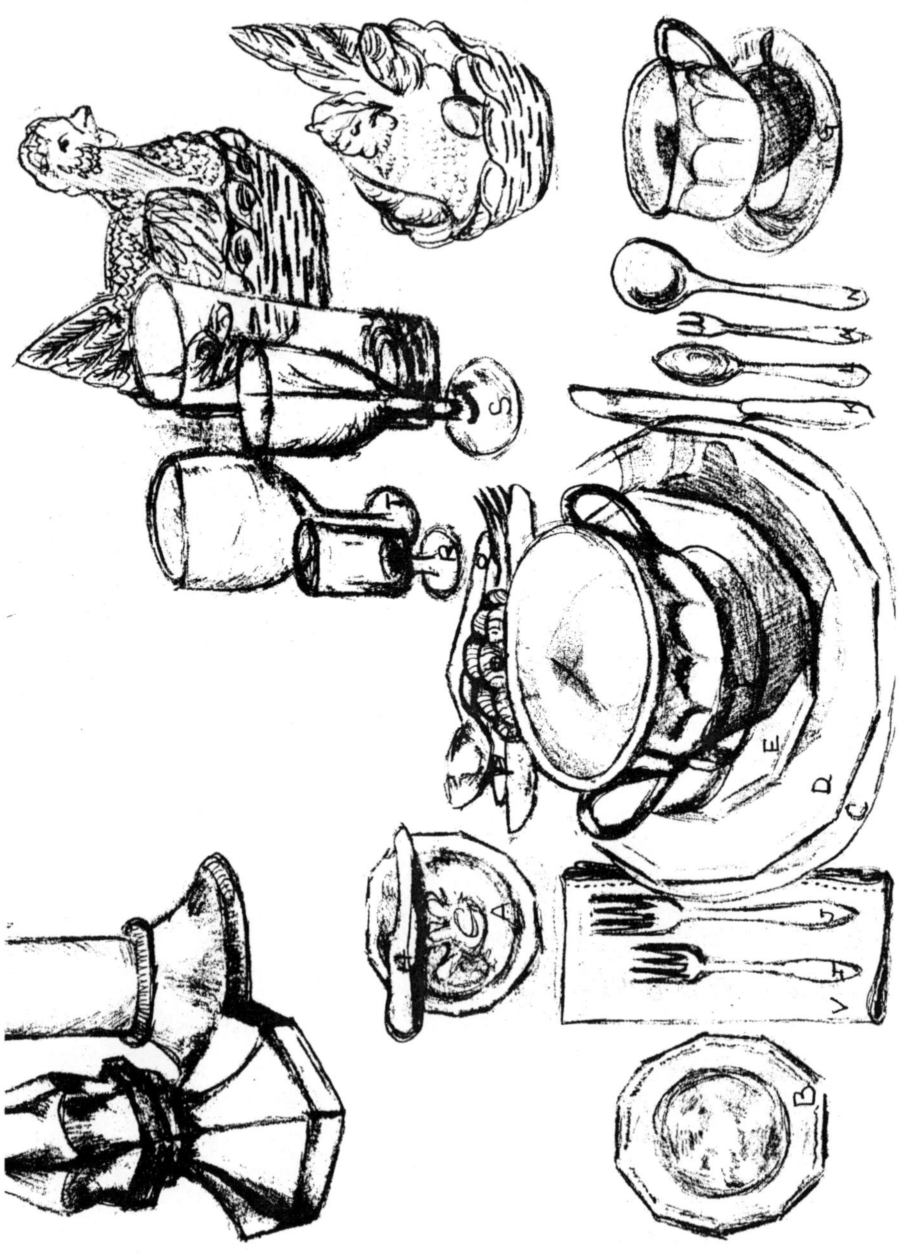

A- Butter plate
B- Salad Plate
C- Charger
D- Dinner plate
E- Serving plate
F- Soup bowl
G- Cup & saucer
H- Butter knife
I- Salad fork
J- Dinner fork
K- Dinner knife
L- Teaspoon
M- Seafood fork
N- Soup spoon
O- Dessert spoon
P- Dessert fork
Q- Name card holder
R- Juice Glass
S- White wine glass
T- Red wine glass
U- Water glass
V- Napkin

Use the diagram to refresh your memory if you forget what goes where. Even if you have a casual setting of a table you can use this formula for the placement of items. It makes it comfortable for the diner and the table looks inviting when it is completed. For the little bit of effort it takes to set an appealing table, the rewards outweigh the time spent. It helps children learn and gain confidence when it's time for them to be out in the world. It gives them a sense of importance that they will appreciate the fact that you cared to give them a little bit of gentealness that is sorely missing in today's world. Large corporations are bringing in professionals to teach their executives table manners. Your children won't have to be taught as adult's given a little bit of exposure to table etiquette as a child. Get them to set the table as you instruct; it is an easy way to learn.

CHAPTER THREE

THE WEDDING

I finished this book, and I was waiting for the different editing of *Ma & Me,* the pictures, the artwork and the written part to be completed. In the middle of July 2002, Nicole approached me with the news that Anthony Weal had proposed. They wanted to be married in October of 2003. Then she sprang a request, that they have the reception in our garden and would I please cook the dinner! And by the way don't tell anyone just yet, not until there was a ring and a formal announcement!

Well, of course, the planning began. We settled on the wedding and the reception in the garden. Nicole loves candles, so the use of candles and torches were a given. To make these things most effective, the time was set at 5:00 for the ceremony and the reception to follow. By the time dinner was served, it was dark and all the shimmering light was very dramatic.

The planning took on a life of it's own. There were magazines to browse, websites to surf, people to talk to. Suggestions came from many sources. I, of course, went to my computer and began to write down ideas and make lists. I would e-mail the plans to Nicole and she would say "yea" or "nay" and that would be recorded in my program, entitled "The wedding." A 3 ring binder began to grow with ideas, price booklets from rental agencies, and other printed material one can find in this wedding industry.

The planning of a large event, we invited 150 and planned for 130, takes a great amount of time. The phone calls and the inquiries go on and on. I am fortunate that a lifetime of entertaining small and large groups have given me the experience to plan a beautiful affair for Nicole and Anthony. We measured and remeasured the yard to be able to locate all the space we needed to fit everyone for the ceremony and the reception. Planning a wedding in the garden required us to create the spaces and formulate the whole event from the beginning.

On November 1, 2002, Nicole received a beautiful marquee cut diamond ring, set in a gold band. The plans for an engagement party were made and written in the program. We were excitedly shown the ring, for Saturday after Thanksgiving was the date. for the party. The aunts, uncle, grandmother, groom's family, and maid of honor were all invited (Anthony had not chosen his best man yet). We had a lovely evening with eager questions about the engagement, the wedding and all the details wanting to be known. It was a chance for the families to meet each other. We had nice sandwiches, savories, and an assortment of sweets to munch on as we chatted, laughed and watched the couple open their gifts brought by the guests.

The Garden

If the bride had not chosen to have the wedding in the garden, for me, the wedding planning would have been a snap. But this location is what made the planning much more difficult. Raking some leaves and cutting the grass was not going to do it. The yard and gardens needed a lot of work. Part of the fence had been crushed by a large limb of an Oak tree, a new one had to be installed. A new garden had to be made to act as a background for the ceremony. So each Sunday, from mid-March to mid-August Anthony, Nicole, George, and myself worked on the property. Sometimes some help came from George Jr. and an occasional friend. At the end of August, we were not going to get everything done so we called in some professionals to do some heavy jobs. In September, we made all the final touch ups to be ready for the big day. All of our work turned out a beautiful setting for a lovely wedding, plus we have the making of a beautiful garden for years to come with just some maintenance.

About the Couple

Nicole and Anthony seem to be matched well; if one's personality is stronger in one area, the other compensates with being stronger in another area. Though the long years of being together, they have done the hard work of working out the details of living together. In the everyday, small details that can make or break a relationship, question's of who does what, what their combined goals are, and the like, have been worked out. The families were excited about the couple's union. They loved the wedding and the fact they could contribute and participate in the nuptials.

This wedding was a United Nations Wedding of sorts. Both Nicole and Anthony have American Indian heritage. Nicole's great-great grandfather (paternal) was from the Black Foot nation from the Dakotas and Canada. Anthony's grandmother was from the White Face nation in South Carolina. The Weal name came from his great-great grandparent, who was slaves of a Dutch slave owner. Nicole is Caucasian, and Anthony is African American. Lorrieanne, Nicole's Maid of Honor, is Philippine, and many of the invited friends are from places like, Portugal, India, Puerto Rico, and others have a heritage from other parts of the world. The guests' choices of philosophy differ widely, the ages vary from their younger friends in their twenties to Nicole's grandmother, who turned 88 the day after the wedding. The foods we choose have different cultural flares as well as some of Ma's recipes. All and all a well-rounded affair I think.

Food

The cooking of the wedding meal became quite a project to tackle. First of all, I said I would be glad to do the cooking but I would need a staff to heat, serve and clean up, as I wanted to enjoy the day. George's sisters all were willing to pitch in and help, as they usually volunteer to do when the family is in need. Friends volunteered to pitch in to run errands to help in any way they could. I set up a menu for the couple to review and many changes were made and discussed and we came to a final menu. The consideration of a menu that would be tasty but be able to hold up under being prepared a few days in advance and then to be served cold or reheated was the challenge. The food preferences of the couple was another consideration, the cost of the supplies was another.

I followed my usual plan of attack to arrive at a satisfactory meal. Also I used my experience, cookbooks, and Martha's experience in the restaurant business to arrive at the size of the portions to figure quantities of food to purchase.

In April we had a trial dinner. I made the menu ahead of time. We invited a couple of friends and some of the family to critique the choices. The menu was a success, so our choices were a go! That day, we also reviewed all of the chooses that had be made up until this point and set up some mock tables to see what the settings and centerpieces looked like. All the songs that were to be sung on the wedding day were chosen.

The Gown

Nicole did not want something too plain or a dress too heavily decorated. After trying on many styles, Nicole settled on a halter neckline with an A-line to the dress. The dress she chose was a cream peau de soie fabric with a band at the neckline that was bordered on each edge in lavender seed beads. In between the borders' are lavender flowers embroidered with pale green and lavender seed and long beads enhancing the embroidery. The same pattern was on the halter strap around the neck. The back of the dress was decorated with small white fabric covered buttons, running down the length of the dress onto the train, where it was met with a triangle at the point of the train. Inside the triangle was the lavender embroidery and beading found on the top border.

Lorrieanne made the fingertip veil and it was worn attached at the back under Nicole's hair, piled on top of her head and decorated with flowers. Nicole bought see-though, platform, high heel shoes to complete the look.

She carried a mixed colored flower bouquet featuring small calla lilies, with a cascade of ivy falling to the edge of the gown.

Nicole follows in the tradition of my wedding and Ma's wedding of carrying calla lilies and roses. When Ma carried her flowers they were picked out of the fields and the white lilies and wild roses were what were available. So too, when I was married, there were only large white lilies but now the calla lilies come in many sizes and colors. Nicole carried lilies in her bouquet of multicolored flowers. I had my reception outdoors and Nicole had both her marriage and reception in the garden. She and I both wore ivory gowns.

Ma's presents was felt in this wedding event. Her recipes were part of the event as well as her teaching of entertaining skills and making the guest feel at home. One of Ma's great-grandchildren, Alice, is a flower designer, and her talent was used in the design of the wedding flowers. George's niece, Katie, also a flower designer, worked with Alice and the two women's work was beautiful. Ma's influences are still seen many, many years after her passing and into generations that have gone on without her, but not without her being remembered.

The Maid of Honor wore a crushed velvet dress. The dress had an asymmetric hemline and spaghetti strap neckline. The shoes she wore were plum high heels with straps that wrapped around her ankles. Lorraine carried a bouquet of cream assorted flowers.

The men wore black tuxedos with a longer length jacket. They also wore plum vest, the groom wore silver and a brooch tie to complement the look of the women. My dress was very easy to find. It was one by the designer Karen Miller. It is a sheer, silver blue formal gown. The lined dress is made to look like two pieces, a blouse and long skirt. The bodice has small straps that are beaded in clear crystal beads, as is the rest of t he top. The sheer jacket is beaded as well, down the front, around the bottom of the jacket and sleeves also. I wore simple jeweled combs in my hair as I wore it pulled to one side. Sliver blue sandals completed the outfit. I wore no flowers, so as not to distract from this lovely dress.

Barbara Ann Weal wore an ethnic gold dress and coat with a pillbox-matching hat. She looked lovely as the Mother of the groom.

The Cake

I don't know about you, but I have had really bad wedding cake! Often they are dry or the icing is too sweet or not sweet enough; sometimes the icing tastes like shortening. Because the cake is so bland, sometimes a dessert is served in addition to the cake. Well, as you may have read, Nicole's favorite cake is cheesecake. So what would be better than a cheesecake wedding cake? A local restaurant makes a lovely New York style cheesecake, so we had them make the cake. The cakes were plainly iced with white butter cream icing and served with a raspberry sauce. It is not possible to stack a cheesecake four layers high, so we displayed three layers on a metal flower stand; the fourth layer sat on the table. These cakes were decorated with mini fresh bouquets, a different one on each layer. It took ten 10" cakes to serve the 130 guests, and they loved every forkful!

The Decoration and How the Wedding was Planned

After much pondering we decided that the theme of the wedding would be the apple. The wedding was in the fall, so the apple fit right in. The dark color of apples was just right with the colors of the wedding, plum and ivory. The yard having an abundance of ivy, we include that and Nicole's gown being satin that completed the theme. Apple, ivy and satin are what she choose. We used satin in the ribbons decorating the tables and the tent, ivy and apple were also included.

The round dinning tables were dressed in plum lines. The centerpieces consisted of a one-foot square mirror raised up on a square of Styrofoam with its edge wrapped with cream satin ribbon. Three cream pillar candles of varying heights, wrapped at their base with plum ribbon, sat on the mirror. Sprigs of ivy and three apples were tucked in among the candles. A fresh apple hollowed out to hold a votive candle, was at each place. The tables were set with white china, and cream napkins tied with plum ribbon that held the flatware. Over each table, there hung two large white Japanese paper lanterns.

The bride and groom sat at a sweetheart table facing their guests. The round cake table skirted with a plum cover was to the right, and a display of white mums in a different container, as well as cream pillar candles on assorted candle stands dressed the other side of the couple. A large screen of plum and white stood behind the sweetheart table.

We live on a hill, so our yard is terraced. The couple was married on one level, which acted as a stage, under a green gazebo. The guests sat one level below the event, so they could witness the play! On each side of the gazebo was a tiki light, shepherd hook holding a white mum, and a pail of apples with candles floating on water to decorate the area. Other mums surrounded this area. The couple came up over a hill, pass a pond, and a hosta garden, then stepped on fall leaf shaped walking stones approaching the gazebo and faced each other. The mayor faced the couple as they exchanged their vows.

Putting It All Together

As I detailed in this section of the book, the key to planning this wedding is just that, planning! Between the months of July 2002 to October 2003 I compiled a loose-leaf notebook of more than 50 pages of details, notes, schedules, and lists. I used my computer to keep track of everything. I up-dated all aspects as I communicated with Nicole for her ideas and comments. When dealing with the serving staff, I had a detailed list of times and order for the food to be heated, served and removed. This was very helpful to keep the event going and moving on time without me being in the kitchen. There is no practical way of pulling off any party successfully without this kind of devotion to planning. George Jr. did the job of the General Manager. A schedule was invaluable to carry off the day. It allows you to look as though it just happed. I will not bore you with 50 pages of details, but I will share the menu and the timeline of the day as the final results of our wedding adventure.

Menu

Appetizer

Whole Gouda and Large wedge of Sharp cheese, Crackers, asst'd Mustards, Apple Wedges, Grapes, and Salted Nuts

Beverages

Fruit Punch Champagne Punch
Coffee Tea

Dinner
Sparkling Apple Cider for toast

Cold
Cold Baked Salmon Pacific served w/ cucumber sauce
Deviled eggs topped w/ caviar & shrimp
Mixed vegetable salad w/ vinaigrette
Onion & cheese rolls Butter
Hot
Boneless Pork Loin Roasted w/Apple Cider and Onion Sauce
Boneless Chicken Breast Tarragon

Spiced Chunky Applesauce
Pancit[4]
Yellow Rice
Harvard Beets
Honey/Ginger Baby Carrots

Wedding cake: Cheese Cake w/ White Butter Cream Frosting topped with Raspberry sauce

4 Pancit is a Philippine dish made with rice noodles, a variety of meats, seafood and Asian vegetables with a sauce that had a bit of spice and soy sauce.

Wedding and Reception Format

Appoint George event manager to carry party forward and handle schedule.

- ❖ Have small backyard set up in auditorium style
- ❖ Married on upper yard under green gazebo
- ❖ Fall leaves walking stones for walkway

❖ 3:45 Bridal party arrive before at home for late lunch

❖ 4:00 Car Attends and servers arrive

❖ 4:15 George be ready to greet guest
George greets guests and shows them to places

4:30 Light torches and candles at pond & gazebo

❖ 4:50 George close back gate
Mary enters from garden, takes place and begins with songs

❖ 5:00 George escorts Mothers to place
Official enters
Groom and best man take their place
Bride, father and maid of honor to side of house
Music
Procession across walkway (Bride on the right)
Marriage. (See page 23 for ceremony details) Bridal party recession to another part of the yard for pictures
Parents recess to patio and greet guests
Guest recess to patio so chairs can be rearranged.
Beverages and appetizers while pictures are being taken

6:00 Music begins

6:15 Bridal party assembles at top of walkway step to be announced
Bridal party mingles among guests
Have someone light candles in tent (start at front and work towards back)

- ❖ 6:30 1st dance bride & groom
  Father and bride
  Mother and groom

- ❖ 6:45 Undo ribbon on tent
  Guest invited to take their place at table
  Appetizer table reset to cold table
  Toast and announcements

- ❖ 7:15 Bridal party served
  Then rest of guest, by table
  Couple moves among guest to greet them after dinner
  When guests are finished dinner, music begins
  Remove cold table, move hot table back for dancing
  Clear tables
  Drinks still available

- ❖ 9:30 Cake cut and served to hot table
  Dancing continue

- ❖ 10:00 Staff leaves

- ❖ 10:15 Throw bouquet
  Garter throw
  Couple changes clothes
  Hand out birdseed

- ❖ 11:00 Bride and Groom leave for honeymoon
  Guests throw birdseed
  Music stops

CHAPTER FOUR

MENUS

For most of my married life I have kept a small, loose-leaf notebook of my parties and holiday menus. It has been helpful to keep this record because it reminds me of what I served on a previous holiday and whether or not I want to repeat it. I sometimes keep note of the recipe I used for a particular dish. I also keep a file of where I can find my favorite recipes in what cookbook and page I will find it. It saves time trying to track down a recipe I know I used but can't remember what book I found it in. I have a file box of recipes I have gotten from people who have been kind enough to share them with me. All of this helps me do research for many of my menus. I have downloaded and printed out recipes from the Internet seen on TV cooking shows. (I have organized them using my computer and made an index.) I am sure I will never cook all of the recipes I have copied, cut out or saved or that can be found in my many cookbooks. They just become a part of my library to give me input regarding ideas, quantity, combinations, etc.

Cooking has become a hobby to me, as my cousin Peg once pointed out, and I enjoy all aspects of it. Too bad I didn't inherit Aunt Ruth's talent for gardening for it could be a well-rounded hobby, grow it and cook it. I try to use the gardener's fresh vegetables, herbs, fruits, and flowers to make a pleasing table, laid with the good things nature provides for us.

Real Menus

These are some examples of my menus I have served over the years. Most of the recipes are contained in this book. Use them as a guide and devise your own combinations.

New Year's Day
Cream of Butternut Squash Soup
Roasted Center Cut Pork Loin
Sauerkraut
Spoon Bread
Mashed Potatoes
Applesauce
Lemon Meringue Pie

Because I don't eat pork, sometimes I add
A Pot of Black-Eyed Pies
Steamed Collard Green

Winter Lunch
Cream of Mushroom Soup
Cucumber/Onion/ Orange Salad
Linguine with Pesto Sauce
Lemon Squares
Coffee

Winter Dinner
Tossed Salad
Grilled Cornish Hens
Potato Cakes
Broccoli
Creamed Corn
Cranberry Sauce
Garlic Bread
Lemon Pie

Valentine

Cranberry Scrub
Baked Ham
Sweet Potato and Apple Casserole
Creamed Celery
Cranberry and Apple, Gelatin Salad
Harvard Beets
Fresh Baked Bread
Cherry Cheese Cake

Saint Patrick Day Dinner

Carrot and Raisin Salad on Lettuce
Corned Beef
Cabbage
Mashed Potatoes
Chunky Apple Sauce
Irish Soda Bread
Apple Pie

Easter Morning

Fruit Salad
Kielbasa and Eggs
Home Fries
Toast
Coffee
Hot Cross buns

Easter Dinner

Eggnog
Roasted Boneless Lamb
Roasted Boneless Pork Tenderloin
Mint Jelly
Baked Curried Fruit
Rutabagas Chunks
Scalloped Potatoes
Broccoli Casserole
Baking Powder Biscuits
Bunny Cake
Desserts brought by guests

Bridal Shower Brunch

Champagne Punch
Quiche Lorraine
Quiche with Broccoli
Tossed Salad
Pasta and Seafood Salad
Carrot and Pineapple
Gelatin Salad
Rolls and Butter
Bakery Cake
Coffee Tea

Mother's Day Dinner

Watercress Salad with Walnuts
Chicken Cordon Bleu
Twice Baked Potato
Scalloped Tomato
Sautéed Swiss Chard
Raspberries Parfait
French Bread/ Butter
Coffee

Father's Day Brunch

Cantaloupe Wedges
Blueberry Pancakes
Blueberries Sauce
Bacon and Pork Roll
Scrambled Eggs
Home Fries
Croissants Butter and Jelly
Coffee

4th Of July

Barbecued Chicken
Deviled Eggs
Corn On the Cob
Tossed Salad
Asst'd' Dressings and Toppings
Potato Salad or

Pasta and Tuna Salad
Baked Lima Bean
Watermelon
Miniature Cherry Cheese Cakes
Homemade Ice Cream
Ice Tea Punch
Soda and Beer

Summer Picnic
Barbecued Ribs
Burgers
Cheese and Toppings
Potato Salad
Coleslaw
Corn on the Cob
Tomato/ Cucumber/Onion
In Oil and Vinegar
Rhubarb and Strawberry Pie
Ice Tea and Lemonade

August Veggie Dinner
Gazpacho or
Cucumber in Yogurt with Dill

Fried Eggplant or Eggplant Parmigiana
Fried Tomatoes
Corn on the Cob
Steamed Green Beans
with New Potatoes
Steamed Zucchini and Yellow Squash
Peach Cobbler
Blueberry Cobbler
Ice Tea and Coffee

Fall Lunch
Orange and Onion Salad
Poached Salmon
Parleyed Small Red Potatoes
Sautéed Pea Pods and Julianne Carrots

Fruit Salad
Cookies
Coffee

Fall Dinner
Waldorf Salad
Chicken with Apple Stuffing
Whole Cranberry Sauce
Whole Green Beans and Carrots
Rice Pilaf
Pinwheel Cake
Coffee

Halloween Party Dinner
Gory Menu
Congealed Blood with Spider Legs
Burnt Fowl
Dinosaur Eggs in Green Slime
Over Yellow Worms
Skunk Cabbage with Rotten Fruit Juice
Golden Spongy Gourds
Lizard Eyes and Smelly Roots
Stale Crusty Dough and Grease
Dirty Haystacks
Poisoned Apple with Worms
Bubbling Hot Brown Brew

Real menu.
Shredded Picked Beets and Onion
Blackened Chicken
Hard Boiled Eggs In Cheese Sauce
Over Buttered Noodles
Kale in Balsamic Vinegar
Acorn Squash Rounds
Peas and Onions
Bread and Butter
Chocolate Hay Stacks
Baked Apples with Vanilla Ice Cream
Coffee Tea Soda

Thanksgiving

Onion Soup
Roasted Turkey
Sage and Onion Stuffing
Giblet Gravy
Scalloped Oysters
Mashed Potatoes
Baked Sweet Potato
Creamed Onions
Brussels Sprouts
Cranberry Relish
Greens, (Collard, Kale, Beet) or
Green Beans with Almonds
Pumpkin, Mince, and Sweet Potato Pies

Christmas Eve Buffet

For about 25-35 people, these are some themes.

Breakfast

Orange Juice with Asti Sumuti
Egg Casserole
Bacon/ Sausage/ Ham
Home Fries
Pastries
Etc.

Summer picnic with check cloth and all the fixn's

Barbecued Brisket of Beef
Fried Chicken Wings
Pieces of Corn on the Cob
Potato Salad
Baked Beans
Etc.

Soup Supper
3 Soups
Salad
Bread and Butter
Lots of Desserts

Here are two complete menus.

Menu #1
Hot Hors D'oeuvres
Fried Ravioli
Swedish Meatballs
Bread and Cheese Rolled in Bacon
Chicken Wings

Bowl of cold Shrimp with
Cocktail Sauce
Cheese and Crackers
Lebanon Baloney Stack
Smoked Fish
Liver Pate
Raw Vegetables and Dip

Vegetable and Barley Soup
Lunchmeat and Cheese Tray
Lettuce, Tomato, Onion

Rolls and Asset's Breads
Cole Slaw
Potato Salad
Pickles and Olive
Asst'd Holiday Sweets
Coffee

Menu #2
Fish Chowder
Caesar Salad
Hot Roast Beef
Horseradish Sauce
Broccoli Casserole
Rolls
Vegetables and Dip
Cheese and Fruit Tray
Pepperoni

Fruit Salad
Holiday Cookies/Candy
Nuts
Hot Cider / Coffee

Christmas morning
Orange juice
Fruit salad
Eggs benedict
Christmas Stollen
Coffee

Christmas Dinner
Salad
Roasted Duck with Orange
Baked Ham
with Pineapple
Baked Potatoes
Asparagus with Hollandaise Sauce
Peas and Onions
Relish Tray
Rolls and Butter
Pumpkin, Mince and Coconut Custard or Pecan Pies
Coffee

Ethic Style Menus

German Dinner
Onion Pie
Sauerbraten with Gravy
Sweet and Sour Red Cabbage
Peas and
Small Dumplings
Fried Apple Rings with Brown Sugar
Scalloped Tomatoes
Pumpernickel Bread
Baked Apple with Custard Sauce

Indian Dinner

Split Pea Dal
Rice
Tomato Chutney
Cucumber Ratia
Eggplant Salad
Pita Bread
If you don't want a vegetarian dinner add a
Chicken or Lamb Curry
Farina Pudding
Green Tea

Greek Dinner

Soup Augdomobo (Chicken Soup)
Small Greek Salad
Moussaka
Garlic Beets
Roast Chicken
Stuffed Grape Leaves
Pita Bread
Baklava from the bakery
Espresso

Japanese Dinner

Miso Soup with Tofu
Cold Asparagus with Sesame Sauce
Or Salad with Ginger Dressing
Sushi and Sushi Rolls
Salmon with Miso
Japanese Cucumber Relish
Vegetable Tempura with Dipping Sauce
Rice
Tea
Fresh Pineapple

Chinese Dinner

I ordered all take out this is an idea of the menu. the amount of each item depends on number of guests. This party was for 16 people.

Egg Rolls
Chinese Pizza
Cold Sesame Noodles
Pu Pu Patter
Cabbage Salad
Shrimp Toast
Soup
Egg Drop
Won Ton
Hot And Sour Or Dragon
Main Course
Beef and Broccoli
Shrimp Szechuan Sauce
(2 orders)
Shrimp Egg Fu Young
Lemon Chicken
(2 orders)
Mu Shu Pork, Extra Pancakes
Pork and Shrimp Fried Rice
Fortune Cookies—Almond Cookies
I supplied
Orange Wedges
Canned Lechi Nuts
Rum Raisin Ice Cream
Tea

New Orleans Dinner

Creole Cabbage Salad
Seafood Gumbo
Jambalaya
Creole Okra
Kale
French Bread
Warm Bread Pudding
Whiskey Sauce
Coffee

Italian dinner
Madge's Spinach Soup
Antipasto Salad
Chicken Ravioli With
Butter and Parmesan Cheese
Roast Beef
Roasted Potatoes
Steamed Zucchini
Sautéed Mushrooms
Italian Bread
Cheese with fruit
Cappuccino
Italian Ice Cream

I like to consider a balanced menu, such as vegetables, meat, starches, and accompanying foods. A balance of flavors is most interesting such as, sweet, sour, rich, delicate, light and filling. Some flavors go better with others. Asian cuisine particularly pays a lot of attention to balancing and complementing flavors in their selection of foods. I like to take a page from their book and follow their tradition.

BEST WISHES

Good planning, inventive cooking, relaxed entertaining, making your own fun is the plan. The tradition goes on, and I pass it to you.

EPILOGUE

I began this book in the fall of 2000 and struggled with a very cantankerous computer. There was much meditating and working with the photos and the drawings consumed a lot of time. Things began to change.

Months after the wedding, Nicole and Anthony had a beautiful, healthy baby boy, born January 20, 2004, Dante Nicholas Weal. The name Nicholas goes to another generation. Nicholas goes through each side of our family and Nicholas is his grandfather's middle name and Nicole is named for him also.

After the wedding Mother became ill and it was evident that she could not stay by herself anymore, so she then came to live with George and myself. The house she lived in for 68 years now had to start a new life with a new family. Mother never wanted the house to go out of the family and since Nicole and Anthony were the only grandchildren that did not have their own home, they were going to buy the family home. They would be the fourth generation to live there and Dante would be the fifth. Unhappily when the house was evaluated by a home inspection team the cost of bring it up to code and repairing damage caused by the mold, termites and asbestos, made the cost of the house, property and rehabbing the house way outside of the kids budget. The only thing to do was to sell the house and properties. Mother made arrangements for her granddaughter, Nicole, to get a large piece of the property so she and her family could build a home there, on the land and sell the rest. Well the story goes on and on, with wills, lawyers, evaluations, surveys and much time. The house was sold and is being rehabbed and three homes are being built on the rest of the property. Nicole and Anthony's home is being built and will delivered at the end of February 2007.

In the mean time on December 15, 2005 Kayla Ruth was born to the Weal's. This is the fourth regeneration of Ruth as a middle name. Aunt Ruth was really Virginia Ruth, I am Myrna Ruth, Nicole is Nicole Ruth and now the new baby. She is as beautiful as her brother is and of course, being grandparents, we just love them to death.

Sadly during all the back and forth of buying and selling, Mother became very ill in 2006 and passed away in September of that year, one month shy of her ninety-first year. My brother and I were there with her along with Alice, one of her granddaughters and her companion for 3 years, Elaine. George Jr. had just left after saying goodbye. She left the way she wanted to end her life, peacefully with her family with her in her yellow room with a dog she loved under her bed. So ends the cycle of a homestead and the long line of a family.

My brother and myself are now the older generation with our children and grandchildren as the generations left to remember the past and hand it on to the generations to follow. I give my ideas to them, to the few cousins remaining and to their children, grandchildren and great-grandchildren. Best wishes and all my love.

Myrna

FOOD INDEX

C

D

E

F

G

R

S